The Wisconsin Father's Guide to Divorce and Custody

ADVISORY

This book is meant to assist men and fathers in winning custody of their children and maintaining their fair share of marital assets at divorce. It is for informational purposes only and is not to be considered as legal advice or a substitute for having an attorney who can deal with all the specifics of your particular case.

This book is designed to help those experiencing a difficult period in their lives to understand the legal processes required to meet their needs and to provide insight and information on resources available to them.

The Wisconsin legislature made changes in family law in 1999 for cases filed after May 1, 2000. The 2nd edition of this book covers these substantial changes. Check at the State Law Library for updates in Chapter 767, which covers Actions Affecting the Family.

The Wisconsin Father's Guide to Divorce and Custody

James Novak

PRAIRIE OAK PRESS

A subsidiary of Trails Media Group, Inc
Black Earth, Wisconsin

Second edition, first printing 2001
©1996 by James Novak

Library of Congress Catalog Card Number: 2001032725
ISBN: 1-879483-81-5

Editor: Jerry Minnich
Book Production: Kathie Campbell
Cover Design: Todd Novak

Printed in the United States of America by McNaughton & Gunn

06 05 04 03 02 01   6 5 4 3 2

Library of Congress Cataloging-in-Publication Data

Novak, James, 1945
The Wisconsin father's guide to divorce and custody / James Novak.
p.   cm.
Includes bibliographical references and index.
ISBN 1-879483-81-5 (pbk.)
1. Divorce — Law and legislation — Wisconsin — Popular works. 2. Custody
of children — Wisconsin — Popular works. 3. Fathers — legal status, Laws,
etc — Wisconsin — Popular works. I. Title.
KFW2500.Z9N68 1996
346.77501'66—dc20   96-8258
[347.7506166]   CIP

Prairie Oak Press, a subsidiary of Trails Media Group, Inc.
P.O. Box 317 • Black Earth, WI 53515
(800) 236-8088 • e-mail: books@wistrails.com
www.trailsbooks.com

Contents

Introduction

This is a Wisconsin father's guide to going through divorce—choosing a good lawyer, getting a fair shake from the courts, and, most of all, doing right by your children. *Read this book before you choose a lawyer.*

I have helped many Wisconsin fathers fight and win custody of their children, and this is the main focus of this book. But even fathers who do not expect to be the custodial parent—who only want to win for themselves an appropriate amount of parenting time—will find much of value in this guide.

This book considers the laws of, and practices in, the State of Wisconsin. While many concepts are similar among all states, Wisconsin has its own specific statutes and case history that determine custody outcomes. We will consider not only what the statutes say, but also those common practices that are not spelled out in the law but are critical in determining custody cases.

Parenting Continues

Divorce ends marriages, but divorce does not end parenting responsibilities, and it should not end the joy of raising one's children. The end of a marriage is filled with loss of expectations and lots of blame. Often it is difficult during the beginning of a divorce for a father and mother to realize that their children need both parents, and will need both in the future. Children fear what changes the divorce will bring in their daily lives. And the anger and blame exhibited by the parents often get in the way of the cooperation that divorcing parents should have in helping their children cope with their fears.

I believe that there should be a presumption of equal placement when both parents are fit. Unfortunately, this is not the reality in Wisconsin today.

I deplore Wisconsin's adversarial system of divorce that forces parents to oppose and often belittle each other, each coming to battle with their attorneys. Children have the right to the love and guidance of both parents after divorce, and each parent has a natural right to association with their children. An important theme of this book is that

THE BEST PARENT IS BOTH PARENTS.

Consequently, this book will help you to win those battles necessary to maintain your proper parenting role now and in the future.

The best time to read this book is before litigation, *before the divorce action begins*. If you are the parent initiating the divorce, you will have the time to use this guide at a studied pace in preparing a thorough offense for winning custody. The responding party will then be at an initial disadvantage. However, if you are the parent reacting to a summons served by your wife, then you have a limited time to respond. Then it is important to use this book as a *crash course*. Too many fathers enter into divorce proceedings with alarming innocence and naiveté, blindly trusting their lawyer to take them by the hand and do what is best for them. *And too many fathers thus lose custody of their children.*

Gender Bias in Wisconsin

This is a father's guide. A father who wants custody needs a special attorney and a well-designed strategy to prevail in Wisconsin's courts. Attorneys perfectly able to defend women clients often fail when their clients are men. Gender bias in the courts is a fact in Wisconsin. It has been documented by numerous studies, including the Gender Bias Committee of the Wisconsin Supreme Court. The bias against fathers can be found in the public media, in family court counselors, in judges, in guardians *ad litem*, and, yes, even in your own attorney, who holds the same cultural expectations, yet who is supposed to represent you vigorously.

The gender bias against fathers is one reason why you must be extremely careful in your choice of an attorney. It is perhaps the most important choice you will make during the divorce. Substantial time and study should go into this process. I have devoted an entire chapter to the best way of selecting and *directing* an attorney (and yes, you must learn to *direct* your attorney to do the things *you* want done!) because the attorney you select will be crucial in your prevailing in a custody dispute.

Fighting Gender Bias

You must remain aware at all times that gender bias against fathers is operating among most parties in a custody fight. You must learn to recognize when judges and court counselors are working under gender bias presumptions that discriminate against the father. You must never underestimate gender bias against fathers in custody cases. Twenty years ago, feminists said that, in order to succeed in the male-dominated workplace, women must be twice as smart and work twice as hard to get half the pay. Today, divorcing fathers must be twice as good a parent and work longer and harder, to get one-half the consideration as a mother for winning custody.

Realize that a father's battle for custody is an uphill battle. It must be fought not merely for the self-satisfaction of the father. The literature is clear on the subject. Children raised without fathers suffer significant social maladies and maladjustments. Children raised in homes headed by single mothers suffer in contrast to children raised by both parents. Your struggle for custody of your children is important because kids need fathers for their very survival.

A Female Judge?

Many fathers believe that the appointment of a female judge dooms their custody case. Just the opposite is likely. My experience shows that the worst judge a father can get is a successful 55-65 year-old white male judge. This judge often has a stay-at-home wife whom he has long supported. He lives in an Ozzie-and-Harriet world. He thus views a young divorcing mother in his court as a "daughter" whom he must protect, as if she were his very own. He may not order her to seek employment, even though fairness would seem to indicate that course. Further, fearful of being called sexist, he vigorously affirms the young mother's rights at every opportunity.

A female judge, on the other hand, has broken through the stereotypes of what society believes a woman should be. She has faced gender-based adversity and overcome it. She is not afraid to issue tough "seek work" orders to mothers. She knows that a woman can make it in the working world, and she is not afraid to make women contribute on a basis of equal responsibility and equal rights. Simply put, a female judge often figures that if she can make it, your ex-wife can and should make it, also. There are no guarantees when it comes to judges—but a female judge is often more likely to rule fairly for fathers than a middle-age male judge.

The roles of men and women have changed dramatically in the last 25 years. It has become more difficult to find Ozzie-and-Harriet families. More than 65 percent of women are now in the workplace. The average middle-class family can stay in that class only because there are two wage earners. It is estimated that men now do more than 40 percent of the housework. The sight of a father with his children in the grocery store, in the park, at doctors' offices, has become commonplace. Stores and restaurants now have baby-changing stations in men's rooms as well as in women's rooms.

The reality is that we are in a major transitional period in which men's and women's roles are not clear-cut. But Wisconsin family law is still grounded in the Ozzie-and-Harriet model, and that means custody of the children is often given to the mother systematically, unless she can be proven to be unfit. In a winner-take-all system, you have to be especially alert that you are not relegated to the 1950s model of justice. You must insist that your child-rearing role after divorce is at least as great as it was during the marriage. *It is up to you to see that this happens.*

Stipulation is Best

While this book is oriented toward custody under adversarial conditions, I advise fathers that it is best for all parties to settle divorce and custody questions by mutual agreement. Custody lawsuits are brutal to all parties, not the least the children. Inviting the state into your most personal life is a humiliating and rage-provoking event. Strangers are asked to make decisions that will affect the rest of your life.

Stipulated (mutually agreed upon) arrangements will cause the least amount of havoc to your emotional and financial life. Most people who litigate to trial spend $10,000 to $15,000 *each*. They deplete a child's college fund and they end up unhappy in the long run. Litigated decisions, made by the courts, have a tendency to create further litigation. Stipulated agreements, on the other hand, are more likely to be followed by both parties because both have an investment in creating them. You and your children will be better off if you can stipulate rather than litigate.

Going to Mediation

One of the ways in which men and women in conflict often

find common ground is through mediation. Family Court counseling offices, which exist in most Wisconsin counties, can help in mediation. Private counselors are also available if both parties can agree in selecting a counselor. Since the cost of mediation is considerably less than attorney fees during litigation, and since the decisions reached are far more likely to be honored by both parties, I have included a chapter on how to use mediation to win an appropriate amount of parenting time.

Last, this book contains information on obtaining sample forms, for those who cannot afford the costs of traditional legal action. While I believe that any father is better off with a good attorney, many fathers do not have the resources to retain one. In general, there is no available free legal service in a civil action such as divorce and custody. It is better to stumble around *pro se* (representing yourself) than to lose your rights through inaction.

In the appendices, also, I include a bibliography of available books and other literature, a list of organizations that provide helpful services in Wisconsin, a glossary of commonly used legal terms, a model joint custody agreement, selected sections of Wisconsin Statute 767 (which controls family law), and the whole text of WDW 40, the rule that spells out in detail Wisconsin's child-support obligation. The WDW 40 document includes a worksheet that you can use in determining child support in your specific case.

Use the resources in the appendices to empower yourself by self-knowledge and lower your dependence on your attorney.

CHAPTER ONE

What Does It Mean to Win?

When men think of "winning," they do so in reference to sports, where there are definite rules. In a baseball or football game there is a decisive winner and loser. When asked who won the 1967 Super Bowl, you can say with certainty it was the Green Bay Packers, 35-10, over the Kansas City Chiefs. No question about it.

Winning custody, however, is not like winning a football game. There is no decisive winner. Neither is it an exact tie. In most cases, each party is a good and fit parent and decisions are close. *Both mother and father have a statutory right to parent their child in Wisconsin.* Your children's mother is not going to go away. She will have the right to return to court on a number of issues until your children reach the age of majority. You will have to cope with your ex-wife's presence at school events, sporting contests, award ceremonies, at-school emergencies, holidays, birthdays, and eventually your children's marriages and your grandchildren's events. Your ex-wife normally does not disappear. She probably will be part of your life for a long time to come.

To win means to get what you want in parenting time. To win means not to become the economic slave of your ex-wife in providing child support, maintenance, and post-divorce income sharing. To win is to recognize that no matter how much you might dislike your ex, your children love and need the parenting she provides. To win is to see your children happy. To win means to keep the government out of your life as much as possible, now and in the future.

Winning means that you will not allow yourself to be exploited by financially enabling your children and ex-wife to continue their lifestyle as if a divorce never took place. Winning means that your ex-wife must be equally responsible for all obligations in raising the children, and totally responsible for taking economic responsibility for her own needs, although there are a few exceptions where maintenance is justified. Simply put, winning means that *divorce ends your marriage as an economic contract.*

Winning becomes more clear when the specifics of your needs are stipulated in a *model joint custody agreement.* Such an agreement is included in the appendices of this book. It is crucial that you fill in these details by getting proper counsel even before hiring and talking with your attorney. Many times, a father has told me that his wife and he were close to a stipulated settlement on their own until her attorney advised her how much more she might gain if she litigated. Even when this is unintentional on an attorney's part, it is in the attorney's financial interest to extend litigation. *The interests of the attorney and the family are often in basic conflict, and it is the mother, the father, and the children who suffer because of it.*

Many people who litigate custody not only squander all their net assets but leave the courthouse owing their attorneys still more money. Winning is being able to keep your life intact as much as possible after divorce. If revenge is your goal, consider the advice of one of my friends:

THE BEST REVENGE IS TO LIVE WELL.

Let your ex-wife suffer from seeing your happiness and prosperity.

When Love Doesn't Die

In the United States, women initiate divorce in approximately two-thirds of all cases. Often, at the time the man receives his divorce papers, his wife has already psychologically divorced him and has made a firm decision to live her life apart from him. Often, this comes as a surprise to the husband, sometimes as a shock.

I always ask a man who seeks my counsel if he still loves his wife. This is an important question for *you* to answer, since you are about to face one or more of the following: to have all your property laid out in public and carved up for redistribution; to have your children possibly taken from your protection, your house taken away, your retirement account plucked and redistributed, child support ordered as an extraordinary percentage of your take-home income, and maintenance ordered for an extended period for a wife who may despise you.

The only person who is ripping your life asunder is your wife. Neither the judge, her lawyer, nor a guardian *ad litem* is the one who brings a case or continues a case. Only your wife is your legal adversary. *When a man is still in love with his wife, even after she has served him with divorce papers, he is in big trouble.*

Man as Family Protector

Men are acculturated—perhaps even biologically predisposed—to protect and take care of their families. To do so was necessary for the survival of the species over eons of time. How can a man then defend himself in court when his only adversary is his wife, who he, in the very fabric of his being, is devoted to protect and support? Often, while his wife is already psychologically divorced, a man is still hoping for a reconciliation. While she is advancing and solidifying her adversarial agenda against him, he is still trying to be protective, fair, and hopeful for a reconciliation in the marriage, which he believes will benefit himself and their children. *A man still in love is a sitting duck in a divorce action.*

A man in love needs first to be aware of this disability—and at this point it certainly is a disability—and then overcome his own inner feelings just to survive the initial battles. Since most lawyers are not comfortable in dealing in this area of a man's defense, a father will benefit from outside help, possibly from a men's group which can help him get his head straight so that he can properly prepare to defend himself. *This issue is so important that, if it is not openly dealt with at the outset, a father will surely fail in a custody fight.*

Rules of the Game

Males learn how to play sports early in life. By age seven, they have learned that all games have rules. Learning these rules and adhering to them is how men define what it means to be fair.

Divorce and custody disputes similarly have statutes and administrative rules. Normally, these rules of play are observed when applied to legal procedures. However, the central legal rule in custody decisions is "the-best-interest-of-the-child" standard. This central rule has no objective meaning and is interpreted by each mother, father, court counselor, guardian *ad litem,* and judge within each's own personal understandings, references, suppositions, standards, prejudices, and agendas. It happens that the best-interest-of-the-child standard is used to award custody to a prostitute with a drug addiction over an alcoholic with a drunk-driving problem. This is considered to be in the child's best interest, even though both are nearly or totally unfit parents and even though the best-interest standard, as ordinarily used, chooses one normal, good parent over another normal, good parent.

The best-interest-of-the-child standard allows innuendo to become as valid as fact. One Madison family law attorney described a custody trial as "trial by innuendo." Images count! "Facts" to show why one good parent is better than the other good parent are specious at best. Adversarial law is primitive in pitting parents against each other. However, fathers lose when they play according to the rules as they exist in Wisconsin. *Fathers need to create their own agenda and thus some of their own rules in winning custody..*

Custody, Power, and Justice

Men who play fair often lose their custody fights. They are fathers who learned the rules of fairness on the fields of play and believe that objective standards and fair play are part of the American justice system, indeed of the American Way of Life.

They are wrong. Our justice system is not about fair play. It is not even about justice as the term is normally used. The term justice has a legal and a moral meaning. From a legal point of view, justice refers to receiving one's due as limited by statute. This does not mean that the statute is fair or equitable. Legally, justice also refers to receiving a fair hearing and having equitable due-process rights.

When most fathers think about justice, they refer to a sense of what is right, of equity based on a sense of human dignity, of being just, fair, and impartial. The very fact that laws are the result of various powerful interest groups exerting pressure on the body politic as a whole speaks to the limitations of the concept of moral justice in custody disputes. Laws are enacted not out of moral imperative, but as the result of political and economic power exerted on the legislature.

A custody fight to trial is like a marathon race. Never in one's life does one exert so much energy and feel so much tension. A father in a custody fight will feel like his stomach is a cement mixer spinning a heavy, ever-falling load of tension and fear. He wakes up at three a.m. sweating in panic. He becomes obsessed with thoughts about losing his children, of their living their lives without him. At work he is distracted by these obsessions. All the money he has worked so hard to earn and save gets swallowed by huge attorney fees. But like a marathon runner, the spouse who keeps spending, who keeps running, who bears the load of tension and fear, wins over the spouse who must stop due to exhaustion. The spouse with the most stamina wins. One spouse must continue to drive the other until one cracks from sheer exhaustion. It shouldn't be this way, but in Wisconsin it is.

If you want to gain custody of your children, or even to gain appropriate parenting time, you must communicate to your wife, to the guardian *ad litem*, to the court counselor and the judge, that you have unlimited stamina to litigate until you get justice. Then you are even more likely to prevail.

Judges, guardians *ad litem*, and court counselors are bureaucrats. They dislike custody cases because they are tense and unpleasant. They recognize that there often are no winners. They do not know to whom to give custody when there are two good parents in dispute. They wish the case would go away as they get snagged in the thicket of the parents' divorce. Bureaucrats don't make waves. They attempt to solve difficult cases with as little effort as possible. This often works against fathers for whom fairness is an important part of their personal code.

Mother as the Natural Parent

A mother often feels that the couple's children are her sole personal property. The children grow in her and are born from her body. She nurses them with milk from her breasts. Society teaches mothers that they have natural instincts that make them superior parents. Little girls play with dolls, boys with trucks. Women in custody fights often simply declare themselves the "natural" parent in front of all parties and get away with it.

They declare, in no uncertain terms, what they expect as the divorced mother and how the fathers should adjust to provide for their needs. *They declare themselves the winners while the fathers are still waiting for the starting signal!*

Most officials are intimidated by the mother's declarations of parental superiority. In evaluating a custody battle, one would think that the party with the more inflexible stand would be called upon to bend and compromise. However, the opposite is true. The bureaucrats will apply greater pressure on the father to yield because, since he has learned the rules of fairness, he is more apt to be flexible and easier to push. When you have a problem without a good solution, it is easiest to push the more flexible party. *The more fair and flexible you are, the more you can expect to lose.*

A father seeking justice must play a Marine game of drawing a line in the sand. First, he must clearly know what it means for him to win, and what his bottom line of compromise will be. He must communicate clearly without anger that he will litigate for the next ten years or until the child reaches the age of majority if any party attempts to push him over the line he has drawn. Clear communication to all parties about what will be acceptable and unacceptable are an important part of this winning strategy. If the bureaucrats sense that you are a no-nonsense person who says what he means and means what he says, then they begin to adjust to your agenda rather than to your spouse's. This is an important lesson to learn about how the system works, how the game is played. *This leads to winners who get what they want and need out of their divorce.*

Now, before you go on to the next chapter, go back and re-read the last paragraph. Memorize it. Remember it.

CHAPTER TWO

The Importance of Fathers

I t's hard to imagine that there should be a need to write a chapter on the importance of fathers. The need to do so, however, shows how far our society has declined and how calloused we have become to the lessons of history and genetics, lessons that have shown the need for a strong parenting role by fathers.

Society is amply ingrained with the sanctity of motherhood. We commonly hear that something is "as American as motherhood and apple pie." Say something nasty about one's mama to a ghetto black or a Latino and be prepared for a serious fight. We hear the praises of Mary, the mother of Jesus, and fail to recognize St. Joseph as the unsung hero who raised a son who was not his offspring. The best-interest-of-the-child standard is an extension of the tender-years doctrine, a gender-biased view of the nurturing that mothers perform.

We sanctify motherhood and virtually ignore fatherhood. Feminists have written and spoken volumes in recent years, crying out that fathers are not only lacking in many areas, but are actually an unnecessary and inconvenient family appendage. Some gender feminists spew outright hate about fathers. The newspapers have published countless articles on irresponsible "deadbeat dads." We are now in the fourth decade of a period in which men and fathers have been berated and vilified by the press, and this has had a profound influence on our courts, and thus on our families.

Life Without Father

In recent years, however, a small turnaround has begun. *The New York Times Magazine,* in a 1989 article called "Children after Divorce," began the serious reexamination of fathers' issues. Robert Bly writes on the role of fathers in the development, or lack of development, of their sons. In 1990, *Parade Magazine* featured an article, "Can a Man Raise a Child by Himself?" To even feel it necessary to pose such a question shows how far we have fallen. In 1995, *U.S. News & World Report* ran a cover story entitled, "Why Fathers Count." In this article, Nicholas Davidson spelled out that "life without father" is America's greatest social tragedy. In 1998, Wisconsin Gov. Tommy Thompson started the Wisconsin Fatherhood Initiative. In the last five years, virtually every major magazine and newspaper has jumped on the bandwagon, running at least one major article on the importance of fathers.

The most outstanding work on the issue is a book, *The Garbage Generation,* by Dr. Daniel Amneus, in which he documents the negative effects on children raised in families headed by single mothers. The movie *Boys in the Hood* portrays the destruction of black ghetto youths without fathers.

Some might think that this single-mother syndrome affects only black ghetto youths. With the U.S. divorce rate at approximately fifty percent of the marriage rate, however, it should come as no surprise that children of most races are affected by being raised in fatherless homes. The National Fatherhood Institute estimates that more than half of all children will spend part of their childhood in a fatherless home. Thirty percent of all children are born to unmarried women, some of them separatist-feminists who so despise men that they feel it is better to conceive children without the direct sexual participation of men and to raise the resulting children without fathers.

Among African-Americans the illegitimacy rate is 68 percent. The black family in America is not merely in crisis, it has disintegrated within the past few generations at a rate unsurpassed even by the institution of slavery, leaving a permanent underclass. Many middle-class black parents do not want their children to associate with families in this underclass, out of fear for their safety.

Much recent literature has cast fathers in the light of absenteeism, focusing on the harm to children when their fathers are not present. The writers have usually focussed on economics, hoping to convince governments that if only more money were spent on welfare, families would thrive. But, although we have ample research on the effects on children who are raised without fathers, we have yet to develop the necessary models of good fathering. Popular movies such as *Mr. Mom*, or *Mrs. Doubtfire*, or *Kramer vs Kramer*, while instructive and sympathetic towards the plight of dads, casts them into the role of super mom, a parental anomaly. These movies do not define good fathering. This is an area that is ripe for research and development. Judges need to be instructed that the criteria for custody is not one in which a dad "out-mothers" the mother, but instead is a competent and loving father.

Women in the Workplace

The last two decades have seen a revolution in bringing women into the workplace. As women work outside the home, however, much work traditionally performed by stay-at-home mothers has been brought into the marketplace, becoming part of the gross national product. This work extends from child daycare to housecleaning, food preparation, and restaurant service. The development of convenience foods and even wrinkle-free clothing is a result of women entering the workplace.

Our economy has, almost without our knowing it, developed into one in which it takes two wage earners to provide a middle-class lifestyle. Life is good for two-wage-earner families. Children raised in these homes rarely experience poverty, while children in single-parent homes are likely to spend at least part of their childhood below the poverty line. In today's economy, the notion of easy no-fault divorce may be attractive to some parents, but it certainly has not been a boon to children who see a lowering of lifestyle.

One might respond that if fathers would only pay child support, then children would escape poverty. However, divorce does not increase family income, and it usually results in a less affluent lifestyle for everyone—mother, father, and children. With the same income as before, there are now two households. Two telephone bills. Two rent or mortgage payments. Extra bedrooms are needed to accommodate children at two residences. Extra beds, furniture, toys, gifts, and clothes must be bought for children. The concept in the state administrative rule (WDW 40) that a judge should attempt to make awards based on the family's past living standard is patently absurd and mathematically impossible in most cases, and should always be legally challenged as such.

If there is any reason for you to struggle through the indignity of a custody fight and the injustices of the family law system, it is that your children desperately need their father in their lives in order to survive. Notice I did not say to get along, but to *survive*. In the next few pages, I will describe what it means for children to be raised in a fatherless home. The negative effects are overwhelming and cover just about every social ill that befalls children.

Nicholas Davidson, in his article "Life without Fathers," documents the following effects on children raised without fathers:

(1) They have lower IQs and lower grades in school. This is true regardless of income or of race. Research for the National Association of Elementary School Principals concluded that "One-parent children on the whole show lower achievement in school than that of their two-parent classmates."

(2) Children from single-parent homes have higher rates of mental illness. Boys deprived of their fathers may suffer deep trauma. Various studies from diverse nations report that anywhere from 50 to 80 percent of psychiatric patients come from broken homes.

(3) Most gang members come from female-headed households. It is difficult for one parent to establish behavioral controls. Studies have established a statistical link between single parenthood and virtually every major crime, including mugging, violence against strangers, car theft, and burglary. Eighty percent of the million men in America's prisons come from single-parent families. Of this 80 percent, only 2 percent of these prisoners come from families headed by fathers. Sixty percent of violent rapists and 75 per cent of adolescent murderers come from mother-headed families.

(4) A UCLA study showed that the number of children who used drugs was 50 per cent less in homes with fathers versus mother-dominated homes. Numerous studies have found higher adolescent drug use as a result of divorce or separation, and in these cases mothers receive custody 90 percent of the time. Judith Wallerstein has documented a loss in children's self esteem and their fear of entering into long-term committed relationships when they emerge into adulthood.

In the *Garbage Generation*, Daniel Amneus points out that (1) more than one-third of children from female-headed homes drop out of school; (2) children living in female-headed homes are ten times more likely to be beaten or murdered; (3) young girls are more likely to become pregnant in their teen years, and young men are more likely to commit crimes, when they live in female-headed homes.

Awful things happen in the lives of children who are raised in fatherless homes. Any father would do whatever was necessary if one of his children needed an operation, yet many fathers do not understand that it is a life-or-death decision for them to fight for custody of their children.

I have written many negative things about single-mother headed households. This does not mean that every single mother is irresponsible or incompetent. Many mothers head families because of circumstances beyond their control, and many are valiant heroes who try their hardest to be both mom and dad to their kids. The negative effects I listed are not meant to berate these women, but are addressed to those women who purposely deny fathers to their children when it is unnecessary to do so.

What Fathers Do

So far, my case against fatherless families has been based on their negative effects upon children. But when you are in a custody fight, you must present *positives* as well as negatives. To the court counselor, the guardian *ad litem*, and the judge, you must present reasons why those officials should recognize *you* as the custodial parent. This is a gray area, at best, so I shall try to offer some ideas about what it means for a father to carry out an active parenting role.

First, it is obvious that men and women are more alike than different. We are both human beings who work, play, eat, and sleep. Most of our biological functions are the same or similar. We are 90 percent the same and only 10 percent different. Fathers and mothers parent in 90 percent the same ways, too. You know what it means to parent, but if an judge calls upon you to reel off all those parenting duties, you could be caught unprepared, even if you've been performing them all for years. So here is a partial checklist. Go over it every couple of days until you've memorized it. It may come in very handy:

- Bathing
- Dressing children for school
- Taking children to the doctor and dentist
- Shopping for clothing and food
- Talking to children about their problems
- Cooking and cleaning
- Taking children to school and for lessons
- Taking children to sporting events
- Comforting children when they get hurt
- Encouraging them to excel and do their best
- Reading to children
- Teaching young children to read and count
- Teaching morals and taking children to church

This is only a short, general list. If you were involved in a custody case you would be making a very specific list containing at least fifty items, all ways that you and your spouse nurture your children in similar ways.

It is the 10 percent difference in how fathers parent that is vital to our children's lives. While I believe that the 10 percent difference is both genetic and environmentally caused, it is difficult to separate the two influences with certainty.

A Bridge to Adulthood

Fetuses grow in their mothers until they are born as babies. Mothers thus view their children as an extension of their own bodies. This genetic factor in large part explains why mothers tend to view children as their personal possessions. Fathers view a newly born child as the *other*, to use an anthropologist's term. A father ascribes a *person* to his newborn, and does not see the baby as an extension of his body. Fathers grow to love and bond with their children as they get to know them. Mothers tend to protect their children as they would protect their own bodies, since they see their children as an extension of themselves. This protection of children during the first years of life is the maternal drive that helps young children survive, but it often leads to harmful overprotection if carried out too long.

Mothers offer unconditional love. This love brings needed security, especially in a child's early years, but eventually it can smother a child. Fathers, on the other hand, give *conditional* love to their children, a love based biologically, of course, but also, in part, in response to the child's good behavior. Children learn the concept of conditional love from fathers, and they learn how to earn it. This knowledge serves them well as they move away from the family into the outside world. How to earn approval, acceptance, and love is something that children must learn eventually. Teachers and playmates do not give unconditional love, and neither will friends, workplace associates, or a spouse in later years. *A father's conditional love is the model for success in mature friendships and marriage. Fathers are the bridge for a child moving into adulthood..*

What Fathers Teach Children

Male success in our culture is defined by our educational level, our profession, and what we do. As men, we are what we do. Men teach their children *what it means to be accepted* in our culture. We teach *independence* versus dependency.

Men learn to play sports early in life. We learn to be competitive, but we also learn *excellence* from competition, and the quest for excellence is carried over into other areas of life.

We teach our children rules of competition. From the rules our children learn how to play fairly.

As males who are defined by our actions and accomplishments, we provide our children with *role models and skills*. We teach our children how to *solve mechanical and mathematical problems,* how to *repair cars,* how to use *carpentry* to create new items for life. We teach them how to *grow gardens or run a farm,* revealing the miracle of plants growing from tiny, dry seeds. We teach our children the skills that give them the confidence they need to *survive and succeed* in this world.

Men have forty percent more body mass and are stronger than women. We teach our children that they can be safe, and that their father can be relied upon to keep them safe. This may be an illusion in an unsafe world, but an illusion that gives young children needed internal security. Fathers teach children physical restraint. The exercise of restraint when one has more power than an opponent is the stuff of *justice.*

To my surprise, recent research has pointed out that children learn empathy from their fathers. It is my conjecture that those who have social positions of power are forced to act judiciously, and that one result of that process is empathy.

Men's testosterone levels promote physical action. Most young men can tell yarns about driving an old car to 100 miles per hour, jumping from one rooftop to another, or performing other dangerous feats without much purpose. As we mature, this same energy allows us to take *heroic action.* Most heroic action in our culture is carried out by males. It is parallel to the *civic duty* that Robert Bly has described in his writings.

The above items in italics represent some of the qualities that fathers specifically offer their children. There are some mothers who can and do provide these qualities, but they are commonly provided by fathers as a matter of course.

Fathers and Social Disintegration

There is no justification for fathers who irresponsibly flee their families, leaving single mothers dependent upon social welfare. However, this is not always the case for single-mother-headed families. The government is searching for ways to solve the huge social problems caused by the disintegration of the family, but is blinded to one obvious solution. Many of these problems can easily be solved by utilizing the most inexpensive, yet effective, solution readily available—a loving father. Why should any government agency allow a mother to go on AFDC welfare if there is a fit father available to take custody? Are a hundred thousand more police needed on the streets, or do we need a hundred thousand more fathers who enforce discipline, set rules and limits, and tame the wildness of adolescents and teens? Are more daycare centers needed, or is the solution to the daycare shortage more equitable physical placement schedules? Are more repressive government intrusions needed to collect child support, or simply greater access to children by their fathers? We know that fathers with joint custody (fair placement) have a 90 percent-plus rate of paying child support.

In the face of a society declining rapidly in safety, security, and traditional family values, it has become obvious to many that the family agenda of gender feminists—based on welfare, daycare, and single-mother-headed households—is an abject failure. Fathers are not the evil persons that many of these feminists have taken delight in portraying, but instead are the medicine that can heal one of society's great lingering ills.

CHAPTER THREE

The Legal Process
in Custody Disputes

Over the years, many fathers have come to me because they are in the dark over the process of a custody dispute. They seem to be advised by their attorney about the next step, but have no idea about all the steps that will take place throughout the custody process and how each step leads to the next. This chapter will give you a quick summary of the overall process.

Summons and Temporary Restraining Order

Generally, a man knows when a divorce is imminent. There are fights with his wife. Their values are in conflict. They sleep apart and sex is infrequent or absent. She visits her parents' house frequently or on holidays by herself. She keeps financial matters to herself, including what her pay level is, her savings and checking account balances, and she files a separate income tax return. If these things are happening, a man should not be surprised if he receives a divorce summons from the sheriff. However, a man often receives the summons with a divorce petition with no prior warning, and this can come as a shock.

The shock can be even more overwhelming if she is a dirty fighter who also petitions the court for an *ex parte* restraining order, which says that her husband has abused her and she fears for her safety. The order bars the husband from entering his own home, even to get his wallet, money, personal effects, clothes, or credit cards. Some lawyers and their female clients deceitfully plan this initial move as a first-round knockout blow. One thing you can be sure of is that this kind of initial attack signals a nasty divorce, so plan accordingly from the start. You will need an experienced, firm, no-nonsense attorney to counter such an aggressive opening move.

Response to a Summons

One person begins the divorce process by hiring an attorney who prepares a summons, notice, order to show cause, and the divorce petition itself. The person who initiates the filing is called the *petitioner*. The person being served is called the *respondent*. A case number and the name of the trial judge will be on the papers, which are served to the respondent by the sheriff.

After receiving the petition, the respondent (generally, you) is given notice that he has twenty days to respond. A response can be very short, such as merely affirming or denying the allegations in the complaint. However, if the initial papers include an order to show cause, then you must begin to prepare immediately. A common problem for men is that women are the petitioners in two-thirds of the cases. Even if the marriage has not been going well, it is still a shock to have the sheriff arrive at your door or at work and serve you legal papers informing you that your spouse is divorcing you.

Finding an Attorney and the Initial Hearing

Many men remain in denial for days after receiving the summons and filing for divorce, delaying the process of finding legal help. They put off finding a fathers' rights group or an attorney. Finally, a few days before their initial temporary hearing, they begin to call around to find an attorney and, to their surprise, find that many attorneys are busy and fail to return their phone calls promptly. In panic, they proceed to call other attorneys randomly from the yellow pages. They often end up hiring any lawyer who will see them, with no knowledge of the lawyer's reputation or experience. Finding an attorney only a few days before the end of the twenty-day response limit is not automatically a disaster, unless there is also a petition for an *order to show cause*, which results in an imminent hearing. In this book, an important chapter concerns the initial hearing before a family court commissioner. Although this initial temporary hearing is one of the most important events in a custody dispute, few fathers and attorneys prepare adequately for it.

The initial court hearing determines who will live in the house, who will get legal and physical placement of the children, and how much time each parent will have with the children. This hearing also freezes the ability of each party to create new debt or irresponsibly dispose of assets, sets maintenance and child-support payments, and imposes any other initial remedies needed to avoid abuses. Any *ex parte* restraining order will be dealt with at this time. The order from this initial hearing seems unlikely to change substantially, once in place.

De Novo Hearings

If you are unhappy with the results of a hearing before the family court commissioner, you are entitled to a *de novo* hearing. This is a hearing in front of the judge to which the case is assigned. A *de novo* is to be heard without prejudice from the temporary hearing that was held previously by the court commissioner. However, lawyers often fail to alert their clients to the option of a *de novo* hearing. They tell their clients that they could lose more, even though a client may clearly be unhappy with the result of the previous hearing in front of the court commissioner. A father has only ten or fifteen days after the court commissioner's hearing to ask for a *de novo* by the judge. (Actual time varies; check your local rule.) One of the advantages of a *de novo* hearing is that you will previously have heard the positions taken by your ex wife, and will be able to address these positions in the *de novo* hearing. Significant planning can take place between the initial hearing before the family court commissioner and the *de novo* hearing that could lead to a reversal of the earlier decision.

Mediation

When there are disputes over custody, each party will be ordered to go to mediation. Most counties in Wisconsin now have family court counseling services that provide the mediation services that are required by law. There is a $200 mandatory fee ordered by statute, which normally is shared equally by husband and wife. Any party can end mediation by going to one session and declaring the process a failure. By going to one session they will have fulfilled the statutory requirement. If the parties seem to show that they are capable of coming to some conclusions without extended litigation, a family court counselor will work with them to find a stipulated settlement (one agreed to by both parties). If there seems to be no promise of reaching a stipulated settlement after two or three sessions, the family court counselor will withdraw..

Appointment of a Guardian *ad Litem*

If mediation appears unable to accomplish a voluntary agreement in a custody dispute, the court will appoint a guardian *ad litem* (GAL), an attorney to represent the best interests of the child. Be aware that the GAL does not technically represent the child, but the child's best interest. This is one of the inherent conflicts of interest that exist in family law. GALs are semi-autonomous and can abuse their power. They can cause harm to all parties and substantially increase legal fees. Often, they are inexperienced young attorneys who have not learned the complexities of family law, custody, or complicated divorces. Some attorneys have adopted the GAL role as a kind of specialty. They often think like social workers and can be as abusive and aggressive as social workers are with welfare families. It is virtually impossible to get rid of a GAL, once appointed by the court. Be careful, because they have the legal power to make your life difficult.

Family Study

In the next step, the family court counselor will begin a family study to determine who is the better parent to be given permanent physical placement of the child or children. The court counselor and GAL often work as a team in this effort. If one parent has accused the other parent of having special problems such as mental defect, alcohol or drug problems, a proneness to violence, or simply a lack of parenting skills, the court will order psychological tests for each party, including the child. Generally, the family court counselor will develop a family history, which will also be used in the study. Each party is asked to name family and friends who can attest to their personal and parenting skills. This is a strongly adversarial stage that can bring out the worst in people.

One must be careful with family court counselors and GALs, since they will work together to recommend to the court who gets custody. In about 90 percent of cases, the court follows their recommendation. With one lazy male judge in Dane County, a trial is virtually useless because he only wants to hear cases that he does not have to judge. Some judges seem to consider only the recommendation of the family court counselor and GAL. Many judges dislike even being assigned these cases. As a father, you must be careful in how you relate to these people, since they are able to play God in your life and determine your future as a parent.

The Recommendation

After the psychologist has done an evaluation, the interviews of all parties are finished, questionnaires from family and friends on the parenting skills of each parent are received, and any other pertinent data given to the court counselor and GAL have been gathered, they develop a recommendation. Normally, the court counselor and GAL work together to develop a common recommendation, but occasionally they each make a separate conclusion about the parents. A split recommendation is likely to result in a trial.

Pressure to Settle

After a recommendation has been decided, it is written up and sent to all parties. Given the high number of judges who follow the recommendation by the family court counselor and GAL, the parties are under considerable pressure to stipulate. The family court counselor and GAL will generally start to pressure and even threaten the parent who, on their recommendation, will get less visitation time and lose custody. They often go after the man, because he is usually more flexible. They will also pressure him to give up other rights. This is the time when a man's own lawyer sometimes betrays him, telling him that this is the best deal he can expect to get, or that the consequences of not accepting this bad deal will lead to an even worse one. This is an important moment to recall "the line in the sand" that a father has developed at the beginning of the divorce process.

The truth is that the court has difficulty in forcing a father to accept a custody agreement that he is firm in not accepting. They know this! But—you are scared! Your children are the high stakes in this game of brinkmanship; you do not want to lose them.

At this time, you should know that their worst nightmare is a firm and determined man who rejects any attempt to destroy his role as father, and who will litigate for ten years to preserve it, if necessary.

Determined fathers who draw the line in the sand, who are willing to litigate, and who won't give up, are most difficult to deal with. All parties know that the best-interest-of-the-child standard is ambiguous and without objective standard. No party using this standard wants to be held accountable for their recommendations, as they have no idea what the future might bring. They are merely making a guess, and they know it. One judge in Wisconsin stated from the bench, "You fathers who want custody are a real pain in the ass." We can guess where his gender bias lies.

The Trial

If the cajoling and pressure from the GAL and the family court counselor fail, the last process is to go to trial. Only a few percent of cases actually go to trial. Most people are exhausted and financially broken from attorney fees after a year or two of custody litigation. Most cannot cope with the stress. But a day or two before trial, all the attorneys, including your own, will again try to get the case stipulated. The GAL, court counselor, or psychologist will again try a combination of persuasion and threats to get the parties to agree to a stipulation. The most pressure is always on the party who is on the short end of the recommendation that will be made to the court. This makes sense, because once the professionals have decided who will get primary custody, they can hardly reverse themselves. Consequently, even on smaller remaining issues they will pressure the prospective loser (father) to give up even more of his rights, essentially rubbing salt in his wounds. They will continue to assert pressure right up to entering the courtroom for the trial.

As a side note, several years ago, I had a lunch meeting with

Judges Moria Krueger, Jack Aulik, and Robert Pekowsky in Dane County. I accused the judges of gender bias, using the argument that mothers get primary physical placement of the children in 90 percent of all cases. They reminded me that fathers stipulate in most cases and that fathers should give the judges a chance to make fair decisions. Their conversation seemed to hint that fathers might do much better by going to trial than by stipulating to unfair and harmful conditions

It takes a man with an intelligent lawyer and a strong constitution to withstand these pressures and to go into court and still win. The fear and stress are overwhelming. They eat away at the strongest of us. But this is where having the stamina of a marathon runner is essential.

The trial ends the case for many people. Many judges are fair, but with a recommendation against a party, it is difficult to prevail in court. Good judges recognize that their job calls for the judgment of Solomon when it comes to custody decisions. Smart judges recognize that if the case has gone this far, it may never go away. Court-imposed decisions have high return rates. Good judges may give concessions to the non-custodial parent, hoping to mitigate further litigation. Judges know that cases decided by trial are likely to come back to them over and over again, unlike custody disputes settled by stipulation

The best advice is to put your energy into prevailing in the trial court without recourse to the appeals court. The appeals court offers only an outside chance for you to become a winner in divorce.

Appealing the Decision

When a father gets a decision by the trial court that is clearly out of line with the statutes, or where there is abuse of the court's discretion, there is the possibility of an appeal. In Wisconsin, every party has the right to have the trial court's decision reviewed by the court of appeals. Normally, this costs about $3,500. In family law appeals, the court of appeals finds error in about half of the cases. This is not surprising, given the lack of objectivity in the whole process, from the best-interest-of-the-child standard to the personal agendas of court counselors and GALs, the gender bias permeating the system, and the inability of anyone to favor one loving parent over another loving parent within Wisconsin's adversarial system. However, even though the appeals court finds high rates of error in family law cases, only rarely is the original finding regarding primary physical placement remanded back for review.

The best advice is to put your energy into prevailing in the trial court without recourse to the appeals court. The appeals court offers only an outside chance for you to become a winner in divorce.

CHAPTER FOUR

How to Choose an Attorney

C*hoosing a divorce attorney may be one of the most important decisions you make in your lifetime.*
This choice is difficult because it is an experience that you, hopefully, will make only once in your life. The stakes are high. Due to gender bias favoring mothers, wide discretion given to the court, the best-interest-of-the-child standard, the primary placement standard, and an adversarial system, parents are necessarily pitted against each other in a "winner takes all" jackpot of possessing the child and receiving child-support payments.

The adversarial system in a child custody suit promotes parents' fighting over their children as if the children were property to be divided. The winner remains a fully empowered parent who can expect a monthly check for up to eighteen years and does not have to account for how it is spent. The loser (the father) becomes an Uncle Wallet, a "Disneyland dad" who visits his child when the custodial parent thinks visitation is "reasonable." The loser essentially loses most parental liberty and constitutional rights. The loser becomes a non-parent and suffers socially and emotionally from being disenfranchised.

The studies are clear! Children raised in families headed by single mothers suffer enormously: higher rates of suicide, alcoholism, and mental health disorders; poverty and all its concurrent effects; higher rates of teenage pregnancy and juvenile delinquency; lower grades in school; and higher rates of incarceration, in which prisons attempt to perform one of the roles specific to fathers. These are the consequences for children raised without fathers!

Most people find an attorney by looking through the yellow pages and finding a nice name, others by seeking advice from a casual friend. Chief Justice Warren Burger, addressing the American Bar Association, stated a few years ago that 90 percent of attorneys are incompetent. We know that only a few attorneys are competent to make a father a winner in adversarial family courts. Even fewer attorneys are qualified or capable of representing fathers. It is wholly a different experience to represent a father than a mother in our court system. Because of gender bias there is a presumption that a mother is a competent parent, while fathers are deemed incompetent to raise children, especially when the children are young or female.

Choosing a Competent Attorney

Most attorneys are incompetent in family law. It is your job to find a competent attorney.

How does one find a competent attorney? Who knows who the competent ones are? Judges don't tell, although they often know. Other attorneys, who keep losing to successful attorneys, also know, but are unlikely to tell you, else you would not hire them. Wisconsin Fathers for Children and Families, a men's group, knows a few good attorneys whom they recommend to their members.

Immediately upon receiving legal notice, the first step is to decide what you want or what it means for you to win. Then, with these preliminary goals, begin your search to find a competent attorney. Don't be pressured into hiring the first attorney with whom you meet.

What if you are trying to find an attorney in your town, but don't know any? How do you do it?

Go shopping. Get a list of three to five recommended attorneys. Your first list can be made by asking some people who have prevailed in custody matters, or from recommendations from fathers' rights groups, or references from an attorney you might know personally.

Call these prospective attorneys and set up an interview with each of them. Each interview should last from one-half hour to one hour, and should cost you nothing. Check beforehand to see if the initial interview is free; if it is not, then cross that attorney off your list. Develop a list of pertinent questions that will allow you to judge whether this attorney will actually represent you well. Your interview of the attorney is exploratory; make it clear that you will not be hiring him or her on the spot. After interviewing all five attorneys, evaluate them on how they meet your objectives for winning. Take some time to consider how you feel about each attorney as a person. Give this considerable weight. Ask yourself whether this attorney will be a good team member with you,so that your energies will be synchronistic. Ask the attorney for references. Then check out the references and ask others what they know about your potential choice before you make a final decision.

Checklist for Finding an Attorney

The best attorney will be legally competent, moral, humane, experienced in family law, firm but fair, anti-confrontational but tenacious (with your adversary) if necessary, dedicated to representing you, willing to allow you to make the decisions about the case for which you may have to pay a lifetime of consequences, empathetic, have good negotiating skills, and be connected (in good standing) to the child custody bureaucracy in the courthouse. The following is a checklist of some measures by which to judge an attorney.

1. Does the attorney advocate shared parenting?

2. Will the attorney continue to represent you zealously once your money has run out?

3. Does the attorney understand gender bias against fathers in the courts?

4. Will the attorney represent you and consider your children only secondarily? (The children will be represented by a guardian *ad litem*.)

5. Does the attorney know the judges, court commissioners and counselors, and the professional guardians *ad litem*? Does she know how they operate and what their values are?

6. Does the attorney discuss the options for your consideration or does he talk down to you?

7. Does the attorney listen? Is she attentive? Is she courteous, not interrupting you while you are speaking?

8. Does the attorney show a sincere interest in your case?

9. Does the attorney suggest non-adversarial approaches to winning the case without compromising what it means for you to win? This is a high priority item.

10. Are the fees fair and reasonable?

11. Does the attorney have a caseload that allows him to have sufficient time and energy to represent you reasonably?

12. Has the attorney taken many custody cases to trial? How many were successful?

13. Will the attorney provide you with references from clients whom she has taken to trial successfully or with failure? Why was there failure?

14. Do you have a gut-level feeling that this attorney will work with you, not exploit your vulnerability and fear, and allow you to be a partner in your case?

15. Will the attorney sign an agreement spelling out the rules by which you engage him and the agreed-upon fee structure for various services?

Yes, these are many qualifications and they can eliminate most attorneys. That's good, because you need only one attorney—the *best* attorney. If your custody case goes to trial you may well spend $8–20,000. You and your children deserve the best. For many men this sum of money will represent all their remaining net assets. It took years for you to save this money, so spend it intelligently. Your children are worth it!

Interviewing for an Attorney

An interview allows you to get a sense of whether this is a person with whom you can form an effective team. It allows you to get direct knowledge about the attorney's knowledge and experience. An interview will allow you to feel in control and develop confidence.

*You hire an attorney to give you counsel, not to make your case decisions for you. You must make it clear that **you** will make the decisions, because **you're** the only one who has to live with the consequences.*

The attorney will be paid and long gone while you have to live with the long-term outcome of this case. The attorney's role is to counsel you, listen, and present options—but *you must remain in control of your case.* The following are some key questions to ask when interviewing an attorney:

1. Where did you go to school? What did you specialize in?

2. How much of your practice is in family law? How many years have you practiced family law?

3. How many custody cases have you taken to trial? How many of those have you won?

4. Who do you consider the toughest attorneys to confront? Why? What is your strategy in prevailing over them?

5. Will you act as a mediator?

6. What is your view regarding the first hearing with the court commissioner?

7. Do you recommend arbitration?

8. What is your knowledge in child psychology, marital relations, and negotiations?

9. Do you know the specific judge assigned to this case and what his attitudes are concerning father custody?

10. What is your attitude toward shared parenting and joint custody?

11. How will you work with family therapists and mediators to reach a settlement?

12. Are you divorced? Who has custody? Who was your attorney? How was the case settled?

13. What are your fees? Fees for research? Fees for letters or phone calls? Terms for payment? What will you do if I run out of money?

14. What would your strategy be in my case?

15. Will you be personally handling all aspects of my case?

16. What is the range of the costs for this litigation from start to finish?

17. If you (the attorney) were getting divorced, which three attorneys would you consider to represent you? Why? (See whether these other attorneys turn up on your list; if so, consider interviewing them).

18. What special attributes do you believe that fathers offer in parenting children?

19. What is your usual strategy in representing fathers?

20. What is your advice in dealing with guardians *ad litem* and social workers?

21. Will you sign a client-attorney agreement?

It would take hours to answer all the above questions. Choose those which you believe are most relevant in your case, and *don't be afraid to ask!*

Attorney Fees

Everyone who performs a service deserves just compensation for their labors. While the term "just" is open to honest debate, in this context it refers to the billing of attorney hours at a reasonable market rate for hours of work diligently performed. Some tips:

1. Agree on an hourly rate that will be fixed throughout this action. A typical rate in the Madison area is presently $100–$175 per hour. Expensive attorneys are not necessarily good or effective attorneys. Conversely, inexpensive attorneys are not necessarily bad or ineffective.

2. Avoid flat-fee arrangements. No custody case can be accurately estimated. If underestimated, a low flat fee will encourage insufficient attention to your case when you most need high diligence and interest. Also, if you should have to dismiss your attorney in mid-action, you may encounter a crisis over fees already paid.

3. Avoid giving large retainers. The retainer should fit the circumstances. Evaluate how long the case may take and negotiate a retainer accordingly.

4. Do not reveal your assets before deciding on a fee structure. Some attorneys unscrupulously charge a rate according to what they believe you can pay.

5. Get quotes for the following services: research; telephone calls; office time; travel fees; court appearances; photocopies; secretarial time; law clerk hourly rates.

6. Billing should be monthly with detailed descriptions of services in tenths of an hour. Net 30–45 days. If you do not have much money, negotiate terms for time payments.

7. All legal services are negotiable. Negotiate even if you are impressed with the attorney, but do not nickel and dime over rates. Be reasonable in your negotiations; it will earn your attorney's respect.

8. Put your fees into an agreement (see page 00) which both attorney and client will sign.

Attorney Control

Many fathers lose custody cases because their attorneys take control of their case and negotiate away what the father has set as his goals for winning.

It is obvious that when you hire a person with specialized skills, you respect their advice. But remember, this custody case is *your* case; you pay all the consequences. Your attorney should present you with options and the probable consequences of those options. However, it is your prerogative to take the option which best secures your interests. Your attorney has an ethical responsibility to promote your interests zealously, unless you request something illegal. Do not let your attorney become your boss. Do not let her berate you or act in a paternalistic way. The consequences of losing your children are too great for you to lose control of your case. Here are some guidelines:

1. Consider taping all meetings and conversations. This will give you the opportunity to review your conversations and options discussed.

2. Keep a diary of all important conversations, ideas, and objectives.

3. Keep a diary of all contacts with your children, wife, and guardian *ad litem.* Tape all conversations with them even if they are unaware that you are taping. It is legal to tape conversations in which you are a party.

4. Keep working on developing a partnership relationship with your attorney, so that the skills of each of you can complement each other and form a more effective team from the start.

5. Identify all the steps in the legal proceedings and set a target date for accomplishing each step.

6. Check at least one week ahead to verify that your attorney has prepared or will be preparing for any court or legal pro-

ceedings. Ask her what could go wrong and prepare for that. Always be prepared for both the expected and the unexpected.

7. From the start make it clear to your attorney that she may not negotiate any settlement without you. Have the attorney bring options for a resolution to you without having made any commitments. Only *you* should make the commitments.

8. Check with your father's rights organization before accepting options to resolve cases. Many of their members have paid high prices for stipulating to poor conditions. Many fathers are sadder but wiser regarding stipulations and their consequences.

9. Instruct your attorney that she may not attend an in-chamber hearing of attorneys and the judge without your presence and participation. Often, repugnant deals are made there, and you will be the bad guy if you do not accept them.

10. Insist that your attorney give you copies of all items that are placed into your file. Your own file should at all times be a duplicate of your attorney's file. In this way you will never be in a position in which your attorney attempts to delay turning over your file if you have a billing dispute, or should you want to dismiss her.

11. Instruct your attorney that only you may sign stipulated agreements or significant court papers that have significant future consequences.

Danger Signals

Whenever you get a feeling that your attorney is working against you, instead of with you, accept that as a clear danger signal. Give credence to this feeling, because most often it is accurate. Sensing danger signals is important because it means your whole case could be in jeopardy. Look out for the following danger signals:

1. Your attorney fails to promptly return your calls, gives ambiguous or rambling responses to questions, or always

seems to be busy.

2. Your attorney says, "Don't worry, this is only a temporary hearing." (That could, in itself, be cause for immediate dismissal of that attorney.)

3. Your attorney talks down to you or tries to run your case.

4. Your attorney is not listening to you or is diverting you from your original goals of what it means for you to win.

5. Your attorney gives pat answers and uses phrases such as, "Trust me," or "This is how it works," or "You can live with this."

6. Your attorney threatens you by saying he will quit your case if you will not do it his way. This is not to suggest that you should not carefully consider your attorney's counsel (otherwise why would you pay so much money for his expert advice?).

7. Your attorney fails to follow your written agreement. Tell him promptly in writing of this failure.

8. Your attorney is not providing you with a copy of your file, or it is not promptly and completely updated.

9. Your attorney has negotiated on your behalf, met with the opposing attorney, attended a formal or informal hearing in chambers, or entered into an agreement or stipulation when you were not present.

10. Your attorney has not insisted that a court reporter be present for a hearing of record.

11. Your attorney has failed to offer you prompt, detailed explanations or options for your consideration and decision.

12. Your attorney appears to be unprepared for your meetings or for any informal or formal hearing. An experienced attorney should be able to anticipate many situations that would escape an inexperienced attorney.

13. Your attorney seems to be impatient with you or your goals of what it means for you to win and remain a parenting father.

14. Your attorney has failed to research an issue or has no idea how he could prevail on an issue. Your attorney lacks ingenuity.

15. Your attorney suggests settling before trial because it's "the best you can do," or, worse, wants to settle because you have run out of money. This happens often, but is rarely acknowledged.

16. Your attorney's attitude seems to be one of grudging tolerance, impatience, laziness, or overconfidence. Anything can happen in a courtroom, especially if the judge has had a personal marital spat that morning. There is no substitute for preparation, especially preparation for the unexpected.

17. Your attorney keeps acting like a guardian *ad litem*, talking about the best interests of your children, instead of representing your interests. This is a matter of degree, but an attorney who acts like a social worker for your children can harm you irreparably.

18. You *feel* your attorney is manipulating or controlling you and your case, leading to a detrimental outcome.

Any one of these may be sufficient reason to dismiss your attorney. Remember, however, that these are general points for consideration, that attorneys are only human, and that they have communication problems and make mistakes like everybody else. If you notice any of the above warning signs, talk about them immediately with your attorney. Don't wait, and don't let resentments or doubts fester within yourself, or allow your case to be harmed by them.

Remember, you are ultimately in charge of your case and you must pay all the consequences of your attorney's mistakes or failures, as well as your own.

Dismissing Your Attorney

If you believe your attorney is incompetent or negligent in representing you, act firmly and shrewdly. Gather data:

1. Keep tapes of conversations.

2. Begin documentation of what the attorney is doing wrong or in disregard of your agreement.

3. Confront your attorney with data that may be cause for her dismissal.

4. If you are *sure* that your attorney has been incompetent, demand a return of your retainer and any billed fees associated with incompetence or lack of adequate counsel.

5. Demand your file or a copy of it.

6. Inform the court that you have dismissed your attorney.

7. If you believe the attorney's behavior is unethical, report her to the Board of Attorney Professional Responsibility and to the judge assigned to your case. Return of retainer or fees could become an issue. Consider civil action.

8. Your attorney cannot quit your case without your prior permission. If she wants to quit the case, demand that she return all fees. Allow the attorney to quit only if it is in your best interest. Consider a malpractice civil suit against any attorney who attempts to quit without a good or ethical reason. Don't underestimate your power. A client can be very dangerous to an attorney in a situation such as this, and every attorney knows it.

Your relationship with your attorney should not be adversarial, but should it become so, protect your case no matter what happens to your attorney. It's your ex-spouse who is your primary adversary. Don't lose sight of the big picture.

A Wisconsin Supreme Court justice has stated that at least some of the bias against fathers in family courts is due to the poor performance of their attorneys. The justice has recommended that fathers direct their attorneys to represent what they wish from the family law dispute. Numerous gender-bias task force reports from around the country recognize that fathers' lawyers often push them into stipulated agreements that result in far less than they would get had the father gone to trial.

The purpose of this chapter is not to encourage an adversarial relationship with your attorney. It is to examine what you want and need as a father who has a disadvantage in family courts, and how to get it. Its purpose is to help you set ground rules and understandings with an attorney so that you will be able to combine your skills and energy in prevailing in your case. This chapter is a guideline to give you a more equal footing in your negotiations in finding the right attorney for you. *It is meant to help you win!*

Do not walk into an attorney's office with this chapter. It is for you, not for your prospective attorney. Only the following "Client-Attorney Agreement," is meant for you to share with your attorney.

Good luck in your desire to remain a parenting father!

CLIENT-ATTORNEY AGREEMENT
Date _____

_____ agrees to act as legal counsel for _____
Attorney   Client

in Family Law Case Number _____
subject to the following agreements and conditions:

1. While the attorney is legal counsel, she is not authorized to have power of attorney. The attorney has no authority to enter into any agreements, court orders, or stipulations unless approved and authorized by the client in advance. Without such authorization, it is agreed that only the client shall approve and sign all such agreements.
2. The client shall be present at all negotiations, conferences, formal and informal hearings, court appearances, and the like in or out of chambers and all court appearances.
3. All negotiations, conferences, and informal hearings will be tape recorded; all formal hearings, court appearances, or meetings of record shall have a court reporter present.
4. The client shall at any time be provided with the original court file and a copy for any other attorney. The client will receive prompt copies of all pleadings, correspondence, and other relevant documents, sent or received.
5. The client will at all times have access to the attorney's file, including notes, and shall have the right to copy the same.
6. All negotiation proposals, calls, and correspondence received shall be promptly relayed to the client. Attorney will keep the client fully and completely informed at all times.
7. Services will be billed monthly and will include a detailed description of all billed hours to the tenth of an hour.
8. All modifications to this agreement will be in writing.
9. Fees are as follows:
   a. Hourly fee for attorneys time   _____
   b. Hourly fee for law clerk   _____
   c. Hourly fee for secretarial services _____
   d. Per copy charge for copies   _____
   e. Per page copy for transcripts   _____
   f. Telephone charges per unit   _____
   g. Hourly fee for research   _____
   h. Hourly fee for travel   _____
   i. Hourly fee for court appearances _____

All spaces above should be filled in with dollar amounts, units, or marked no charge.

Signed and agreed to,

_____   _____
Attorney   Date   Client   Date

CHAPTER FIVE

The Importance of the First Hearing

A Temporary Order provides a structure for the dissolving of a marital relationship. For spouses who cannot, on their own, create order in their post-separation lives, a Temporary Order hearing before a Family Court Commissioner is often necessary. For spouses who are able to plan cooperatively for their future, a hearing is unnecessary: Until they are divorced they can function without a Court Order outlining their rights and responsibilities, or they may "stipulate" to the entry of an Order adopting their plan for handling their affairs on a temporary basis.

Many attorneys file papers requesting a Temporary Order hearing at the time the divorce petition is filed. The advantage—and the disadvantage—of this strategy is that it catches the adverse party off-guard. Reeling from the recognition that divorce is inevitable, the spouse "served with papers" is likely to react with fear and defensiveness to being summoned to Court in a matter of days. (A "motion" for a Temporary Order hearing requires five days notice of a hearing date, excluding weekends and holidays. An "Order to Show Cause" to appear for a hearing may require as little as 48 hours notice.) The spouse who files the divorce petition and requests the hearing is in the driver's seat, having already retained an attorney and charted the course of the proceeding.

Many attorneys choose to take one step at a time and refrain from scheduling a hearing date at the commencement of the proceeding, believing that the spouses may be able to work out an arrangement with the assistance of their counsel if hostilities are downplayed and cooperation is fostered. A hearing can be scheduled at a later date if negotiations prove futile, but any short-term advantage gained by rushing to the courthouse may engender such ill will that the family suffers a long-term loss.

Before requesting a Temporary Order hearing, an attorney should determine that the hearing is necessary by analyzing the client's marital history, family relationships, financial circumstances, and likelihood of success. The attorney should also clarify for the client the anticipated expense for taking the case to Court. (Negotiating is usually less expensive than litigating.) If the client is certain that legal custody of children (decision-making authority) or physical placement (where children live) will be contested, the attorney should request the appointment of a guardian *ad litem* prior to the hearing. A guardian *ad litem* is a Court-appointed attorney whose fees are paid by both parents and who represents "the best interests of the children." The guardian *ad litem* will need sufficient time to meet the parents and children to prepare an argument for the hearing. If the case presents complex financial issues, the attorney requesting the hearing must take sufficient time to understand those issues well enough to explain them to the Family Court Commissioner.

The spouse receiving notice that a hearing has been scheduled may request postponement of the hearing to afford time for selection of an attorney, negotiation, or preparation. Postponements are granted routinely. If a Temporary Order hearing is unavoidable, a spouse is well advised to appear with counsel if the other spouse is represented. The respondent's counsel should request appointment of a guardian *ad litem* if the petitioner's counsel has not done so. The respondent's counsel must become intimately acquainted with the client's case, as well, to forecast the likelihood of success at the hearing. The danger for each client is the attorney's failure to ask the right questions during client interviews—or the client's lack of perception as to the true nature of the marital relationship. With the wrong slant on the case, the attorney can waste precious funds and time in pursuit of unattainable goals.

The Commissioner serves as the gate-keeper to the Court system for divorcing couples, presiding over Temporary Order hearings and pre-trial conferences and certifying the case for final hearing. The Commissioner's office will schedule the Temporary Order hearing for the amount of time requested by the moving party—from a minimum of 40 minutes to a maximum of several hours. Counsel requesting the hearing must gauge the amount of time required for the Commissioner to consider carefully all issues in dispute, or face a bifurcated hearing. If the hearing is continued to another date, the Commissioner must rely on notes to refresh the recollection of the evidence presented initially.

Hearing procedures vary from county to county. In Dane County, Wisconsin, the process is informal (the Commissioner hears "offers of proof" of how the parties would testify under oath) or formal (the Commissioner hears "sworn" testimony of the parties), at the option of the parties or their counsel. In other counties, the Commissioner may prefer that counsel provide offers of proof, and the Commissioner may question the parties personally. Representation by a local attorney is preferred, not only because that attorney will be familiar with the practice in the county, but also because out-of-town counsel may charge fees for travel time.

Attorneys and clients should consider the case from the perspective of the presiding Family Court Commissioner. The Commissioner can rule only on the case as presented. *If attorneys do not present the facts of the case accurately, the Commissioner cannot be expected to issue rulings that fit the parties' circumstances.* To appear before the Commissioner unprepared is a waste of the client's money and the Commissioner's time, and an embarrassment for both attorney and client. The Commissioner is expected to rule on a wide variety of issues with no advance knowledge of the parties, since exhibits are rarely submitted prior to the hearing, and there is not much time for in-depth consideration of the facts presented. Consequently, the client's financial statement must be precise, and the presentation of the family dynamic must be clear and compelling. Attorneys may request that the Commissioner "take matters under advisement" and issue a decision at a later date, to afford the Commissioner time for reflection. Since the Commissioner is responding to the client's perceived need for immediate relief in scheduling the Temporary Order hearing, the Commissioner will invariably rule "from the bench."

The Commissioner is statutorily empowered to order temporary joint legal custody and will do so in most cases, unless there is evidence presented of spousal or child abuse. Presently, there is no statutory presumption in favor of joint physical custody. However, at the Temporary Order hearing the Commissioner will strive to maintain an equal balance of power with respect to decision-making for children, unless the evidence indicates that the children's best interests would not be well-served by this approach.

The guardian *ad litem*'s recommendation as to temporary physical placement will carry great weight. If a guardian *ad litem* does not appear at the hearing, the Commissioner will decide temporary physical placement based on the Commissioner's perception of the evidence presented regarding the family history of child-rearing. Upon request, the Commissioner will refer the parties to the county counseling service/human services department for mediation of their dispute and appoint a guardian *ad litem*. If mediation fails, an in-depth study of these issues will ensue.

The client who has not participated actively in child-rearing is at a significant disadvantage in proving at the Temporary Order hearing that the children will be best served by a dramatic shift in the family's pattern of care-taking. The spouses may have divided family responsibilities so that one spouse works while the other serves as the at-home parent. If that is the case, the Commissioner will try to avoid abrupt changes for the children, who are already suffering from the marital breakup. The Commissioner will be sensitive to the fragility of the family's financial circumstances at the early stages of divorce and will prefer that the higher income-earner continue to function in that capacity. The economic reality of the family's situation may militate against substantially equal periods of physical placement for the clients. Perhaps through the course of the divorce proceeding, the client may demonstrate that "it's a whole new ball game," that children of a non-intact family need both parents as equal caretakers, and that both parents must henceforth work full-time to support the family.

Usually, the Commissioner will apply the state guidelines for the determination of child support in light of the temporary determination of child placement. In allocating disposable income between the parties following the determination of child support, the Commissioner will consider the debts that must be paid in order to preserve the marital estate. The Commissioner may discern that income tax withholding can be revised to maximize available income. However, thorough analysis of the parties' tax status is not possible at the initial Temporary Order hearing, since the Commissioner cannot predict whether the parties will divorce in the current tax year. In ruling on a request for temporary maintenance, the Commissioner will consider each party's child-support obligation and responsibility for the payment of debts, in light of the prevailing concept that marriage is a partnership with each partner "owning" fifty percent of marital income (unless a premarital agreement dictates otherwise).

Ultimately, property division is the province of the Judge (unless the clients submit a stipulation dividing property by agreement). The Commissioner will rule on the temporary use of personal property and real estate and will issue Orders restraining the parties from selling, encumbering, or otherwise disposing of property while the divorce is pending, to preserve the marital estate until the final hearing.

Clients who are displeased with the Commissioner's rulings may seek a *"de novo* hearing" (a new hearing before the Judge to whom the case is assigned) by filing a request for hearing within a certain number of days of the Commissioner's decision. Legal fees generated by preparation for and attendance at the *de novo* hearing may exceed the amount charged the client for the Temporary Order hearing. In most counties, the Commissioner's ruling must be reduced to writing and is available to the Judge for review. Before requesting this hearing, it must be considered that the Judge presides over a variety of legal matters and may not be as expert in family law cases as the Commissioner. The Judge may give great weight to the Commissioner's decision, despite the fact that the hearing is intended to be "from the beginning." It is rare that *de novo* decisions are appealed to the Court of Appeals.

The importance of the Temporary Order hearing is that a new status quo will be created by the Commissioner's issuance of an Order based on the evidence presented. If the evidence is flawed due to faulty preparation, the Commissioner's Order will be poorly-designed for the family. Parents rearrange their lives and begin to conform to the dictates of the Order, by necessity. Children become accustomed to the custody/physical placement arrangement designed by the Order. By statute, the Temporary Order "may not have a binding effect on a final custody determination." (Section 767.23(1)(a), Stats.) However, swimming upstream is easier than overturning a Temporary Order adverse to the client on custody/physical placement issues.

If the case goes to a contested divorce hearing, Counsel will utilize the Temporary Order rulings to assist clients in analysis of the Judge's potential rulings. Particularly if the final hearing is scheduled many months after the Temporary Order hearing, the Judge may see little reason to interrupt the "new status quo." If the child-support/maintenance payer has adjusted his/her lifestyle to accommodate obligations set by the Temporary Order, the Judge may rule that the magnitude of such obligations is manageable by the payer. The parent whom the Commissioner has ordered to leave the family home rarely returns to residence there.

One should approach a Temporary Order hearing with extreme caution, armed with carefully prepared evidence, clear insight into what makes sense for the family, and the ability to distill the essential ingredients of a fair decision in the limited time available at the hearing.

CHAPTER SIX

Setting the Agenda: Establishing the Best Interest of the Child

Protecting Assets

Whether you are the petitioner or the respondent, you must do everything you can to *set the agenda* In the legal procedure.

At the outset of a divorce, the first agenda-setting issue is control of assets, documents, and the home. One of the advantages in planning and initiating the divorce is that you, as the petitioner, can set an agenda to control these from the very beginning. Once your agenda is set, the respondent can do little more than scurry, trying to catch up. If you are the petitioner, for instance, you can use your charge card to do some serious shopping, and the charges will become part of the marital debt before divorce proceedings begin. As the petitioner, you will cancel all credit cards on filing, so that the respondent will not be able to create new marital debt for which you might later be held accountable. As petitioner, you can guarantee that you will have cash available. You will take half the money out of your joint checking account, then open a checking account in your name only. Having access to cash is essential for paying an attorney's retainer fee. As the petitioner, you will make sure you have keys to all jointly-owned items, including the autos and vacation cottage. There are advantages in being the petitioner, if you expect custody to be contested.

Having control of important documents is also critical. Get possession of your children's and your own passports, birth certificates, social security cards, tax returns, business documents, bank statements, stock certificates, and any other pertinent documents or records needed to carry on after your spouse and you no longer live together. If you have a premarital agreement or any other stipulated document that will affect divorce or custody, make sure that you place these outside the reach of your spouse. Joint safe deposit boxes should be emptied and cleared of all documents and valuables, except for personal items that obviously belong to the other party. Make sure that all important mail will reach you; a post office box will guarantee that checks and documents come to you and you alone.

I am not recommending that you take any of the marital assets due your spouse. The move to take control of assets and documents is defensive in nature. It is to make sure that in the event that your spouse goes a little crazy on hearing that you want to divorce her, that you will have the things you need to function. It is difficult to get possession of most of the above items if they have been snatched away first by your spouse. Be ethical! Know what is yours and what is hers. Make sure that she gets what is hers, but be sure to protect what is yours.

If, on the other hand, you are the one who is served the divorce papers, make sure that you attend to the above issues *immediately*. Often, the petitioner has not considered all these items and there is hope that you will be able to get control of your property if you act without delay.

Leaving the Marital Home

Another pre-divorce agenda item is to make sure your spouse is the one who leaves the marital home. Often, the husband volunteers to move out because, still being psychologically married, he feels that he should continue to protect his wife. This sets up the man to be perceived as the one who abandons his home and children, even if his wife is the one initiating the divorce. The children will perceive the parent who has remained in the home as the faithful parent and the one who moved out as having abandoned them.

Defining the Best Interest of the Child

Earlier, we stated that there is no legal definition of "best interest of the child." This is a problem, because without an objective definition, innuendo and gender bias are likely to have a significant and irrational influence on your case. The current outmoded social perceptions of male and female roles are likely to be a subtle but powerful influence in custody cases. One's community and its influences affect a judge's perceptions, just as they do those of ordinary citizens, even though the judges' positions require them to be faithful to the statutes.

The current 2000 family-law reforms attempt to define more aspects of what is in a "child's best interest." These include items such as the presumption of joint legal custody, defining a physical placement standard, including further criteria for custody, and setting sanctions for violation of placement orders. However, be aware that some Family Court Counseling Services, such as that in Dane County, are following their own political and philosophical agendas, ignoring the policies as set forth in the statutes.

We know that the standard in Dane County is effectively different from that in Sauk County. We know that if you draw one judge in Rock County, you might be treated fairly as a father, while another judge is likely to award sole custody to the mother without just cause. In another Wisconsin county, the judge deciding between a mother and father seeking custody of their young children actually stated, "I've never seen a young calf run after a bull." This was all the proof he needed to rule that it was in the best interest of the child to be with the mother. Fortunately, most Wisconsin judges are more sophisticated than this judge. However, many judges still carry their own hidden biases.

Whoever sets the agenda determines the issues to be negotiated. One of the advantages to the person who psychologically divorces and legally initiates the divorce is the opportunity to develop a game plan. The initiator of the divorce does not formally have a legal advantage, but obtains an advantage by planning and developing the issues that influence the custody decision. By *investing substantial time and by preplanning*, the initiator of the divorce is able to set an agenda to which the other party must respond. In the process of responding, the other party is likely not to have the time or energy to initiate their own agenda. The initiator takes the offensive and often maintains it.

Dirty Fighting

The resolution of these issues can stay within the bounds of fair fighting or veer to dirty fighting. Both are effective. Dirty fighting includes getting Temporary Restraining Orders (TROs), unfairly professing a fear of the other person. Naturally, this is a tactic used most often by a woman. When divorce is imminent, it is normal for people to fight and feel threatened by each other. This does not imply that either party would physically harm the other. Judges, however, almost always grant a TRO in the name of taking the safest route. They would be blamed if, after denying a TRO, one party put the other into the hospital. The net effect of a judge's granting a TRO against the father is to deny him his home, assets, records, and access to his children.

Other forms of dirty fighting include false physical or sexual abuse accusations against one's spouse, stealing all liquid assets and records, secretly moving out with all the assets and the children—with or without leaving a forwarding address—or a combination of any of the above.

By using any of these tactics, a wife can not only effectively set the agenda but unilaterally put in place a new living arrangement which a father must then convince the court to alter. The obstacles to altering this arrangement can be overwhelming, if false accusations of physical or sexual abuse of the children is part of a wife's dirty agenda. Fathers have spent a year or more and thousands of dollars just trying to prove that they are "not guilty" of abuse accusations, falsely made, before even beginning to address routine custody issues.

Quiet Agendas

Wisconsin Sec. 767.24(5), Stats., spells out the "factors in custody and physical placement determinations." There is a list of "a" through "k." After much thoughtful analysis, father-rights leaders have come to the conclusion that most of the criteria are quietly ignored, and that "k" actually becomes the battleground for determinations of custody.

Item "k" reads, "Such other factors as the court may in each individual case determine to be relevant." The statutorily mandated specifics too often are given less weight or even ignored. Often, the court ignores the wishes of the child, or the effects upon the children upon being uprooted from their schools or community. "Best interest" often is perceived as the wishes of the parent who has effectively set the agenda for consideration, or the parent whom the family court counselor or guardian *ad litem* favors after a quick first impression.

The issue of setting the agenda in defining the best interest of the child can be spelled out by a few examples. Who is the nurturing parent—the one who teaches the child how to play football, teaches rules, teaches fairness and social interaction, or the parent who washes the child's dirty football uniform? Is it the farmer-father who tills the soil, plants the vegetable garden, and harvests the food that feeds his family who is nurturing, or the mother who cooks the meal for the children? Is the nurturing parent the father who, with his child, builds a tree house, a tire swing, and a soapbox racer for Cub Scouts, or the mother who pushes the child on the swing and takes him to his Cub Scout meeting?

Gender Bias

It is my contention that one of the greatest examples of gender bias in family law is the underlying assumption that the mother's traditional roles are considered to be nurturing, while the father's are ignored or perceived as unimportant. When we see dysfunctional children, we see children affected by a father's absence and lack of father nurturing. Often, I hear family court counselors, court commissioners, and judges using the traditional mother's role as the sole criterion in determining the best interest of the child for custody purposes. These role functions often will include who does the grocery shopping, who cooks, does the dishes, watches the children during the day, gives the children baths, takes the children to the dentist or the doctor, and goes to parent-teacher conferences. These most certainly are skills needed to nurture children, but are associated with the most traditional role model of mother as a stay-at-home wife. Using these criteria to form the hidden subjective agenda in defining the best interest of the child should give an advantage in most cases for mother custody. For this reason, the family law reforms of 2000 sought to purge gender bias from custody disputes.

An early agenda item that a father must overcome is his being absent from the home more often, since he more often contributes the majority of outside income used to support the family. The argument is used that the mother should get custody because this continues what she has been doing, and that the past family history should be a determinant of the custody decision.

Using Historical Roles as Criteria

A father must address the status quo argument for mother custody in two ways. First, he must argue that a divorce is a radical change of circumstances in which the voluntarily accepted roles of a mother and father within marriage are not the voluntarily accepted roles in divorce. A man who lives alone must cook, keep house, do laundry, etc. to carry out a normal mode of living. Even if a divorcing man had no children, his role would change, since these are the new tasks necessitated by changing circumstances. A mother who has had a traditional stay-at-home role as wife must now have a paying outside job in most cases, and this means that the more traditional roles which she played within the marriage will no longer be possible. The new working mother is more likely to buy frozen entrees, use child care, take the kids to fast food restaurants for supper, and have clothes cleaned at the dry cleaners or laundromat—much as the father is likely to do if he were to be named the custodial parent.

Simply put, a father must legally challenge any attempt to make custody decisions on the basis of past marital roles which are no longer possible after the radical changes necessitated by divorce. A father must legally challenge any attempt to use past role functions exclusively in determining custody, because this is a form of gender bias *and it is not permitted by law*.

Second, if the court is going to use past experience as a criterion for custody, a father should argue that since he has had physical placement time with his children every day of their lives that the court should order daily placement with him, using the same historical argument. A father should challenge the court to use the same historical criteria for both mother and father in placement or be accused of gender bias. This should almost always result in some form of shared parenting at divorce, since gender bias is against the law.

The traditional nurturing role of the mother is a fair area for evaluation in a custody decision. The problem is that the areas in which fathers nurture their children will not be considered seriously unless they are put forward as being just as important as the mother's role in determining custody. This can be a difficult challenge for a father. The new criteria for custody give consideration to the life-style changes that are adopted by a family when it splits into two units, necessitating role changes for both parents.

Father's Criteria List For Custody

I suggest that fathers develop a list of all the specific things they do in nurturing the development and care of their children. If this list is less than fifty items, go back and think of some more until the list is at least that long. After you have developed a thorough and complete list, ask for appointments with the guardian *ad litem* and with the court counselor. These should be two different appointments. You do not want a two-on-one situation.

At each of these meetings, discuss the criteria that each of them will use in determining their recommendations for physical placement. Ask them exactly what are the specific criteria that they will use in arriving at a recommendation. Finally, give them a copy of your list and ask them to consider not only the things that mom does, but also what dad does in nurturing the children.

Watch their reaction carefully to see if they are in sincere agreement with the criteria you have presented. Ask them to put in writing that they agree that your list is genuine and pertinent in determining the best interests of the children. If the guardian *ad litem* or the family court counselor seems luke-warm, or refuses your list, or is unwilling to put in writing that your list will be used equally as criteria for determining the best interest of the child, then it is time for your attorney to file a motion with the court asking the court to accept your list as criteria in determining the best interest of the child. This is an assertive legal move, as it forces the court to be on record as to the meaning of "best interest of the child" in your case.

Remember this: *If the best interest of the child is not defined, then it is likely to be based upon the unstated and gender-biased definition relating to the roles mothers have performed traditionally in marriage; it is likely to be based on the personal values and prejudices of the family court counselor and the guardian ad litem.* If you do not define "best interest of the child" in your specific case, then you will be forced to attempt to win custody based on your effort to "out-mother" mom. This is generally a losing game for fathers.

Parents Are the Only Guardians of the Children

A father has just as much right as a mother to determine what will be the best interest of his children. Either parent has a greater right to determine what are in the best interests of their children than a family court counselor or guardian *ad litem*. Do not be afraid to challenge either the family court counselor or the GAL in determining the criteria used for custody. *The guardian ad litem does not know your child, does not care for your child, and does not love your child.* The GAL and family court counselor have only one reason to be involved in your case, and that is because it is their job and they get paid for it. They are mercenaries placed by the law and the court into your life. If your children are sick, they will not take care of them. If your children need to be picked up from day care, they will not pick them up. If your children are hungry, they will not feed them.

Often, guardian *ad litems* are inexperienced young attorneys without a developed law practice. What the guardian *ad litem* will do is present you with bills for thousands of dollars in legal fees for representing your child's best interest, thus depriving your child of college education funds. This may seemed cynical, but it is the simple truth which no guardian *ad litem* can deny, when challenged. I'm not suggesting being combative with the GAL, just that you realize who they are and what their role is in your life and the lives of your children. The answer to custody surely flows logically from the criteria used in determining a recommendation for custody. Work hard to make sure your criteria for the best interest of the child are used in determining custody. Lose this battle and you will have more difficulty prevailing in the custody battle ahead.

When you set the agendas in a custody fight, the other person's energies become dissipated in defending against your agenda, and it is difficult for them to ever gain the offensive. The person who sets the agenda often gets much of what he wants.

CHAPTER SEVEN

Child Support

Parents are Responsible

Wisconsin statutes state that both parents are financially responsible for their children. Each parent is morally responsible to support their children. If parents won't take care of their children, who will? Welfare subsidizes while it entraps both mothers and children into a system that keeps them in poverty and steals human dignity.

Why is there so much resistance from non-custodial parents to pay child support? The answers are not difficult and are well known. Female supremacists and government bureaucrats have entered into an unholy alliance to create a system in which fathers are treated as wallets while being deprived of parenting rights. Fathers resent becoming "Uncle Daddy" to their children.

Why Do Fathers Resist Paying?

Why is it that parents, during marriage, are willing to work themselves to death, taking awful jobs, to support their families, yet after divorce their attitudes change? At a large gathering, I once asked a group of fathers how many resented paying child support, and most hands went up. I then asked the group how many would resent paying court-ordered support if they knew with certainty that their child-support dollars would go exclusively to their children, and no hands went up. I continued by asking how many would pay even more child support than was ordered if there were certainty that it would go to their children and about a fourth of the hands went up.

From this experience, I have learned that one of the primary reasons that non-custodial parents resent paying child support is the lack of *accountability* for use of their hard-earned money. The State of Wisconsin does not care about accountability for child support paid by non-custodial parents. However, if a family has a foster child and they receive state funds, the state asks for the family to fill out a form twice a year, accounting for the funds which they spend on behalf of the foster child.

We often hear the term "deadbeat dads." The term is sexist, insofar as most fathers pay their child support as ordered by the court. It is sexist in that women who are non-custodial parents have a far lower rate of compliance in paying child support than fathers. The U.S. Census Bureau numbers are as follows, for dads: 50 percent pay in full as ordered; 25 percent pay part as ordered; and 25 percent do not pay. But 14 percent of the 25 percent of "deadbeat" dads are not *deadbeat* but actually *dead*. Yes, they have died, but their child-support record is still carried on the books.

However, fathers are excellent payers when compared to mothers. Only about 25 percent of mothers pay support when ordered to do so. These percentages regarding fathers are skewed, in that they were compiled by asking women only about the payment of child support by fathers. When the male payer was asked about his payment of child support, compliance numbers increased substantially.

When fathers have primary physical placement, many do

not ask for child support. Men take pride in self-reliance and are not comfortable asking for handouts. Not only do custodial mothers not have any accountability for child support which they receive, it is questionable how much they voluntarily contribute to the daily needs of their children. WDW 40, the rule that interprets Wisconsin's child-support statute, states that it is presumed that the parent who has primary physical placement will share their income with the children. So, not only is there no accountability for the money that the father pays a mother in child support, there is no accountability that she will spend any of *her* earnings on the children. When we keep reading about cases in which mothers spend child support funds on new cars, alcohol, drugs, a non-working live-in boyfriend, or additional children, it is no wonder that fathers resent paying child support.

A few years back, there were national headlines about a father who owed more than $550,000 in child support. He was called America's number one deadbeat dad. The press in their usual ignorance did not think to ask just how was it possible that any child could use or need more than a half million dollars to live well. The mother remarried into wealth, yet on television berated the father and proclaimed how happy she was that he had been jailed. The message to every father was that child support is the new alimony. Too often, child support has been the means of transferring income from one parent to the other after the marriage contract has been nullified. This makes fathers cynical and destroys the credibility of the state. Ultimately, the state harms children when it fails to develop systems of accountability for child support.

Child support is no small amount. If you did not pay child support, you could be investing that sum of money to earn a fair rate of return compounded annually. At 8 percent compound interest per year, $100 per week payment over ten years would yield a return of $112,000, and over 15 years a $247,000 return. A $150 per week child-support payment accumulate $57,000 over 5 years, $235,000 over 10 years, and $453,000 over 17 years. For most fathers, this is big money, making it well worth the effort to litigate in court until the other person is exhausted, going the route through the appeals court, if necessary. If you are a conscientious and persistent litigator, everybody will try to avoid further rounds of legal sparring with you. This could tilt any post-divorce hearings your way.

Who Pays and Who Doesn't Pay

Statistical profiles demonstrate that fathers who have access to their children pay child support at overwhelmingly high rates. The U.S Census Bureau found that 92 percent of fathers who had joint physical placement paid their child support, and that 75 percent of fathers who had any placement time with their children paid. It is only logical that when fathers can actually parent their child, they remain emotionally attached. Fathers pay even without financial accountability when they can be intimately involved in their children's lives.

The number-one reason why fathers did not pay child support, according to an Arizona study, is that the fathers had *lost their jobs*. The second reason was that they did not have *access to their children*. If our government spent a fifth as much time on enforcing physical placement orders as it does on child-support enforcement, we would have wealthier and happier children and fathers.

Dead Dads

As I said before, 14 percent of those called deadbeat dads are actually dead. My own brother's son, who had been paying child support, died four years ago. My brother continued to receive threatening letters addressed to his son from the child-support office, in which they continued to compound new payments and interest. He informed them more than five times that his son had died. I suggested to my brother that he send the child-support office a change of address to the cemetery where my nephew rests. These dads who are dead are used by unscrupulous politicians and feminists to create false figures that depict fathers as "deadbeats."

Being in prison, unable to earn a living, is also not accepted as an excuse for not paying child support. One million men in the United States are in prison. Many of these men are fathers with child-support orders. These men will have a hard time taking care of themselves economically when they are released. A child-support order with interest compounding year after year, while the debtors are in prison, will be virtually impossible for them ever to pay.

What You Need to Know
About Child Support in Wisconsin

To play any game, you must know the rules. WDW 40 is the rulebook for child support in Wisconsin. WDW are the initials for the Wisconsin Department of Workforce Development. The Division of Economic Support, Office of Child Support, has written this rule. The rule was specifically modified about six years ago. At the public hearings for these minor changes, fathers and second wives showed up *en masse* to protest the rule and to ask that it be substantially rewritten to make it fair to both parents. Fairness is not what is desired in Wisconsin, however—just more money, and the ability to collect it by using the police powers of the state. The Division of Economic Support is ruled by women who ignored what amounted to a revolt by the citizens and who rammed through their minimal changes without considering public input or protest.

I have included WDW 40 in the appendix. If you're going to play the child support game, it is absolutely necessary for you to read the rule, study it as if you were going to have a college exam on it, and know it so well that you can plan your custody strategy around its terms. *I assure you that your spouse and her attorney will be doing the same.*

Be aware that in Wisconsin, one parent is a payer of child support and the other is a receiver. The payer is the parent who has the child less than 50 percent of the time. This is an exact number! If you have your children 49.5 percent of the time, you are a payer. The measure of time you have your children is measured by *overnights*. One man who had negotiated his parenting time at 48 percent thought he had equal time until I advised him that unless he has his children exactly 50 percent of the time, he would be a payer. Since there are 365 days in a year, no parent can have their children exactly 50 percent of overnights, so parents who want joint custody normally write into their stipulations that even though their parenting time may be slightly different, it is their intention that the time be considered to be exactly 50-50.

You should be aware that whether you are a payer or a receiver of child support, there are two reduction tables found in WDW 40. One table stipulates a slight reduction for those who have placement for 31 percent to 40 percent of the time, and the other offers more relief for those who have placement from 41 to 59 percent of the time. In theory, parents who have their children between 40 to 60 percent of the time are both payers, but the percentage standard is so skewed that the declared primary placement parent pays a disproportionately small amount of what should be allocated, based on the actual placement time. The absurdity of the reduction tables is that if you are the parent without primary physical placement, and you have your child 59 percent of the time, you would still have to pay 3.43 percent of your child support obligation.

WDW 40 "expects that the custodial parent shares his or her income directly with the children." This means that one parent is held accountable and the other is not. This also means that when you pay $800 per month in child support and your children come to you in dirty or ragged clothes, there is nothing you can do to ensure that your support payments are being used to buy clothes for your kids. The law provides no obligation of accountability for the spouse who receives support payments.

Child support is taken directly from your paycheck by your employer, so you do not even see it. In reality, child support is no longer the loving act of a father for his children. It is a tax!

If you are self-employed or unemployed, Wisconsin may charge you child support at a rate that presumes that you earn minimum wage. If you have lost a high-paying job via downsizing, the court may rule that your former high income is your potential income, and will not change your child-support amount or accept the reality of the job market and lowered salary expectations.

By federal law, past-due child support may not be dispensed by any court, once ordered. Fathers who have lost their jobs often feel they cannot afford an attorney. Here they are in a "Catch 22." If they do nothing, their child-support arrears grow not only for missed payments, but payments with compound interest. *If you lose your job and are entitled to lower child-support payment, immediately write a letter to the family court commissioner asking for a hearing.* You can get relief from your present order only from the time that you filed for a revision of your support order.

Child support is normally an open issue, which means that either parent can reopen the issue with ease. Federal law fosters the reexamination of child-support awards every three years. This appears to be a difficult job. However, if your ex-spouse wants more money, and you are the payer, she can haul you back into court each year, asking to see your year-end federal tax returns to verify your income. Child support follows a percentage standard, but is usually expressed in a court order both in the percentage and a dollar amount. Your child-support order will not increase unless your ex-spouse takes you back into court, and then the judge will apply the percentage standard to your new and often higher income.

Many spouses hesitate to go back to court if there has been a nasty divorce. After a year or two, wounds begin to heal, and all parties hesitate to reopen issues that will restart hostility. Fathers who litigate vigorously are less likely to see child-support issues revisited, since the other parent knows that he is likely to resist, and may reopen another whole list of issues once litigation is reopened.

Base for Child Support

Wisconsin has a percentage standard: 17 percent of wages for one child, 25 percent for two children, 29 percent for three children, 31 percent for four children, and 34 percent for five children. This percentage amount is based upon your *gross* wages, not your take-home pay. This means that if you make $500 a week and your take home pay is $325, and you have five children, your support payment will be $170 and your net take-home pay will then be $155 a week. You pay the taxes on your child-support payments.

For most fathers, the base used for child support is their income from work. But income can also be imputed a payer's assets and all real or personal property over which a payer can exercise ownership or control. Interest, dividends, self-employment income, trust income, worker's compensation, private or military pensions, unemployment insurance payments, personal injury awards, and any other income can be taxed for child support.

One issue that many fathers do not understand is that their bonuses and overtime wages are also liable for the child-support tax. Many fathers think that only their regular wages can be used as a base. The child-support tax is so unjust that tens of thousands of fathers have entered, in one form or another, the black market economy of cash payments, thus avoiding all forms of taxes. Some fathers felt this was necessary because they were not able to survive the heavy tax burden when it included support payments.

One standard established in the preface of WDW 40 is based on the principle that a child's standard of living should, to the degree possible, not be adversely affected by his or her parents no longer living together. This principle is a major cause of oppression of fathers. Earlier, we stated that a family's standard of living goes down because of the inefficiencies of divorce. Certainly, expenses increase when two separate homes must be supported instead of one. The standard-of-living principle is thus a mathematical fantasy, and WDW knows this. In effect, it means squeezing more than what is fair or possible from the child-support payer, no matter how miserable his life may become. Fathers too often accept this burden because men in our culture have been taught that they should be the providers and most will attempt to continue to provide, even if it kills them. Fathers have been taught to "take it like a man" and suffer in silence. This is changing, however, as fathers realize and feel the injustice of the system.

How to Calculate Your Child Support

At the back of WDW 40 is Appendix B, which is a worksheet to help you calculate a child-support award. You should be using this worksheet to calculate your child-support payments, given different time-sharing arrangements. Money is important. While we all want our children to be cared for, we must also take care of ourselves. Your children's mother was equally responsible for them in the marriage, and since the child-support law is irresponsible for continuing this obligation, it is up to every father to litigate to insure that the custodial parent will be accountable. It is difficult to overcome the discrimination built into the law, but your persistence in litigation can tire out all parties until justice is achieved.

Limits on Child Support

There is no limit on the income base for child support in Wisconsin. This means that if you make $500,000 per year and have two children, you are still obligated to pay 25 percent, or $125,000. Normally people in this income bracket can afford to litigate for 18 years until the children are the age of majority, so stipulations almost always occur. However, if you are in an income category in which child support is so obviously above the real costs of raising the children, consider a stipulated settlement which will put much of the funds into a trust or college education account for them. Make sure that you are the trustee, so that your ex-spouse will not try to steal these funds as the custodial parent.

Other Tips

Always pay some child support, even if you are unemployed, even if it is only $10 a week. It shows good will and may let you avoid a criminal action.

If you pay child support directly, always make a copy of the check, keep the canceled check, or get a receipt. This has been an area of grief for fathers, especially if one gets involved in litigation for support paid many years in the past.

Make a list of all expenditures that you make when the child is with you, especially if they would be considered joint expenses. Keep receipts whenever possible. You may want to use these records in some future court hearing.

The parent who has primary physical placement, according to federal Internal Revenue Service rules, receives the child exemptions on federal taxes unless the court directs otherwise. *Always ask the court that you be allowed to have the child exemptions on federal taxes when you divorce.* Use the arguments that the other person may not be able to use them or that you are the one paying child support and so the exemptions justly should go to you. If there is resistance, split the deductions or agree to take them every other year.

Another gender bias against fathers is that the law allows banks to consider your child support as an expense when you are trying to get a mortgage after divorce. The banks do not consider the number of children or the costs to raise them as an expense when a married couple applies for a mortgage. Mothers who receive child support may count the child support as income when applying for a home mortgage, while a father who pays child support has a decreased ability to purchase a home after divorce. A father needs to be aware that any child-support award can preclude him from buying a home after divorce, or may force him to buy a less desirable home. There are grave tax implications, as this often means that a father will have to accept the limitations of the short-form tax returns.

When Does Child Support End?

In Wisconsin, child support lasts until the child reaches the age of majority, which is 18. If the child is in high school, parents are responsible for child support until June after the child's eighteenth birthday. A father is not legally responsible for paying child support for a college-age student unless he has so stipulated in his divorce decree. While he may stipulate to paying child support or to contribute to college expenses, a judge is not allowed by Wisconsin law to order payments after 18.

Every father has a moral obligation to support and raise his children. This does not mean that a father has an obligation to pay child support to another party with no assurance that the money will be used to support his children. A father's goal in divorce should be to maximize his time in raising his children with solid moral values and to personally direct his financial resources to his children's needs. This goal is worthy of extensive litigation.

New Developments

Legislation has been introduced to reform DWD 40 by removing it from an administrative rule under the Department of Workforce Development and again making it part of the statutes to be administered solely by the legislature. This is because the DWD and its predecessor, Health and Social Services, have resisted reasonable and fair changes. Reform of child support has strong supporters, but powerful political forces resist change. Billions of dollars in child-support transfers are at stake in Wisconsin. WDW receives an incentive reward from the federal government for all child support which passes through its hands. A more equitable child-support standard would mean less money and personnel going to the agency. This money could better be spent on children's benefits than bureaucrats' salaries.

The proposed changes may be summarized as follows:

1. The child-support percentages should be more closely related to the percentage of actual placement time.

2. The income both parents should be considered.

3. Similar child-support resources should be available in each household.

4. There should be an upper income level to which the child-support percentages can apply.

These above changes are meant to ensure that child support is used to support children and is not a new form of alimony. Pressure needs to be applied to legislators to support these common-sense changes. Wisconsin currently is one of only two states that does not consider the income of both parents in awarding child support.

CHAPTER EIGHT

Wisconsin Family Law Reform-2000

O n October 27, 1999, Wisconsin Gov. Thompson signed into law significant family law changes. The reforms were championed and sponsored by State Senator Gary George. They were included as part of the state budget bill with bipartisan support between both Democrats and Republicans. A coalition of parents groups, the Association of Court Commissioners, and the Family Law Section of the State Bar worked to reach consensus for change. Each party gave a little and took a little to reach consensus. The Association of Chief Judges, the State Department of Health and Social Services, and the domestic abuse coalitions opposed the changes.

The reforms, summarized below, are far-reaching, although not complete.

1. There will be a rebuttable presumption of joint legal custody. The exceptions were weakened to reach consensus, but are specific by statute.

2. Placement time for each parent shall be regular and meaningful, maximized to each parent. This reform does not

reach our goal of a presumption of joint placement, but effectively should move most cases into joint parenting.

3. The best-interests standard remains, but begins to be defined. Less discretion is left to the judges and court commissioners.

4. Domestic abuse protections are maintained.

5. Temporary orders shall follow the guidelines for the permanent determination of custody. No longer will the temporary orders be discretionary without the statutory guidelines being followed for custody.

6. Paternity children shall be treated equally as children of divorce before the law, rights given to each parent. Courts are required to give paternity fathers placement time at the same time that child-support orders are issued.

7. Parenting plans must be submitted by each parent early in the action, thus defining the scope of what the parents share in common and where they disagree. The questions asked in the parenting plans are extensive and are defined by statute. These plans narrow the lines of contention and will significantly reduce litigation. Any parent who does not supply a parenting plan will not be able to refute the plan of one who does.

8. The court may require the parties to attend classes on parenting and on ways in which divorce stresses children.

9. Enforcement of physical placement is given teeth. Primary placement parents who intentionally and unreasonable deny placement to the other parent *shall* pay court costs of the petitioning parent. Makeup time for lost placement is required by statute. An injunction may be issued resulting in a fine up to $10,000 and /or two years in jail for unreasonable interference in the determined placement. Parents who fail to exercise their placement time can, upon motion by the other parent, have their child-support order adjusted. Both parents will be held accountable for fulfilling their placement time. No more

getting placement times and then dumping on the other parent. No more withholding kids from their other parent or scheduling events during the other parent's placement time. This has had detrimental effects upon both mothers and fathers. This change is good for children!

10. Interest on back child support shall be reduced from 18% to 12%, in line with the lower interests rates in our recent economy. In paternity cases, child support can be ordered only from the time of filing, not from the time of birth.

11. Paternity orders shall follow essentially the same standards as those for children of divorce. Findings of paternity shall include a legal custody and a physical placement order.

12. A legislative council will be created to study the role of the guardian *ad litem,* to determine whether their appointment should be mandatory in all cases where custody is disputed, and whether non-attorneys might fulfill this role.

13. The criteria for custody includes strong new provisions. (A.) No longer will the psychologist report be so controlling, but will be just one more criterion. (B.) The future role changes, necessitated by divorce, of both mother and father will be considered, not just the historical roles that mom and dad formerly played within the marriage. (C.) A non-cooperative parent will be seen as a factor in awarding custody. (Presently, the court system too often caters to the most obstinate parent.)

14. All the above provisions took place on May 1, 2000. These reforms primarily affect new cases. Where a party with an old case can get into court, overcoming the hurdle of a "change of circumstances," these new laws will be in effect.

These reforms took years to accomplish. We never lost faith that one fine and courageous legislator would come forward to champion common sense and eradicate gender bias. During the past twelve years, we cultivated a fertile climate for the acceptance of these legal reforms.

The changes in Wisconsin Family Law may be found in their original language and in their entirety at the following Internet site: http://www.legis.state.wi.us/1999/data/acts/99act9.pdf

This is a long law, because it is part of the budget bill. Look at pages 627-639. The family law reforms are all in Chapter 767.

Below you will find these changes as summarized by the Wisconsin Legislative Reference Bureau.

Budget Briefs
From the Wisconsin Legislative Reference Bureau

Budget Grief 99-2, November 1999
prepared by Richard Roe, Legislative Analyst

JOINT LEGAL CUSTODY
Introduction

The biennial state budget act (1999 Wisconsin Act 9), passed by the legislature and signed into law by Governor Tommy Thompson on October 27, 1999, changes the determination of legal custody and physical placement of children in actions for annulment, divorce, or legal separation. The same provisions, which take effect May 1, 2000, will also apply to paternity cases, custody actions, or physical placement actions in which the parents have voluntarily acknowledged paternity.

Legal Custody Decisions

Act 9 states that, while a custody decision must still be based on the child's best interest, "the court shall presume that joint legal custody is in the best interest of the child." The court may give legal custody to one party only if both parties agree or if one party requests sole custody and the court finds at least one of the following situations: 1) one party is not capable of performing parental responsibilities or does not wish to have an active role in raising the child; 2) one or more conditions exist that would substantially interfere with the exercise of joint custody; or 3) the parties will not be able to cooperate in future decision making for joint legal custody. In addition, the court may not five sole legal custody to a party who unreasonably refuses to cooperate with the other party. Evidence of child abuse, spousal battery, or domestic abuse creates a rebuttable presumption that the parties will not be able to cooperate.

Allocation of Physical Placement

Under Act 9, the court will still be required to allocate periods of physical placement between parties, based on factors specified by statute. The factors currently considered in placement, such as the child's wishes, the relationship between the child and the parents, and the child's adjustment to surroundings, will be continued with few modifications. One new requirement is that parental wishes must be formally indicated by an agreement between the parties, a proposed parenting plan, or a legal custody or placement proposal submitted to the court. A second factor dealing with unreasonable interference is modified to cover questions such as frequent and continuing contact or interference with the continuing relationship between the child and the second parent.

New factors the court will consider in physical placement include: the age of the child and the child's changing developmental and educational needs; cooperation and communication between the parties; amount and quality of time spent with the child in the past; life-style changes needed to spend time with the child in the future; and the need to provide predictability and stability for the child. The court must set a physical placement schedule that allows the child regular and meaningful placement with each parent and maximizes the amount of time the child spends with each parent.

Parenting Plans

Under the new law, if legal custody or physical placement is contested, each parent must submit a parenting plan before any pretrial conference is held. A party who fails to submit such a plan on time waives the right to object to the plan submitted by the other party. The law specifies the information a parenting plan must contain, including who will provide child care, where the child will go to school, the doctor or health care facility to be used by the child, payment of the child's medical expenses, the child's religious commitment, how holidays will be divided, the child's summer schedule, and how the child will be transferred between parties if there is evidence of spousal abuse.

The parenting plan must also include information on where the parent who seeks legal custody or physical placement lives and intends to live for the next two years and where that individual works. If there is evidence that the other parent has engaged in spousal battery or domestic abuse, the parent seeking custody or physical placement is not required to give a specific residential or workplace address, but only a general description of each.

Enforcement

A parent may petition for enforcement of physical placement if the other parent has denied or substantially interfered with physical placement or has forced the party to incur expenses or financial burdens by failing to assume responsibility for physical placement. The court must accept any legible petition and hold a hearing no later than 30 days after a copy is served on the other parent.

If the court finds the respondent parent has denied or interfered with physical placement, the judge is required to order additional periods of placement and reimbursement of reasonable costs. In addition, the court can order specific times for placement if the underlying order does not make such provision. If a parent intentionally failed to exercise physical placement, the court may order restitution to the other party.

When a parent repeatedly fails to exercise periods of physical placement, a court may modify a physical placement order upon petition. The court also may grant an injunction ordering strict compliance with the original physical placement order effective for not more than two years. Violation of an injunction may lead to a citation for contempt of court, punishable by a fine of up to $10,000, two years imprisonment, or both.

Classes on Effects of Separation

Courts may require parties to attend court-approved classes that address child development, how parental separation affects child development, and what parents can do to make the separation less stressful for the child. Class attendance is not a condition to granting a final divorce or paternity judgment, but the court may refuse to hear a custody or physical placement motion of a party who refuses to attend.

Budget Briefs
From the Wisconsin Legislative Reference Bureau

Budget Grief 99-3, November 1999
prepared by Richard Roe, Legislative Analyst

CHANGES IN DIVORCE LAWS

The biennial state budget act (1999 Wisconsin Act 9), passed by the legislature and signed by Governor Thompson on October 27, 1999, makes various changes to Wisconsin's divorce laws. Major modifications in the joint custody and physical placement laws are discussed separately in Budget Brief 99-2, and the other changes are discussed here.

Appointment of Guardian Ad Litem

Prior to passage of Act 9, if a court had special concern regarding a child's welfare of if legal custody or physical placement of a child was contested, the judge was required to appoint a guardian ad litem to represent the interests of the child. Under the new law, the court would not be required to appoint a guardian ad litem in a contested action to modify legal custody or physical placement if: 1) the proposed modification would not substantially alter the amount of time the parent spends with the child; 2) the court determines that the appointment would not assist the court because the likely determination is clear; or 3) the party seeks the appointment solely for a tactical purpose or delay.

Act 9 requests the Joint Legislative Council to study reforming the guardian ad litem system as it applies to paternity, separation, and divorce. Issues to be studied would include: whether a guardian ad litem should be appointed in every case in which legal custody or physical placement of a child is contested; whether professionals, such as child psychologists or child psychiatrists, should be appointed; and the role, supervision, training, and compensation of the guardian ad litem.

Paternity Actions

Under the new law, when the court orders child support in a paternity action, liability for support begins the day after the action is filed, unless the party seeking support shows to the satisfaction of the court that payments should have begun at an earlier date. In those cases, the claimant must prove that he or she was induced to delay the action due to: duress or threats; actions, promises, or representation by the other party; or actions taken by the other party to evade paternity proceedings. The claimant must also show that after the inducement ceased, there was no unreasonable delay in filing the action. Support cannot be ordered for any period before the birth of the child.

Effective May 1, 2000, custody and physical placement orders issued in paternity actions or actions where paternity is acknowledged will be governed by the same provisions as those that apply in divorce actions (see Budget Brief 99-2). At the same time, the law expands the applicability of child-support provisions for divorce actions to paternity cases.

Interest on Unpaid Support

A party ordered to pay child support or family support must pay an interest penalty on any amount in arrears equal to or greater than the amount of support due in one month. Act 9 reduces the interest rate from 1.5% TO 1% per month. The reduction first applies to arrearages existing or accruing on May 1, 2000, regardless of the date of the court order on which arrearages was based.

Visitation or Placement in Homicide Cases

In a divorce action, a court may grant persons, such as grand-parents, visitation rights to a child. If an individual eligible for visitation rights is convicted of first- or second-degree intentional homicide of one of the child's parents, that person cannot be granted visitation rights, and

previously granted visitation rights will be denied. Likewise, a parent may not be granted visitation or physical placement rights if that individual is convicted of first- or second-degree intentional homicide of the other parent. The court may, however, decide to grant visitation rights or physical placement rights in any of these cases if it determines by clear and convincing evidence it would be in the best interest of the child to do so. The court must consider the wishes of the child in making the determination.

For More Information

For copies of the material relating to changes in divorce laws, contact the Legislative Reference Bureau at (608) 266-0342. 1999 Wisconsin Act 9 can be found on the Internet at http://www. legis.state.wi.us/billtest/acts/99acts.html.

CHAPTER NINE

Physical Placement
in Wisconsin Statues

T
he 1999 family law reform includes more specific directions to family law courts regarding the standards for legal and physical placement. As is normal after the legislature acts, the impact of a law is not fully know until it is interpreted in practice by those in the executive branch and lower courts, and interpreted more definitely through judicial review in the appellate courts. Since contested family law cases normally take nine to eighteen months to reach resolution, along with an additional two-year period for appeal court cases to issue definitive rulings, the interpretation of new standards must come from the straight language of the statute.

The family law reforms of 1999 were an outgrowth of Senate Bill 520 and Assembly Bill 442. I mention this because one method to interpret legislation is to ascertain what the legislation intended to say and accomplish. These bills would have eliminated the "best interest of the child" standard rather than the absolute right of each parent to the presumption of legal and physical placement. The legislature rejected the "one formula fits all" standard. The final language of the reforms that passed regarding placement did not specify 50/50 or absolute equal placement to each parent. The legislation eliminated, by the governor's veto, the obligation of the court to accept both parents' stipulated agreement.

What the Law Says

What are the standards under today's statutes? In 767.24, the court is directed to make provisions as it deems just and reasonable concerning legal and physical placement. The court shall presume that joint legal custody is in the best interest of the child, but provided for a rebuttal to this presumption. The court spells out its underlying principle in the allocation of physical placement. Except when a parent "would endanger the physical or emotional health of a child, and after consideration of each case, the court shall set a placement schedule that allows the child to have regularly occurring, meaningful periods of physical placement with each parent which maximize the amount of time the child may spend with each parent, taking into account geographic separation and accommodations for different households." The court shall consider the factors for custody and placement as spelled out in 767.24(5). A court may not deny placement with a parent for failure to pay his or her financial obligation to the child. The legislature then edited and added numerous factors for the court to consider in determining physical placement.

What can we learn from the plain language of the statute? First, the court retains the right, when parents are divided on custody, to allocate both legal custody and physical placement. Legal custody is to presumed by the law unless rebutted by sufficient evidence in court. Not only do *parents* have a *right* to placement time with their child, but a *child* is *entitled* to periods of physical placement with its parents. Both parents, apart from endangerment to a child, are entitled to equal treatment without regard to their gender. Make no mistake—these new statutes were enacted because parents were being discriminated against on the basis of gender, a situation forcefully expressed through testimony in public hearings. The legislature meant to give *specific* directions to the courts in defining the "best interest of the child" standard and in protecting the rights of both parents. The legislature uses *shall*, not *may*, in giving its instruction to the courts as to the principle of placement.

Even before the family law reforms passed in 1999, Wisconsin courts had slowly been recognizing the right of both parents to maintain legal custody of their child. We must remember that when married couples have a child, each of them *de facto* has both joint legal and physical custody. *When a couple seeks a divorce, a court is not giving custody and placement time to one parent, it is issuing a restraining order that takes away the right of one or the other parent to the legal and physical custody that parent enjoyed before the court intervened.*

The legislature recognized from all the facts and studies that have been conducted over the past twenty years that, in most cases, it is in a child's best interest to have two parents active in its life. The legislature recognized that the process of raising a child is hard work, and that Wisconsin children of are not suffering from too much parenting, but from too little, especially those children from divorced families. Thus, the legislature enacted statutes for joint legal custody, maximum physical placement for each parent, and tough enforcement mechanisms to make sure a child will have two loving and caring parents in its life.

The new statutes recognize that geographic separation and accommodation are critical factors in physical placement. If one parent lives far away from the child's school district, that would affect the ability to follow the principle of placement which maximizes the time to each parent. If the dad is an over-the-road truck driver with a different schedule each week, he will not be available to fulfill his obligations for regularly-occurring maximum placement. If mom remarries and lives 125 miles from the children, she will not be able to fulfill her obligation for maximum placement. However, if the standard is regularly occurring, meaningful periods which are maximized to each parent, then, given the limitation of geographic separation, it would seem that the separated parent would be *entitled* to the majority of time when the child is not in school, during holiday periods, long weekends, and summer vacations, when the separated parent is available.

Geographic issues are not a consideration in physical placement in a majority of contested divorce cases. Most parents after divorce do not move far away. The physical placement standard which the legislature enacted is a "soft presumption of joint physical placement." "Regularly occurring" refers to consistently occurring at *fixed and certain intervals.* "Meaningful" refers to having *function* and *purpose.* The function and purpose is for a parent to have the time and opportunity to help bring his child from dependence to a fully functioning adult who will contribute to society.

Finally, since there are two parents, to "maximize placement time" to each parent is to give each fifty percent of placement time. This is a "soft presumption" of joint physical placement, however. That is what the legislature intended without definitively spelling out a "one-size-fits-all," strict 50/50 placement. Flexibility was left for the courts to make adjustments in the best interests of the child.

While the legislature granted only a soft physical joint custody standard, which still maintained the best interests of the child standard, they enacted substantial changes in the factors for custody and placement. These changes were enacted to correct existing biases, to change the weighting of factors, and to address abuses in the family law system regarding custody placement.

In the past, the amount and quality of time spent with a child was a prominent criterion of custody. Considering the traditional roles of fathers and mothers, this often meant that mothers who traditionally stayed at home received priority over fathers who worked outside the home. This alone often determined mom for primary physical placement. The roles of men and women, however, have undergone significant changes in the past 35 years, and the legislature finally caught up with the realities of a changing society. They changed this factor, recognizing that for most middle-class families today, both mom and dad work both at home and outside the home. The legislature recognized that the roles that parents voluntarily chose within the context of a marriage cannot be continued at divorce. Even with child support, most mothers cannot afford to continue as stay-at-home moms. Even coming from a traditional family, dad will have to learn to change diapers, shop, cook, clean house, and wash laundry. The Legislature changed the "factor of custody" that the necessary changes at divorce to the parents' custodial roles and the reasonable lifestyle changes to that which a divorcing parent proposes in order to be able to spend time with their child, one just as valid as that which parents voluntarily and historically practiced while raising their children together within the marital family.

The age of the child and the child's developmental and educational needs at different stages were recognized as new factors. Not only did the legislature recognize the needs of the various children in the family, but it statutorily opened the door to building into a final agreement a future re-opening of placement, based on these new factors. A custody placement order put in place when a child is two years old is not necessarily in its best interest when the child is fifteen.

The need for regularly occurring and meaningful placement

was repeatedly placed among the factors to be considered for custody, to emphasize that a child needs predictability and stability, normally provided best by both parents.

In the past, the most angry, adamant, and uncompromising parent often was given more placement time. It is difficult for courts to deal with uncooperative parents, and the courts often tilted their way to appease them and bring the litigation to a conclusion. The legislature has dealt with that bias. How could this ever have been seen as being in a child's best interest? The new law stipulates that the party who refuses to cooperate or communicate with the other party will be considered in a negative light regarding custody matters. The effort to cooperate and communicate will be rewarded, not the opposite. This addition to the factors considered for custody puts each parent on notice that no matter how angry their feelings toward the other parent, whether they wish to continue an old marital fight, or they simply want vengeance, the court will protect the child and the parent who is trying to reach beyond this life tragedy. The law cannot change the feelings in people's hearts, but it can demand behavior that will promote the the child's long term interest. The pain of a failed marriage has its most intense effects after separation, and too often a custody dispute can be gasoline thrown onto this emotional fire. Good attorneys should now advise their clients to control their anger. Parents should be advised that to curb their raw emotions is now in their own best interest. The addition of this new factor will save many children from the crossfire of their parents' anger.

In the pre-1999 statutes, the reports of appropriate professionals were built into the general text for the determination of custody. These reports held a more statutorily prominent place in determining custody than they do under the new law. The legislature has come to accept that these reports, while valuable, are written by people who have little actual knowledge of the child or of either parent. These professionals know little of a child's best interest. These opinions should not take precedence over the inherent right and desires of the child and its parents. Professional reports are now downgraded from a position of primary consideration to merely one among many considerations for custody determination. Of all the changes in the statutes, the courts and Family Court Counseling Services have seemingly ignored this change. However, the legislature does not make such changes lightly. There was intent in changing the focus of the importance that a court should give to these "professional" reports.

In summary, the legislature significantly reformed the factors for physical and legal placement in Wisconsin. While rejecting a one-size-fits-all model, mandatory 50/50 placement, it posited that children would be best served when they receive maximum care from each parent , insofar as this is possible, given geographic circumstances, physical or emotional endangerment to the children, and common-sense factors that recognize the good will of each parent in loving their child. The legislature meant to partially define what is the best interest of the child by giving specific directions to the courts. Finally, the legislature wanted to remove gender bias as a factor in awarding custody, recognizing that the love and care of one parent is no less than that of the other, and that both are necessary for their children to grow into productive adult citizens.

CHAPTER TEN

Successful Mediation

Mediation or Not?

There is no question that stipulating is far less painful for your spouse, your children, and yourself than prolonged litigation. Litigation is lengthy, expensive, and leaves scars that may never heal. Mediation, on the other hand, avoids win-lose situations, keeps friends from being pulled into one's custody dispute, allows parents to arrive at schedules which they are more likely to keep, and helps fathers to avoid the gender bias often exercised by older male judges.

What is Mediation?

Mediation is a method by which parents who have differences over physical placement of their children may settle these issues without the intervention of judges, lawyers, psychologists, or social workers. Mediation deals only with scheduling issues, not financial issues. The mediator is a family court counselor who is employed by the court. The counselor tries to help the parents focus on settling each person's desire to be with their children without their becoming adversaries in the courtroom.

In Wisconsin, mediation at the outset of a divorce is mandated by statute. However, at the outset of the divorce there often is so much hurt and bitter feeling that parties are more interested in fighting each other than in establishing new life patterns. This makes mediation difficult. Still, mediation performed by the family court counseling office may help the parties settle many, if not all, of parenting time issues.

The current fee for mediation is $350, may be different by county, and is usually split by the two parents. Poor families may receive a fee waiver upon application, if they meet the criteria for eligibility.

Preparation for Mediation Sessions

One of the first things a father should do is find out as much as possible about the mediator, seeking advice from other fathers or from groups whose members know the counselor in that county. Knowledge is power. Discover the mediators beliefs and biases regarding joint custody. Find out what triggers his or her decisions. Find out how the whole process is handled in your county, since different counties may have specific procedures or rules.

Don't try to "wing it" through these sessions. Before you go to your first session, prepare written notes on your most important issues and have them ready to use. Know the issues well so that you can converse with ease on each of them.

Some judges dislike family law cases, wishing they did not have to hear them. They look for an easy way to handle these cases. Thus, judges trust mediators and most often accept their recommendations, knowing that they spend extensive time and energy to gather information and understand the issues of each party. Lawyers mistrust this process because they are not present and their client may say things or make concessions that they would not recommend.

During mediation, a smart parent will always focus on the children's best interest while still getting what they want. A father should bring up the point of separation anxiety in children, and the fact that most children do not want their parents to separate, and that a schedule in which the children see both parents regularly is best for them.

Fathers should remember to have a list of all the ways they have nurtured their children. This list should include not only the nurturing skills that are traditionally ascribed to the mother, but those that are unique to the relationship between fathers and children. Just as in adversarial situations, a father in mediation must define the best interest of the child so that he plays an essential role in post-divorce parenting.

Procedures

The procedures that are followed may be different in each county and may actually be handled in a different manner by the counselor, who may perceive that a specific process may be more helpful in your case. Some counties now use a film that shows parents ways in which their divorce will affect the children. The film stresses that a peaceful settling of custody issues is best for the children. Mediators hand out literature so that the parents may study methods of non-adversarial conflict resolution.

After the initial introduction to mediation, a counselor will normally talk to both parties together. The counselor will usually talk to the children without the parents, and interview them so that she may learn just what the children want without pressure from the parents' presence. The mediator may talk with other health professionals—teachers, coaches, the police, doctors, or any other people who may have knowledge of the family situation.

Mediators are frequently women, and sometimes they act with a gender bias against men. Address gender bias up front, if it is apparent. But be careful in your language and attitude. Do not get angry at the mediator or at your spouse. Don't let your spouse trigger your sore points. Be prepared to respond to any bait from your spouse with intelligent, reasoned, and considered responses, quickly bringing the conversation back to your own agenda items. Concentrate on addressing your most critical issues. Prepare and bring with you less or unimportant points that you can concede in return for your spouse's concession on the ones important to you.

The Ten-minute Presentation

Prepare well before you come into a mediation session. Carleen and Michael Brennan, in their book *Custody for Fathers*, recommend an excellent practice of preparing a ten-minute presentation on your interpretation of the issues. Prepare well so that all the issues just roll off your tongue. Speak in a manner showing that you are familiar with these issues. They are your agenda for the mediation session. If your spouse takes the conversation to other areas, acknowledge her issues, then return as quickly as possible to your own agenda. Whoever sets the agenda is more likely to prevail.

What to Do and What Not to Do

The Brenanns give the following advice on what to do and not do in mediation:

Always be on time. Be clean and neat in appearance. Dress conservatively. Be confident. Speak slowly, and listen attentively. I would add that a father should be firm, but reasonable and concise. Don't quarrel, show anger, over-react, interrupt when the other is speaking, or raise your voice.

Read the above paragraph a second time, because it is packed with good advice.

If your spouse violates any of these rules, call her on it. If she loses control and yells, ask her to stop. If she interrupts you, look over at the counselor for approval and ask her to let you finish. If your spouse is quarrelsome, remind her that you are here to find solutions and not to fight. In the process, you will appear to be the more reasonable, peace-loving parent, and your opinions will be given more respect.

Stay Positive and Focused

Be positive in mediation sessions. Focus on how good a parent you are. Speak with knowledge about what the children need during this period of insecurity. Shift the dialogue to what the children need and how your parenting is part of the solution for their well being. By preparing your ten-minute presentation, you will be verbally strong, confident, and less likely to be diverted by interruptions. Don't try to be who you aren't. Take all the above advice and adapt it to your own personality. Some of the above will come easily for you, but some issues will call for you to train yourself for mediation. Sometimes you should simply restrain your emotional self.

Audio and Video Tapes

Mediators, like all people; believe more easily what they can see and hear. Your diary and notes about the children are believable, especially if you make daily entries. Letters from doctors, health professionals, teachers, coaches, and police are useful. Taped conversations, especially from disputed encounters, can be extraordinarily helpful. If your spouse is accusing you of making things difficult when you stop to pick up the children, it can be extraordinarily effective when you play a tape in which mom provokes you with screams and obscenities. Before your first mediation session, videotape your presentation and view it with a critical friend who can help you improve the quality of your presentation. A wonderful videotape detailing the interaction of you and your children at play says more than a thousand words. It's authentic and believable. Make use of audio and video tapes and photos to bolster your positions. However, stay on your agenda of why your good parenting skills are needed by the children, without cutting mom down.

Don't Accuse—Correct!

Don't make accusations against your spouse. Instead, use phrases such as: I am concerned ... worry tha ... I am afraid that ... I have a concern that. Accusations will normally elicit a defensive response from your spouse and hurt your credibility with the mediator. Remember, your goal is to get the mediator to accept your agenda as her recommendations.

Mothers have a common habit of referring to the children as *my* children. Many mothers believe in their hearts that the children are their personal property. Whenever mom uses the phrase *my children*, without fanfare remind her, looking at the mediator, that the children are *our* children and that mom's use of *my* children is indeed part of the problem that needs to be solved. In fact, children are neither parent's property. A parent should act as a *good steward* whose primary role is to guide the child successfully along the road to adulthood.

Smart Negotiating

Without appearing not to be listening, stay tuned to the important issues on your agenda. Be firm but fair in your negotiations. Draw the line in the sand on your most important issues and compromise on less important ones. Have some throwaway issues ready. It is smart to give away something you don't care about in order to get something important in return. Whenever you make a concession, always get something in return. Normally, let the other person make an offer after discussing an issue. She may offer you far more than you were expecting, and if you are smart you might even get her to offer a further concession in return for your accepting her offer. Act with reason, yet keep close track of how you are doing on the most important issues on your agenda. Have a mental checklist of your primary goals, and know where you stand in reaching them.

The beauty of mediation is that people who stipulate have

created the terms to which they agree. The commitments parents make under the mediation process are more likely to be followed than those ordered by a judge. Your job is to convince everyone, through logic and good negotiating skills, that what you want is good for the other person and for the children, without ever saying as much.

Preparation the Night Before

In their book, the Brennans present ten ideas for consideration the night before going into mediation:

1. Formulate your plan on paper.

2. Bury your anger and focus your thoughts on your parenting role.

3. Identify the specific applicable issues as they may affect your children's need for continuity and stability.

4. Acknowledge that your children need both parents.

5. Recognize that your children should be shared equally.

6. Devise a plan that meets your children's needs along with yours.

7. Try to keep communication open.

8. Concentrate your focus on the children's needs, not the problems of mom.

9. Allocate time on *what* is wrong and not on *who* is wrong.

10. Get a good night's sleep. Being rested, bright, and alert fosters successful mediation. Wear clean clothes. Be on time. Do all the above with the intention of making an impact on the mediator the next day.

Some Words of Wisdom

A father can fight and litigate and, at first, it makes him feel great to get all the anger out of his system. However, once adversarial litigation builds up steam, it is difficult to stop it. The stress of litigation takes its toll on your health and happiness. A father who is involved in bitter adversarial litigation is not likely to develop loving relationships with other women. Litigation so consumes one that it is difficult to get on with one's life. You and your children can be so hurt that the scars never heal. For this reason, always give mediation a chance, as it is likely to give one the best chance of the best revenge.

And remember: "The best revenge is get on with your life and to live well."

CHAPTER ELEVEN

False Accusations of Child Abuse

A false accusation of child abuse, whether referring to neglect or physical or sexual abuse, is a destructive and all too easy manipulation used by unscrupulous mothers and their lawyers to get initial placement. This is an atom bomb-type opening blow to a parent (usually the father) who faces not only gender bias in family law, but also a public perception that fathers are the primary perpetrators of child abuse. A false accusation is devastating not only to the adult being accused, but to the child who often is subjected to numerous interviews and therapy sessions that hammer repeatedly on an incident that never happened. False accusations are destructive to every party except the person who makes the accusation, who too often gains rather than loses, even after the lie is uncovered.

Statistical Data

From a 1980s report required by the Child Abuse and Neglect Act and submitted to the governor of Wisconsin, the following was reported: First, of the 11,116 Wisconsin cases reported, 8,405 (75.6 percent) were unfounded. That statistic is for all the state's reports of abuse. The percentage of reported false accusations when a divorce is pending is much higher. (It should be noted that "unfounded" does not mean with certainty that the abuse did not happen, but that there was no cause to prosecute.) However, one should also be aware that the state has a very low standard for bringing prosecutions (often just the accusation itself), hoping that most of the accused will cop a plea rather than face criminal charges.

The second item of the report to the governor on child abuse clarifies just who is committing this crime against children. More women are the perpetrators of neglect and abuse, by a ratio of 60.8 percent to 39.2 percent. In sexual abuse accusations, the biological parents are accused in 24.4 percent of the cases. I have read that 87 percent of the accused are males. An additional 9.4 percent of sexual abuse perpetrators are reported to be stepparents, who often are men who live in homes with teenage girls or young women to whom they are not related by blood. Moreover, of all the sexual abuse accusations made against biological male and female parents, 67 percent are unfounded.

Numerous studies have been conducted on the issue of accusations of child abuse within the context of a pending divorce. Consistently, these studies have shown that about three-fourths of accusations are unfounded. Depending on the gravity of the accusation, child services and/or guardians *ad litem* are required to examine and study the facts and report back to the court.

If you are accused, prepare a list of the studies showing the high level of false allegations on child abuse. Give special attention to those studies that show the even higher level of false accusations that occur when divorce is pending. Pass out a summary of these studies to all involved parties.

Half-Lies are Credible
Especially pernicious is a false accusation by the mother that

the father is sexually abusing a female child. This accusation is normally made by the mother in the name of a child who is two to four years old. At this age, the child cannot verbalize whether a sexual act has taken place or not. All mama has to do is suggest that what daddy has done is dirty and bad. The child readily takes the cue.

What has daddy done? Why is the sexual abuse accusation so effective when it involves children of this age? The most effective accusation is filled with innuendoes and half-lies. What happens with accusations involving young girls is that dad does give the child baths and may wash their genital area as any responsible parent would; or children wake up at night scared, and run into their parents beds when all parties may be wearing fewer clothes. Yes, dad did touch his daughter's vagina when giving her a bath, and yes, dad was naked in bed with his daughter. However, these are normal things that happen in two-parent families every day and are no indication of child sexual abuse. However, when there actually is child sexual abuse, these behaviors might be part of a pattern of that abuse. Consequently, fathers are especially vulnerable when mothers make false sexual abuse accusations against fathers who are merely carrying out normal parental duties.

The reason that a false accusation is so effective as an opening move is that judges have little choice but to be conservative in their initial placement. If they take the risk of placing the child with a father who might further abuse the child, the judge would be publicly chastised and run out of office.

David Levy, of the Nation's Council for Children's Rights, suggests that the father call for full psychological evaluations of all parties and that, while the evaluation is going on, physical placement should continue in a controlled situation. Continued visitation will lower the motivation for the accuser to continue the false accusation since it will not terminate the relationship between the child and the accused parent.

False accusations of child abuse fall within two categories—those which are perceived as bad parenting, and those which carry criminal penalties. I say "perceived" because many so-cial workers, family court counselors, guardians *ad litem*, and judges know that large numbers of false accusations are going to be unfounded. However, they are time-consuming and expensive to investigate.

Seriousness of False Accusation Charges

One needs to address the issue of a false accusation against oneself by first determining whether it is a criminal or non-criminal issue. If it is a non-criminal accusation, there will usually be no evidence such as bruises or medical reports. Still, this should be taken seriously, since abuse of spouse or child is one of the statutory factors in awarding child custody.

If you are accused falsely of criminal child abuse, take this charge extremely seriously. You could not only lose custody, but end up doing prison time.

Attorneys representing fathers too often fail to realize how zealous guardians *ad litem*, social workers, and district attorneys can be when there is even the slightest indication of child abuse, even indications that fall within the realm of normal parenting. React immediately if your attorney does not take seriously accusations that have criminal implications.

The atmosphere in America is hysterical on the issue of sexual abuse of children. If you are accused, you are considered "guilty" until you prove your innocence. This is not our legal standard for guilt here in America, but we are in a period comparable to the old Salem witch trials when it comes to this issue. Don't become a victim.

The Best Defense is a Good Offense

I suggest that a father who is unjustly accused of criminal child abuse take an offensive strategy rather than a defensive one. Immediately hire a second attorney who specializes in defending parents in cases of child abuse. Those who specialize in this area usually are very skillful in repelling false accusations.

Lie-Detector Test

Second, I suggest that a father take a lie-detector test, administered by a reputable firm, which will include questions on all issues brought up in the accusations and cover other general issues as well. After the results confirming your innocence are issued by the firm administering the lie-detector test, pass them out to all parties, including guardians *ad litem*, social services, family court counseling, the district attorney, and your spouse's attorney. These parties know that even though lie-detector tests are normally not allowed into court as evidence, they are 85 percent accurate.

Circulating the lie-detector results that the father did not abuse the child effectively changes the presumption that there was sexual abuse in the first place. Rather than all parties continuing to work to try to find you guilty, they may change direction and try to find out why the accusing party made the false charge. The results of the lie-detector test can make the evaluating parties wonder whether the parent making the false accusation is to be trusted, indeed whether she is a good parent.

Follow up your release of the lie-detector results with a written challenge to the accusing party to take a lie-detector test, also. In this written challenge, include the questions that the other party should be asked, knowing that the other party will almost surely fail the test. Be aggressive in challenging the investigating parties to insist that the accuser take a lie-detector test. Just this move alone may make the accuser recant her charges.

The goal of an aggressive defense is not simply for you to be absolved of guilt, but for you to actually gain an advantage after such a horrendous accusation. The net result is that you will be perceived as the more balanced and responsible parent at the conclusion of a false accusation process.

Civil Suit for Damages

Next, I recommend that, if you have the energy and resources, you hire a third attorney to file a lawsuit for defamation of character against the accusing party. This means that the honor and dignity of your name may be restored by financial compensation. The sum asked should be significant, so that it is intimidating to the accusing party. Your attorney in this civil action will be able to operate independently from child services or guardians *ad litem*. You may subpoena records and issue depositions for parties who may be withholding information from you and your other attorneys. Aggressiveness in this civil suit puts all parties on notice, including parties who normally have some level of immunity in the other legal actions.

Moreover, consider filing an immediate malpractice suit against any accusing party such as a social worker or therapist who may have conveniently been used by your spouse to give credibility to a false accusation. A lesser step is to report their misconduct to their professional association. Making therapists nervous by making them become defendants as well as accusers is one way of making them behave more cautiously toward you in the future. This is not a matter of vengeance; simply one of justice and compensation.

Stay in Charge of Your Case

Don't count on your lawyer(s) to be your savior. *Take charge of your case*. Develop files and organize your defense. Develop chronologies leading to the accusation. Prepare reports on false accusation statistics. Evaluate carefully any professional persons appointed to investigate the accusation. Find out as much as possible about them. Find out whether these investigators are believers in the mostly discredited "false memory syndrome."

Check to see whether one of their degrees is in women's studies. Find out whether they are on the board or involved with battered women shelters, or if their practice is slanted toward battered women. Read any professional articles or books they may have written and discover any of their subjective agendas. Investigate whether their academic degrees and certifications are accurate. Check police reports and court records to see whether they were once a battered child, or have a history of being a battered wife. Investigate thoroughly, so that you are confident that the investigating party is an open and fair professional without an axe to grind against men and fathers.

Learn all the procedures and processes that are required by law or rule. Constantly monitor to make sure that all of these are followed, so that abuses cannot be committed by the professional investigators. Check their past history to see whether they have made substantial or procedural mistakes in other cases. Check all applicable standards for the professional process of investigating abuse, and monitor them carefully.

Addressing Fallacies

Two issues on children must be addressed. One is the myth that children never lie. In the past, professionals have held that children never lie about abuse, that their minds and souls are pure and innocent. This belief simply is a product of someone's imagination. Anyone who has raised children know that they often lie when it suits their purposes, and that it is parents who instill the moral principle that truthfulness is good and lying is bad. There is now sufficient research to show that children do indeed lie about physical and sexual abuse. Research this literature and present it to all parties. Many have not read it.

The second issue about children is to make sure that all interviews with the alleged child victim be videotaped. It is now clear that the approach and methods used by skillful professionals can elicit confirmations of false accusations from children. A child, especially a very young one, can eventually be made to comply with repeated suggestive or coercive questioning by therapists. Further, a professional can make interpretations of children's behavior that no normal person would. A jury may find the interpretations of a professional to be ridiculous. It is essential that all interviews be recorded on tape, so that another expert witness can nullify the conclusions, or question the methods, of a professional who has less than an objective agenda.

The accused should also review taped interviews to see whether the therapist spent a sufficient amount of inquiry to determine whether the child was coerced by the mother, who has a vested interest in the custody result, into making statements that may not be true. The therapist should do this, since 75 percent of all cases are unfounded. Finally, the insistence on taped interviews of the child with a professional will make every person involved follow conservative and commonly accepted professional procedures, since their work will be reviewed by many parties.

Legislative Relief Needed

If we are to stop false accusations in divorce actions, the legislature must make changes in the law to include both criminal penalties against the accuser and civil relief for those falsely accused. The following changes would be appropriate. (1) Since the accusation harms not only the father, but the child and its relationship to the father, a criminal penalty of up to one year in jail should be imposed on a false accuser. (2) In chapter 767, false accusations should be included as one of the statutory factors for awarding custody (The legislature has added "unreasonable cooperation and communication on the part of one parent" and this could be construed to cover false accusations, but does not speak directly to the issue.) (3) The falsely accused party should receive specific civil relief in the form of damages along with fees and costs. (4) I further suggest that the court, upon a finding of false accusation, require the accuser to take out an ad in the local paper in which she apologizes to the ac-cused, to her child, and to the community. As long as there are only rewards and no penalties for false accusations of child abuse, false accusations will continue to be used as an effective means of obtaining custody or vengefully punishing a spouse at no risk of personal cost.

A Practical Motion

In light of the slowness of the legislature to respond to any issue of the day, Bruce Gould, an attorney from Washington State, has stated that some matrimonial lawyers have a standard motion that they make whenever there is a divorce involving the custody of children. The motion is that the minor children of the parties to this divorce may not be taken to any therapist, psychologist, psychiatrist, social worker, counselor, or other mental health professional without (1) prior notice to the court, (2) prior notice to all parties to this divorce, and (3) if the children are allowed to go to any of the above, then all sessions with such professional will be videotaped from start to finish with the non-taking party paying the costs of such videotaping and giving a copy to the other party.

The Child Abuse Industry

Last, be aware that the investigation of child abuse has become a very lucrative industry for many professionals. This industry, like any other, must be fueled constantly with new revenue. Many of the professionals in this industry are rewarded only when they put abusers away, not when they find them not guilty, and thus it is in their interests to find evidence of guilt, rather than seek the truth. Many of these professionals operate in a close network and know each other both personally and professionally, all working together with the common goal of exposing child abusers and putting them away. If your spouse or another case worker suggests using therapist A, B, and C, presume that this list is one of such connected colleagues who often support each other. Do your own research, find your own experts, and insist that your or some of your experts be used for the investigation.

Always, always deny the accusation. Do this without rage, malice, or anger. Never cop a plea unless you are guilty. Make the state *prove* you committed child abuse beyond a reasonable doubt. Copping a plea gives them a free ride for cases that they should not win. The consequences of maintaining your innocence are significant, but if you cop a plea, you will *never* get custody.

CHAPTER TWELVE

Property Settlement

W|he Marital Property Act of 1985 made Wisconsin a community property state. This means that, in general, all marital property will be divided equally between the spouses at divorce. There are exceptions to this rule, noted later in this chapter. The controlling law is S.S. 767.255.

Less Litigation

The Marital Property Act has resulted in significantly lessening the amount of litigation over the division of property. In a Wisconsin Fathers for Children and Families' study of all cases filed in Dane County (1987), only about five of two thousand cases went to trial specifically over property division. The reason for small rate of litigation is not difficult to understand. If property is going to be divided 50-50, lengthy litigation means that both parties will most likely get less out of the divorce settlement.

Further, the statutes consider the distribution of property division without regard to marital misconduct. Thus, no matter how hurt one party may be by the other's adultery or unfaithfulness to the marriage vow, there will be no consideration of this conduct in the distribution of the marital property. The law thus reduces the motivation for parties to continue their marital fight when addressing property division issues during divorce.

In general, those who go to trial do so under unique circumstances. Most often these involve cases where there are substantial assets in which the potential gains are substantially higher than the cost of litigation. The net assets of most divorcing families are relatively small, however, and are not worth litigating the property division.

Exceptions to an Equal Division

The three primary exceptions to the equal division of property are *gifts*, *premarital property*, and *inheritances*. While property division may be disputed on the basis of hardship, the primary reason that equal property division is challenged is that property in one partner's name has been co-mingled with the assets of the spouse. This sometimes happens when one person owns a house and then marries. During the marriage, both parties pay the mortgage and house repairs. At divorce, the non-owner of the house then claims the house to be marital property since that party has paid for some of the mortgage and its upkeep. A situation such as this is a candidate for property division litigation. Gifts, inheritances, and premarital property titled solely in your name should never be mingled with assets jointly held by you and your spouse.

Prenuptial or Written Agreements

The other way to consider avoiding litigation over property division is by arranging a prenuptial agreement. However, if you have not done this *before* your marriage has fallen apart, it is irrelevant to your situation at divorce. The beauty of a prenuptial agreement is that Wisconsin statutes state that the court is to presume that any such written agreement before or *during* the marriage shall be equitable to both parties. In the appendix there is a lawyer-reviewed template for a prenuptial agreement that will help you to avoid making the same mistake, should you choose to marry again.

Case Law

In Appendix VI, under Sec. 767.255, Stats., you will find a summary of assorted cases of record that constitute prevalent case law in Wisconsin. If you foresee a property division problem in your divorce, it will be worthwhile for you to read these short summaries to see whether your issue has been litigated previously. If a case seems relevant to your own situation, go to a law library and read the details of the case and bring this issue to your attorney.

The Time for an Easy Division

The easiest way to handle property division is to make a list of all items owned by a couple at the start of the divorce, before lawyers get too heavily involved. Sit down with your spouse before litigation gets heated up, especially if you anticipate custody litigation, and divide up the property according to anticipated *needs*, not according to value. It is often more important to receive the items you need or want than the items that have more financial value but will just take up space in your garage. Giving up a chest freezer that you do not need makes it more likely you will receive the snow blower that you will need, later on. After you and your spouse have divided up all the property, make a short, complete written agreement which you both sign. The court is required to consider this written agreement. Far more important is that most parties who freely enter into a written agreement feel obligated to honor it. To do this before litigation on contested issues is helpful in shaping a smoother end to the divorce.

CHAPTER THIRTEEN

Practical Advice on Paternity Issues

By Atty. Keith Wessel

Paternity of children is established by marriage or, when the parents are not married, by 1) acknowledgment of the parents, or 2) by filling a petition which is followed by a determination in court. Those paternity cases involving custody and placement (formerly visitation) where the parents never married are substantially increasing in proportion to all custody and placement cases in Wisconsin. For the most part, the law of paternity in Wisconsin follows the law of divorce—even more so, since the 1999 revisions. The law of non-marital paternity has evolved to the point that an adjudicated father has the same rights for legal custody and placement as a father going through a divorce.

The issue of paternity arises in many different ways for men. A man may believe that he is the father of a child and seek custody and placement of that child. Alternatively, a man may believe that he is being falsely accused of fathering a child and thus find himself in the position of convincing the state that he has no obligation to support the child. In between these extremes, men may find themselves in the position of not knowing whether they are the father of the child they have been raising while living with the mother, or if he may be the father of a child who will soon be born to their partner or someone they simply were involved with sexually with no commitment for a long-term relationship.

The law makes presumptions about the paternity of children. For example, the law presumes that the lawfully married husband of a mother is the father of her children born or conceived during the marriage. (See Wisconsin Statutes, sec. 891.41, Stats.) The law also presumes that the husband is the father if the child is born before the marriage, if he had a relationship with the mother prior to the marriage, and no other man has been adjudicated or presumed to be the father. Additionally, the law defines the husband as the natural father if he consents in writing to the artificial insemination of his wife. (See Wisconsin Statutes, sec. 891.40.) Prior to April 1, 1998 the law presumed that a man was the father of a child when both the mother and the man signed an acknowledgment of paternity under Wisconsin Statutes, sec. 767.62.

Paternity issues thus become important to married men who suspect they are not the biological father of children born during their marriage or to men who have been involved in relationships with women who conceive and give birth to children.

Legal presumptions can be defeated by a showing of evidence that proves the presumption is wrong. For example, a party may defeat the presumption that a husband is the father if the person can show by "clear and satisfactory preponderance of the evidence" that he is not the father. (The reader should review elsewhere in this book the concept of standards that must be met to overcome the moving parties' burden of proof.)

Genetic testing can be used as an aid to determine whether a man fathered a child. It is most common today to use DNA testing to determine paternity. DNA samples can be removed from tissue inside the mouth or from other areas of the body, including a blood sample. Also, due to advances in technology, genetic testing can be performed on children as young as infants.

For the results of genetic testing to be accurate, it is best to have samples taken from the mother, the child, and the putative (meaning suspected or assumed) father. It is also important to obtain a court order for blood testing. Courts have excluded test results that were conducted without an order.

With ordinary blood testing or DNA testing, a man can be excluded as the father. In other words, the test results show that the man could not possibly have fathered the child being tested. These tests cannot provide conclusive results showing that a man *is* the father. Instead, these tests show the *likelihood* that a man is the father. Whether a man can meet the burden of proof that he is or is not the father of the child will depend on the percentage chance that he could be the father.

Pursuant to sec. 767.48, Stats., a person who is a party to a paternity case may request that genetic testing be conducted. Genetic testing can also be requested by an attorney for the State or a county on behalf of the governmental entity. Once a request is made, the court or family court commissioner shall require the "child, mother, any male for whom there is probable cause to believe that he had sexual intercourse with the mother during a possible time of the child's conception" to submit to blood tests.

A man alleged to be the father may also waive the right for blood testing. Men who do not wish to contest the finding of paternity often waive the right for genetic testing, and a paternity judgment is entered that establishes them as the legal father of the child.

Voluntary Acknowledgment of Paternity

In 1997 the Wisconsin Legislature revised sec. 767.62, Stats., to provide non-married parents the opportunity to formerly acknowledge paternity of non-marital children. Pursuant to sec. 767.62, Stats., non-married parents can sign a statement stating that the man is the father of the child, thereby acknowledging paternity. Unless one of the signers rescinds their signature in a manner that is timely under the statute, then the father is legally determined to be the father once the statement is filed with the state registrar. [See Wisconsin Statute sec. 69.15(3m) for deadline to rescind; currently no more than 60 days after filing the acknowledgment or prior to a court hearing, whichever comes first. Putative fathers should thus closely examine a decision to sign an acknowledgment of paternity.]

Prior to April 1, 1998, if a man signed a voluntary acknowledgment of paternity, doing so only created a presumption that he was the father. Statements signed before April 1, 1998 do not have the full legal ramifications of those signed after that date. This is significant because many fathers have signed these statements either before or after that date and continue to be in intact families with the mother of the child. Should those relationships dissolve, it will be important to determine the date the voluntary acknowledgment of paternity was signed.

To obtain an order for legal custody or placement under the old law, that still applies to anyone who signed the voluntary acknowledgment before April 1, 1998, a father must file a Summons and Petition to determine paternity and pursue the matter in court. He has no statutory right to contact with his children until the court enters a judgment that he is the father. The legal process to do so can take months, particularly if genetic tests are done. Under the new law, a father who is seeking legal custody and placement must file a petition for custody under sec. 767.02(1)(e) and 767.62(3), Stats. Because of the new law, he already has been determined to be the legal father and thus does not need to file an action for paternity. If he files for paternity, his case will be dismissed and he will need to refile under the appropriate law, requiring payment of a second filling fee.

Judgments of Paternity

The Wisconsin Statutes provide a substantial list of interested parties who may initiate an action to have a father determined to be the legal parent of a child, including "a man alleged or alleging himself to be the father." See Wisconsin Statutes, 767.45. Oddly, but nonetheless characteristic, regardless of the evolving understanding of male parenting, the Wisconsin Statutes provide language for a summons and petition to establish paternity that reads as though the man is always responding to the action brought by the mother or the state on her behalf. With some work, these forms can be modified for a man to start the action.

A man may waive or contest in court a finding that he is the father a child. If he is the moving party, he can demand genetic testing be completed before paternity is determined. If paternity is contested, the statute allows the party contesting the matter to request a jury trial. If a jury trial is desired, a request must be made at or prior to the initial appearance or pre-trial. Once paternity is established, the Court enters a Judgment of Paternity and will proceed to the second phase of the trial to determine custody, placement, and child support without the presence of a jury. The court can order sole custody to either the mother or the father, or joint custody with both the mother and the father having joint custody. Actions filed after May 1, 2000, fall under the statutes enacted by the legislature in 1999 that create a presumption for joint custody. See Wisconsin Statutes 767.24. The statute provides grounds for the court to order sole custody only if certain conditions exist. With very minor exceptions, all issues related to custody, placement, and child support are now determined under the same statutes regardless of whether the parties are married. A man involved in a paternity matter should thus closely examine the changes in the law discussed elsewhere in this book. For example, the new law requires parents to submit a parenting plan prior to a pre-trial or waive the right to challenge the other parents' plan. The new law also specifically spells out that child support may only be set prospectively, subject to very specific exceptions related to duress or coercion.

Men should not waive their right to be heard in court at the hearing to determine paternity. It is common that men assume they are the father. They are served with papers notifying them to appear in court to contest or challenge the allegation that they are the father. These papers also advise them that they can waive the hearing and consequently be adjudicated the father. The man who believes he is most likely the father of a child and wants to be determined the father should not waive this hearing unless he makes it clear to the court, in writing, that he desires genetic testing. This will lead to further court hearings before he is determined to be the father. When a judgment is entered by default (i.e., if the alleged father signs a waiver and sends it to the court, or if the alleged father fails to go to the court hearing), the mother is typically awarded sole custody of the child, the father is ordered to pay child support and the costs associated with delivery of the child, and the court orders that placement issues will be resolved by reaching agreements with the mother. Obviously, parents who are separated and suing each other in court may have difficulties reaching agreements. Thus it is important, in my view, to obtain a specific order for placement by either agreement or by decision of the court if placement is contested. Parents can later agree to other arrangements, but during the preliminary stages in this process they should have a specific court-ordered schedule.

Many decisions in the area of family law are made by family

court commissioners. These officers of the court are appointed and are not subject to the electoral process. They serve at the benevolence of elected judges, and any decision they make can be reviewed by an elected judge. See Wisconsin Statutes 767.13(6). Each county creates rules with regard to what issues will be heard in front of a family court commissioner. In paternity matters, if paternity itself is not contested, many counties allow the commissioners to enter paternity judgments and make decisions on custody, placement, and child support. If the father, by waiving or attending the first hearing, does not contest that he is the father and later decides that he is not satisfied with the order for custody, placement, or support, signed by the court commissioner, he may request *de novo* review to a judge. A *de novo* review is like an appeal, but, unlike an appeal where the appeals court makes a decision based on the evidence presented at trial, when a court hears a case *de novo* the court starts from the beginning and hears all of the evidence before making a decision. A person is entitled to *de novo* review pursuant to sec. 767.13(6), Stats., but, be aware that each county in Wisconsin has its own court rules. In Dane County, for example, the court rules require that a request for *de novo* review be made within 15 days of an order made orally by a court commissioner.

Modifications

In family law, judgments can be altered by stipulation of the parties. But once there is a judgment in place, if the parties are not willing to stipulate, modification of the judgment to change custody, placement, or child support can be very difficult. As discussed elsewhere in this book, when these issues are resolved in the context of divorce, there are procedures that provide for temporary custody, placement, and support orders before the final divorce judgment. These procedures allow a couple to experiment with custody, placement, and support issues before they become locked into a judgment. After the judgment of divorce or paternity, the procedures to modify custody, placement, and support issues are defined by statute. A parent must show that there has been a **substantial** change in circumstances in order to change custody, placement, or support. In order to change the custody or placement order during the first two years after the judgment, sec. 767.325, Stats. requires a parent to show by "substantial evidence" that the modification is "necessary" because the current custodial conditions are physically or emotionally harmful to the best interest of the child. After two years following the entry of the judgment, the standards to modify custody or placement are less stringent, but nonetheless difficult to establish. For these reasons, it is important to have a custody and placement arrangement you truly desire before agreeing to stipulate to a finding of paternity and the subsequent entry of judgment.

If a party to a paternity action is not absolutely sure that they want to abide by the conditions for custody, placement, or child support at the time of the hearing to establish paternity, they should ask to court to enter an "interim" or "temporary" order on those issues. By doing that, paternity is established and the parties can then seek modifications of custody, placement, and support at the lower standard of best interest of the child. In other words, they will not need to show that it is "necessary" to change placement to protect the child(ren) from physical or emotional abuse.

Reopening A Judgment

When a man waives paternity judgment by default without having blood tests, he has several options to reopen the judgment. Pursuant to sec. 767.465(3), Stats., he can reopen the judgment one time during the first year and request blood tests. After the first year, if he can show good cause, he can move to reopen the judgment at any time. To show good cause, one would have to present evidence that demonstrates a strong case that he should not have been adjudged the father. Sec. 767.466, Stats., applies these same standards if a man acknowledges paternity without having a contested trial. A man who has been adjudicated the father can also move to reopen the judgment by applying the standards of the generic rules of civil procedure which are included at sec. 806.07, Stats. Although a man can move to reopen the judgment anytime after the first year, it is extremely difficult to reopen the same pursuant to State Statute and case law. Even if a man can show he is not the biological father of the child, he faces an uphill challenge to reopen and may be required to pay child support for the child until the child is 18, or until 19 if the child is pursuing a high school degree or its equivalent.

The Non-biological Father

It is not unusual for a man to have functioned as a parent when he is not, in fact, the biological father of the child. This might occur when the man lives with the mother, she becomes pregnant, and leads him to believe that he is the father when in fact the child was conceived with another man. In another example, a man may move in with a mother and her minor child from a previous relationship, while the couple also decides to have a child of their own. This man may then raise both his own child and his child's half-sibling as his own for a period of years. The law provides opportunities for men in these kinds of situations to allow them to maintain a parental role with the children after separating from the mother.

In the context of a divorce, the non-biological father is protected by Chapter 767 of the Wisconsin Statutes. See sec. 767.245, Stats.. If a father "has maintained a relationship similar to a parent-child relationship with the child" he can move the court to order visitation. If he can show he maintained a parent-child relationship with a stepchild, he can get the court to order visitation if he can show that doing so is in the best interest of the child. The criteria he must meet to have the court consider the question of visitation and subsequently order visitation is spelled out in great detail in *In re Custody of H.S.H.-K,* 193 Wis.2d 649, 533 N.W.2d 419 (1995). *In re the Custody of H.S.H.-K,* provides an opportunity for non-married men to seek visitation of children they have raised who are not their biological children. On the other hand, to seek custody of a non-biological child is a different issue, and a third party must show that the legal (i.e. biological or adoptive) parents are "unfit" in order to get the court to order legal custody, See *Barstad v Frazier,* 118 Wis.2d 549, 348 N.W.2d 479 (1984).

In *In re Custody of H.S.H.-K,* the Wisconsin Supreme Court held that a person who has maintained a parent-like relationship with a child can move the court to order visitation, pursuant to Chapter 767, even if the person has never been married to the child's legal parent. The court held that:

> Visitation law balances a biological or adoptive parent's constitutionally protected liberty interest in determining how to rear a child [footnote omitted] against the best interest of the child. The state not only must respect a biological or adoptive parent's constitutional right, but also must recognize when state intervention in a parent-child relationship is necessary to protect a child's best interest. Visitation law is thus concerned with identifying the triggering events that may justify state intervention.

The court went on to identify the necessary trigger events to be established for a person who is not a biological parent to move the court for visitation rights. First, the moving person must prove the existence of a parent-like relationship with a child by showing that: 1) the biological or adoptive parent consented to, and fostered, that person's formation and establishment of a parent-like relationship with the child; 2) the person and the child lived together in the same household; 3) the petitioner assumed obligations of parenthood by taking significant responsibility for the child's care, education, and development, including contributing towards the child's support, without expectation of financial compensation; and 4) the person has been in a parental role for a length of time sufficient to establish with the child a bonded, dependent relationship parental in nature.

After showing that a parent-child relationship exists, the moving party must show that the biological or adoptive parent has substantially interfered with his parent-like relationship with the child, and that he sought court-ordered visitation within a reasonable time after that interference.

Obtaining Visitation
While a Paternity Case is Pending

As noted above, a putative father does not have a statutory right to obtain an order for visitation of his child until after the court enters a paternity judgment. To obtain a paternity judgment can take months, as a contesting party can demand genetic testing and/or a jury trial. If a father has lived with his child and maintained a parent-like relationship with his child, then he has standing to seek visitation under the courts' equitable powers discussed above. A father should thus pursue his case under both the statute and the case law from the outset of his case. He can move the court, pursuant to the equitable powers set forth in *In re the Custody of H.S.H.-K*, for a temporary order for visitation while his statutory case to be determined the legal father is pending.

Conclusion

The man who faces decisions regarding paternity should thoroughly understand his rights and obligations under the law before consenting to a determination that he is the father of a child. He should never waive his rights to a hearing and allow a default judgment to be entered.

When paternity is established, a judgment is entered which establishes custody, physical placement, and child support for the child. The parents can agree to joint custody or sole custody or they can contest the issue and force the court to decide who shall have legal custody of their child. If a man fails to resolve the custody issue at the time of judgment and later decides he wants to change custody, he will be forced to show evidence under stringent standards to change the judgment if he cannot reach a stipulation with the mother for a change.

Placement (formerly know as visitation) is also established by the judgment of paternity. In Wisconsin, a default paternity judgment usually gives all control regarding placement and custody to the mother. If a man wants to share placement of his child on an equal or some other basis, he should be sure to include language that specifically details his placement time in the judgment of paternity.

If the parties do not agree on these issues at the time paternity is established, they should ask the court for a "interim" or "temporary" order on contested issues. Under a temporary order, revisions are easier to acquire as the test is a best-interest-of-the-child standard. Final orders are subject to a much higher standard, and therefore more difficult to modify. During the first two years, a moving party must show that it is necessary to protect the children from abuse to modify a judgment with regard to custody and placement. After the two years following the entry of the judgment, one must show that there has been a substantial change in circumstances and defeat a presumption that maintaining the status quo is in the best interest of the child.

Once a judgment of paternity is entered, it can be reopened

and/or changed, but doing so can be difficult with the possibility of undesirable results. Therefore, a putative father should be well prepared, know what he wants, and negotiate his best arrangement before he stipulates to being adjudicated the father of a child. Short of negotiating a suitable arrangement by stipulation, he should contest any issues on which there is no agreement by presenting evidence at a hearing before a family court commissioner. If he is not satisfied by the ruling of the family court commissioner, he should ask for a *de novo* review of the decision by a judge in circuit court. The time limits for requesting *de novo* review vary from county to county in Wisconsin, and the father should be aware of those limits before he makes his case to the family court commissioner.

A father can seek an order for visitation of his children's half-siblings under the courts equitable powers set forth in *In re the Custody of H.S.H.-K,*. He can also seek a temporary order for visitation of his biological children under these same powers while his paternity case is pending.

A man facing issues of paternity, whether he hires a lawyer or proceeds *pro se*, must be prepared and understand his rights and obligations before agreeing to waive his right to contest paternity or before going to court for a hearing. He should not depend on the court to guide him to explain what he wants for his child, rather, he must be prepared to show the court that he has formulated a plan that is in the best interest of his child.

CHAPTER FOURTEEN

Maintenance and Family Support

With two-thirds of women now part of the labor force in America, the concept of alimony or maintenance (maintenance is the payment by one spouse to the other spouse supporting them after divorce) is declining as an issue in most divorce cases. Only about ten percent of families are traditional ones in which the father is the sole provider of financial support and the mother is a full-time child-care provider.

Criteria for Maintenance

When the Wisconsin Fathers for Equal Justice did a study of all court cases filed in Dane County for 1987, they found only a handful of cases in which maintenance was an issue for trial. The profile of these cases typically included an older couple where the wife had spent her adult life raising the children as her primary career, where there was a marriage of ten years or more, in which the wife remained dependent upon her spouse for her standard of living, and where there was little indication that the wife could develop a career that would provide a living standard equal to the one she enjoyed within the marriage.

Another scenario is where the spouses are young and one has worked and sacrificed the development of his or her career while the other attained the education for a professional career. The working party, by supporting the spouse who received an education, expected to see benefits later in the marriage. In a recent case, in which I was a counselor, the man had a job, supported his wife through medical school, and was the primary caretaker of the home and a young child. This is often how young couples make their way through the great expense of graduate educations. The wife/doctor divorced while earning a six-figure income while the husband's was far more modest. He was entitled to maintenance.

The criteria for maintenance and family support are found in S.S. 767.26 and 767.261. The courts have been encouraging the economic independence of both parties at divorce. After all, marriage is the end of the economic contract, and both parties should be taking responsibility for their own lives.

The Wisconsin Supreme Court has set criteria for maintenance in its case law. Generally, it has become assumed from case law that marriages should be of some duration before maintenance should be considered; this has in general been assumed to be a marriage of ten years or more. However, the courts make many exceptions based on need and equity. The reader should study the footnotes and case summaries in 767.26 Stats., which can be found at the end of the book. Further, the reader can go to any law library and look up these cases in the *Wisconsin Reports* for full details on each of these cases.

Time Limits Necessary

Rather than order maintenance payments, the court will sometimes divide marital property unevenly so that the less advantaged party receives the equivalent of maintenance in a single cash payment or transfer of assets. Where maintenance payments are ordered, time limits are normally put on the payments. Other awards are a tit-for-tat award, as in the case of education. If one party supported the other through four years of graduate education, the court will award that supporting party the same financial benefit at divorce.

It is unusual for the courts to order a lifetime maintenance award. The courts put time limits on maintenance in most cases. If one spouse has not worked for five years while being a primary caretaker, the court may issue an order in which the dependent spouse will receive three to five years of payments. Or the court may order a declining amount until after the fifth year the payments will stop, e.g., $500 a month the first year, $400 a month the second year, $300 a month the third year, etc. The theory is that by the fifth year the dependent spouse will have developed an earning capacity sufficient to maintain the standard of living that was previously enjoyed in the marriage.

Two Good Options

I believe that if a man is caught in a divorce in which he is liable for maintenance, he should choose one of these two options:

(1) Pay her off up front and avoid monthly payments, which irritatingly remind you of a failed marriage. Under this option, make sure that you get a stipulation in which your spouse permanently forgoes any further claim to maintenance.

(2) The following option is better if you have good earning power but few liquid assets. Choose a declining payment plan over several years, rather than an immediate cash settlement. First, the longer time frame seems attractive to the receiving party; second, your ex-wife will slowly discover that she needs to get a job and work as hard as you do to get ahead in life.

No matter what option you choose, make sure that your divorce decree ends maintenance at a specific time. You don't want to live your life with your ex forever hauling you back into court for more money, many years after the marriage has ended. Make sure that you also put in writing that all maintenance ends upon her remarriage.

Maintenance payments, unlike child support, are taxable to your spouse. **(Jim—Is it a tax deduction for you? If so, say so here. Deductible both state and federal?)**

Family Support and Tax Considerations

Family support is a court-ordered payment that substitutes for child support and maintenance. The advantage to one who pays family support over a combination of child support and/or maintenance, is that the payer may be able to deduct some of what will be used for child support as family support. However, this means that the other party would have to pay income taxes on the amount considered maintenance. The advantage to the spouse receiving payment is that family support is collected by the clerk of courts, like child support. This means that a delinquent payer is under the same stringent guidelines as for child support. Normally, when a payer of maintenance is delinquent, the receiving party must initiate a civil suit without aid from the child-support agencies.

The most important thing for you as a father to remember is that, if you choose family support as your preferred method of paying child support and maintenance, try to get a lower percentage of child support than you would have to pay under the percentage standard, in exchange for a higher maintenance payment. This means you will pay lower taxes and your ex-spouse will pay higher taxes, and this is good for you!

Study Case History

When reading the statute citations for maintenance and family support, look through the summarized case history, and if any of the cases apply to you, go to your county law library and read those cases. Take notes, and discuss any thoughts you might have with your attorney.

The Realities of Family Law

You are one of the twelve million men in America who are facing divorce this year!

You know that women get primary physical placement in about eighty percent of all cases. Affirmative action has entered the boardroom, but not the courtroom when it comes to fathers and custody.

Many men do not bother to ask for custody because they think they will never get it. Other men are discouraged from asking for child custody by their own lawyers, who tell them how difficult and expensive it is to try. But just what is "too expensive" when the reward is to remain the father to your children? Consider also that many men who lose custody end up paying hundreds of thousands of dollars in child support over a period of twelve to fifteen years. Then, some men doubt that they can actually take care of their children as well as their wives have, perhaps because they have learned fewer of the nurturing skills traditionally assigned to women. However, these skills can easily be learned by any loving parent.

Custodial lawsuits are brutal to all parties. Thus, I advise all fathers that it is best to try to reach a stipulated settlement, if at all possible. Stipulated settlements will wreak the least havoc on your emotional and financial lives. Most people who litigate to trial spend thousands of dollars before even going to trial. You and your children will be better off if you can stipulate a settlement while meeting your needs as a parent and father. If that is not possible, and you want to remain a father to your children, then you will need a good attorney, the help and encouragement of other fathers and friends, sound advice, and plenty of emotional support to get you through a harrowing process.

There is some hope for men who want custody. More judges are recognizing their own gender bias against fathers and are starting to treat dads more fairly. Wisconsin family law reforms became effective in 2000. More fathers have a history of raising their children and are confident of doing a good job of it. Other dads have learned the politics of the courthouse and are acting accordingly to overcome gender discrimination.

Let's not get carried away! The problem women faced in the past, in moving into the corporate boardroom, is the same problem fathers now face in family courts. For you, as a father, being good is not enough. Regrettably, you must show that your ex-wife is deficient in her parenting skills, and at the same time demonstrate that you have superior skills. If you don't have the stomach to take the offensive against your soon-to-be-ex, then you should avoid litigation. Unfortunately, litigation is about being adversarial!

Women initiate about two-thirds of all divorces. Their husbands, who are often unprepared when papers are served, find themselves psychologically unable to defend themselves. They still love their wives, and they have been conditioned over a lifetime to protect their home and family. They continue to act as the home protector even as their wives are taking their children from them. You must begin to protect yourself when it comes to child custody if you wish to remain the father to your children.

The "best-interest-of-the-child" standard has little objective legal definition. Thus, its interpretation is open to all those who have power in disputed custody cases. This includes judges, psychologists, family court counselors, and guardians ad litem. Bottom line, none of these people really have any personal responsibility, interest, or love for your kids. However, they often have social agendas that they are willing to impose on you. These people are social creatures with all the gender biases of society at large and, deep inside, many believe that the children "belong to the mother." Be realistic; the state's overbearing interest in child custody cases is to make sure that your children don't end up on the welfare rolls. If this means relegating you to the role of Uncle Dad or Mr. Wallet, they are willing to do just that.

One deciding factor in the award of custody is in judging which parent will give access to and not interfere in the other parent's physical placement. Too often, women act as if the children are their personal property, and they communicate this without the least bit of shame. Gender bias in the courts allows women to get away with self-righteousness in this area. Men should be careful to maintain their position that the children need both parents, and that if you, as the father, are granted custody, you will see to it that the mother has liberal parenting time with the children. By doing this, you will be seen to be magnanimous in your love for your children, as well as the more reasonable and cooperative parent. Still, the objective reality is that your children have a right to a good relationship with their mother.

You must figure out what it means for you to win. To win means different things for different situations.To figure out what it means for you to win will save attorney fees and also help you to focus all your energy on accomplishing your goal. You must view a custody dispute as a marathon race. The person who perseveres wins. The fight drains all the emotional energy that fathers have, and it seems that it will never end. You must be single-minded about winning.

Part of the innuendo game is discrediting your ex. Bring up her sexual relationships, but not as a jealous ex-husband. Tell the court counselor and GAL how her new relationships are upsetting the children and leading to their instability. However, don't do this in such a way that it appears you are controlling or jealous. Keep the discrediting focused within the "best-interest-of-the-child" standard. However, remember that you must come back to raise your child with the other parent. In your adversarial pursuit, try not to burn all bridges unless forced to do so.

One of the ways of discrediting your ex-wife and setting the record straight is to keep a daily written log. Record everything she does wrong and everything you do right. Record all negative things that your children say about their mother. File your journal with the GAL and court counselor on a monthly basis. Do not give a copy to your wife's attorney. Even better, if your wife's behavior is acrimonious, use a hidden tape recorder or video to document her displays of hate or violence. Tape your phone conversations with her. When you pick up the children have a tape recorder in your pocket and tape her nasty comments. Use this data at the right time to impeach her testimony on the witness stand or discredit her at an important hearing or point of decision.

In court, we're not talking about moral fairness or justice. We're talking about your ex-wife's use of the law and of state power to force you to do what she wants. The goal is to WIN! You should approach custody as if you were a draftee in war. You do not want to be there, but if you want to remain a father you must be there. I suggest the same approach you would take if you were in a firefight. Kill or be killed. I am not suggesting killing anyone, just that if you lose, you lose your children, your parenting role, much of your meaning in life, and part of your soul. War is not fair, is not a discussion, is not ethical. IT IS THE DISPLAY OF POWER to force another to do your will.

I suggest some initial first moves. I believe it is important for men to have a tough, smart, experienced attorney who aggressively advocates on your behalf. I recommend a male GAL because too many of the female GALs act less like lawyers than like protective social workers with their own social-action agendas. But beware of all GALs, as they too often act like social workers and not lawyers. Choose an attorney with whom you can act as a team, then you will be able to double your energy and lower your expenses. Always control the actions of your attorney, as this is your case and you must pay the consequences if you lose. You are paying your attorney to represent your position zealously, not to take your hand and lead you their way. Only you know what is best for you. Only you must pay the consequences of your positions! This does not imply that you should not listen to your attorney's advice. But do this with discrimination, and without selling out your fatherhood.

Many fathers become fearful when they find that they have drawn a female judge. But female judges are more likely to recognize the restrictions and dangers of gender bias. A father has a great deal to fear from a 65-year-old male judge who was raised and cared for by an at-home mother, who then married a woman whose career has been raising his children while he has been the sole financial support of the family. An older male judge from an outmoded "Ozzie-and-Harriet" background can be the most insensitive to a father who wants to be treated as one of two equal parents when divorcing.

A temporary hearing should be treated as if it were a trial. What happens in the temporary hearing tends to stay in place about ninety percent of the time. Most attorneys do not adequately prepare for the temporary hearing, and the client, unfortunately and erroneously, often believes that the temporary hearing is indeed temporary. I've seen many men come out of a temporary hearing in shock, and those fathers often never recover.

The GAL and court counselor know little about your family or children. They have their own social agendas. Don't presume that they actually care about your children's best interests. Your children and your relationship to them are unique, but outsiders tend to interpret your situation from their own experience, or from the latest book they've read. Some court counselors discriminate against fathers and do not personally believe in joint custody in any case. To find out if your court counselor is one of these, call other fathers who have had experience with them in their own custody cases.

You must set the agenda for the court counselor, GAL, and custody study. If you and your attorney can set the agenda, you will have a better chance of getting a positive recommendation from them and a better chance of winning custody. You can set your own agenda in subtle ways, but it is necessary to do so, in order for you to win.

One of the advantages a mother often has is that, in marriage, she has had the children more of the time than the father. She will use this history to claim that the children's routine must be maintained, that she has been their primary parent and thus deserves custody. But you must find the weaknesses in her argument. Remember that she will make more mistakes, if only because she has had to make more decisions. You must be aware of these mistakes and use them to show her to be the less able parent. You don't need to lie. Just search out the truth and present it in such a way as to build the kind of impression you want to create. Again, this is a matter of winning, not fairness or justice. Take advantage of your wife's many faults. Exploit them to your advantage. Develop a public relations program for your strengths as a good father. Promote yourself. Moreover, the new family law reforms acknowledge that divorce brings about a sharp change in family circumstances and routines, and that the traditional roles of mother and father may no longer be valid during and after divorce.

Never put your blind trust in your attorney or in a judge. Neither knows every aspect of the law. And even when they know a law, they may not always follow it. Study the statutes yourself, and read pertinent case law. Make sure your attorney presents the statutes and appropriate case law to the court. A trial judge is less likely to violate a statute if your attorney brings the law to the judge's attention and demands that everything be placed on the record. What is not presented will not be part of the record. Don't give your attorney permission to have side conferences in the judge's chambers while you are not present. Deals are often struck there which are not in a father's interest. Keep everything on the record, with you present.

Most studies show that children who grow up in mother-headed families are headed for big trouble. Children from mother-headed families have lower grades in school, teen girls are more likely to become pregnant, teen boys more likely to become delinquents, and both have higher rates of mental illness and suicide. An astronomical 85 percent of those in prison come from mother-headed families. You need to fight to have custody to save your children from the consequences of gender bias as practiced in family law.

Men are accustomed to being independent and taking care of themselves, while women have often depended on various other women and women's support groups, formal and informal. On separation from their wives and children, men often suffer a dreadful feeling of separation and aloneness. Many feel suicidal, as the world they have known and built crumbles around them. This is the time to join a fathers' rights organization such as Wisconsin Fathers for Children and Families, or another such group in your area of Wisconsin. You do not have to endure your pain in silence or accept injustice as a father. Many fathers who have been through this ordeal are willing to listen to you, help you with good advice and suggestions, and share their experiences. You do not have to be alone.

Finally, even if you lose after giving your all, you will not experience an inner sense of guilt that comes from knowing you failed to do everything you could to take care of your children and remain a father to them. When your children become more mature, they will recognize your love for them and the vindictiveness of a mother who kept them separated from their father.

Twenty-five of the Most Commonly Asked Questions

I have been answering the (608) ALL-DADS telephone line for ten years. We receive roughly a thousand calls a year from fathers, second wives, and grandparents asking questions about custody issues. In this chapter, I will try to give general answers to some frequently asked questions. Remember that your situation is unique. The answers given are not meant to substitute for the legal counsel of your attorney, but are meant to give general direction to those in need.

Q. How do I know what my child support will be if I do not have primary placement?

A. In Wisconsin, child support is a percentage standard of one's gross wages and other net income. The percentage standard is 17 percent for one child, 25 percent for two children, and 29 percent for three children. Read the WDW 40 guidelines as found in appendix eight.

Q. Can my child support change?

A. Child support is always an open issue. Since it is a percentage of your income, and incomes normally increase if employment is stable, your child support can also increase if your ex-spouse petitions the court. Child support can also be reduced if your income decreases. A change of circumstances is normally required. Good stipulated agreements can reduce the ability of a parent to frequently reopen the case to increase child support.

Q. My ex-wife won't let me see the kids. What can I do?

A. You have a statutory right to parent your children. First, document her refusal through the use of police reports and witnesses. Tape her phone conversations in which she admits that she will not let you see the kids. If you have a court order with specific times, file a motion for relief under the new statuary changes on interference.. If you do not have a court order specifying parenting time, you will need to file a motion establishing specific court-ordered days and times. The penalties for interfering in court-ordered placement have been increased substantially. They include make-up time, attorney fees, and court costs, and with an injunction up to two years on jail and a $10,000 fine.

Q. My wife has served me with a summons for divorce. How do I find a good attorney?

A. Good attorneys are difficult to find. Get a referral from a fathers' rights activist. Go through the interview process as suggested in this book. Do not call the Wisconsin State Bar for referrals, as they give names selected at random from a list of attorneys who have asked to be placed on that list. Do not get a referral from a friend. Do not pick a name out of the phone book. Research and spend time and energy to find a good attorney for you. This will be the smartest thing you can do.

Q. My attorney won't represent what I want. I'm fighting with him. What can I do?

A. Your attorney has an ethical obligation to represent your legal positions. Confront your attorney if he or she won't zealously represent your position. Be clear that you are the client and that you are the only one who must live with the results of divorce and custody litigation. Put on paper what you want your attorney to represent, so that your position is clear. If your attorney continues to ignore what you want in representation, ask for a refund of your retainer and credit any billing to date.

Q. *What can I do to support fathers and to change laws that are biased against dads?*

A. Join a local fathers' rights group and get involved. Write letters to your state representative, senator, the secretary of the Department of Workforce Development, and the governor. Donate money to Wisconsin Fathers for Children and Families or to Legislation for Kids and Dads. Help a friend in need who is just beginning a custody fight. Write letters to the newspapers when you see biased reporting about fathers. Use your position of power at work to promote fathers' rights whenever possible; the opportunity often arises. Become active and use your time and talents for change. Make the world better for your kids.

Q. *My wife has falsely accused me of child abuse. What should I do?*

A: The best defense is a strong offense. Take a lie-detector test. Publicly challenge her to take one. Hire a separate attorney to represent you on this issue. Show past patterns of lying. Bring the child to a doctor. Take the charges seriously, especially if they include potential criminal charges.

Q. *My wife has custody and is planning to move out of state. What can I do?*

A. Wisconsin State law requires that she give you a 60-day notice. Upon notice, file an objection to her move in court. This reopens the custody issue. The bad news is that Wisconsin courts have been allowing the custodial parent to move for frivolous reasons. Further bad news is that the Wisconsin statutes presume that it is in the best interest of the child to remain with the primary placement parent. This is an area of abuse ripe for statutory reform.

Q. When I walked out of the initial temporary hearing, I was in shock at the injustice against me. I didn't get anything I wanted. Is there anything I can do?

A. File for a de novo hearing in front of the circuit court judge. Introduce evidence and witnesses to bolster your position. Address the issues used by your ex-wife before the court commissioner. County/local rules determine the time limit for a de novo hearing. Often it is fifteen days. Check to see what the time limit is in your county. Meeting time limits is essential to preserving your rights.

Q. My wife and I are still living together. She told me she wants a divorce and says she has an appointment with an attorney. What should I do?

A: Don't go into denial as many men do. Act swiftly! Close all credit accounts in both names. Find a fathers' rights group and get counseling. Take half of all cash from joint accounts and put it in a new account in your name alone. Remove from your home all important documents or any items that might be used against you in a custody fight and put them in a secured place. Stop co-mingling any assets or income. If you get an attorney, pay that attorney from a joint account. Don't have sex with your soon-to-be ex, so that you cannot be accused of spousal rape. Buy a tape recorder and record any pertinent conversations. Tape phone calls. Develop a strategy for joint custody. Be cautious and call 911 immediately if she gets too aggressive and starts fighting; make sure you call first.

Q. I lost my job. Do I still have to pay child support?

A. On the day you lose your job, write a letter to the court commissioner or file a motion for a change of support. Child support cannot be forgiven except from the day of filing for a change. Document that you lost your job through no fault of your own. Pay the applicable percentage standard from your unemployment compensation. Try to get into court as soon as possible.

Q. *Every time I pick up my kids my ex-wife screams at me and starts a verbal fight. If I start to respond she threatens to call the police. What can I do?*

A. Bring a witness with you when you pick up your children. Carry a tape recorder in your pocket and record her aggressive verbal behavior. If you have a car phone, when she starts a fight, call the police and report that she is violent. Ask the police to come help you. Stay in your car until they arrive. If she continues this behavior, file a motion for a restraining order. After documentation, file a motion for interference with placement. The new sanctions can be tough!

Q. *What should I do to prepare for mediation?*

A. Beforehand, get counseling from a professional and carefully plan out your strategy. Be on your best behavior. Set the agenda. Stay focused on the best interest of your children. Don't let your wife egg you into a fight. Be relaxed; get plenty of sleep the night before. Dress well. Listen attentively. Don't bring up money issues. Negotiate smart to reach your essential goals.

Q. *My ex-wife spends the child support I pay her on her new live-in boyfriend, drugs, and alcohol. Is there anything I can do to make sure the money goes to my children? I'm afraid for my kids!*

A. There is no accountability for how child support is spent. This is a shameless irresponsibility on the part of the State of Wisconsin, which has strict rules of accountability for the foster care funds it hands out. Your ex-wife can spend your child-support money on her boyfriend and alcohol. However, if you know that she is an alcoholic or is using illegal drugs, plan a strategy and document her behavior. Do not confront her in anger. Hire a detective to catch her buying drugs, and develop evidence for the amount of time she spends in bars, especially if the children are left alone. Find witnesses to testify against her. Find out if she has a drunk-driving record. Get plenty of evidence before taking her back to court. Try to change custody.

Q. I've been assigned a female judge. Will that work against me?

A. The worst judges men face in court are male judges between 55 and 65 years old. They tend to be the sole wage earners in their families. Their experience of family is a mother who raised them, a wife who has raised their children, and a man who is the financial provider for his family. These older male judges are likely to view your ex-wife as his "daughter." On the other hand, female judges are more likely to be fair. They have fewer stereotypes of what a man or woman should be. They worked hard to get to their position of power, and are more likely to tell your ex-wife that she must get her life together and get a job. Female judges will not fall all over themselves, as paternalistic male judges will, when a woman cries in the courtroom.

Q. My wife, who has primary placement, makes $25,000 per year. Her new husband makes $50,000 per year. I make $20,000 per year. Do I still have to pay child support?

A. Yes! While this is obvious injustice, the child-support guidelines in WDW 40 require only the parent with less than 50 percent of placement time to pay child support. The law does not consider the income of the custodial spouse or the new family. However, if you get back into court for child support, ask the judge to use the alternative method, which considers the economic circumstances of both parties, to determine child support. Wisconsin is one of the few states that does not consider the income of both parents. This is an injustice which cries out for a statutory remedy.

Q. My ex-wife has primary physical placement. My kids tell me that they want to live with me. Is there anything I can do?

A. If your kids are 12 or older, consider reopening custody if you have passed through the two-year threshold. Make sure your kids are firm in their position and are not just trying to please you. Plan a strategy. Try to get as much placement time as you can through mediation. File when the timing is right. A court is very hesitant not to grant a change of custody to a 16-year-old who wants to move in with you, permission of mom or court notwithstanding. Rather than create another juvenile delinquent, a court will more often than not grant a custody change when the child is intent on the change.

Q. *My wife wants a divorce. I still love her. She wants me to move out so that she and the children can stay in our home. What should I do?*

A. First, forget that you still love her. She is now your legal enemy and is about to take your home, furnishings, and children. If you are friendly with her, talk her into moving out, and tell her she can see the children as often as she wants. The children identify the parent who moves out as the parent who deserts them. Let her live in the less comfortable apartment. The parent who moves out has a distinct disadvantage, as the children will not view the new apartment as home. The parent and children remaining in the original home will feel like the remaining family.

Q. *What does "best interest of the child" mean?*

A. The "best interest of the child" is not legally defined. Part of the reforms of 2000 were to define "best interest" and cut down on some judicial indiscretions. For this reason, custody fights are governed by personal prejudices of the parties involved, including judges, court commissioners, guardians ad litem, family court counselors, and the parents. A smart litigator will spend time planning on how he will define "the best interest of the child" in his case, and how he will convince all the other interested parties in the litigation to accept his definition. The father who can set the agenda by defining the best interest of the child in his case is more likely to prevail.

Q. When does child support end?

A. Child support ends at age 18 if your child is out of high school. If your child is over 18 but still in high school, child support can continue to age 19 and graduation. If you stipulated to support your children through college, you are obligated to continue paying until the end of that stipulated period. In Wisconsin, the courts cannot order you to pay child support or college costs after 18, unless you have previously stipulated otherwise.

Q. I owned my house before I got married. I am divorcing after ten years of marriage. During the marriage, we lived in my house. My wife wants 50 percent of the net asset value of the house. Can she get this?

A.: What often happens is that after marriage, the parties mingle their assets and pay house mortgages, repairs, and upkeep with mutual funds. Thus, there has been a commingling of assets and she has a claim on your house. However, you should be able to document how much you put down on the house when you bought it or how much its value was at the time of your marriage. With the help of a good attorney and accountant, there is a good chance that the initial net worth of your home will be ruled as a premarital asset. The danger here is that judges have wide discretion, once assets have been commingled. It is best to have a prenuptial agreement that deals with issues such as these.

Q: Can my divorcing wife get my pension?

A. The amount in your work pension before marriage should be considered a prenuptial asset and is yours. However, any amount earned in your pension plan during the marriage is a community asset that must be split. This is true for her pension as well as yours. Your wife may also receive more than 50 percent of your pension in lieu of your obtaining other marital assets, and vice versa.

Q. My wife has a live-in boyfriend. The kids tell me that he abuses them and hits them. They are afraid of him and hate him. Is there anything I can do to protect my children?

A. The sad thing is that there is nothing you can do except wait for the right moment, even if your children are endangered. Once you have convincing evidence of physical harm to your children, immediately take them to the hospital, call your attorney, and get an ex parte order giving you temporary custody. Call child service and the police and file charges of child abuse. Keep the children with you until there is a court hearing. File for permanent custody of the children.

Q. What's better for a man, a male or female attorney?

A. Evidence shows substantial gender bias against fathers in family law and the courts. I once believed that a competent female attorney was more effective than a competent male attorney in representing fathers. A female attorney symbolically was perceived as a women/mother testifying that a man is a good father. Female attorneys seemed more comfortable with a family law system whose players are more often other women than men. I now believe the system has changed to become fairer to fathers. Rather than choosing an attorney based on gender, choose a competent, experienced attorney who practices family law, one who knows the "players" at the courthouse.

Q. Is there any help for those involved in a custody dispute who can't afford an attorney?

A. There is little or no help for either men or women in civil law. Any person accused of a felony can get an attorney appointed by the state. However a parent who might lose a child in the family law system risks a much greater loss, but can receive no help. Lawyers seldom take pro bono cases in family law because these cases consume too many billable hours. More and more parents are learning to represent themselves pro se, and frankly maybe what we need is a system where lawyers are prohibited from operating in the field of family law. The greatest reform needed in family law is to remove the issue of custody completely from the realm of adversarial law. The present system of pitting one parent against the other is barbaric. Our legislature has a long way to go in true reform in family law. Some counties now have pro se clinics in which attorneys volunteer to help parties fill out pro se forms. You can get some good legal advice through these clinics.

Organizations and People Who Can Help

Reinventing the wheel in divorce and custody issues is an expensive way to learn. The person who seeks out the advice of individuals and organizations that are versed in these issues can save thousands of dollars and mountains of grief and insecurity.

There are not many organizations in Wisconsin that are dedicated to men and fathers. Hundreds of women's organizations exist, subsidized by the local, state, and federal governments using your tax dollars. Parallel to this government funding is volunteer funding from United Way and branches of the University of Wisconsin system. The inherent assumption for all the funding for women is that men are oppressors and women are victims who need societal protection. This assumption is ironic in the area of family law, where men are almost always the ones who face sexual discrimination.

Wisconsin Fathers for Children and Families

P.O. Box 1742, Madison, WI 53701. Tel. (608) ALL-DADS.

Founded in 1987, WFCF is a volunteer organization consisting of about 200 members, about 80 percent of who are fathers and 20 percent are second wives and grandparents. Membership is $30 a year.

WFCF has public meetings in Madison about four times a year. It publishes a monthly newsletter called Today's Dads, which is the only fathers' publication in Wisconsin. Its purpose is inform members about fathers' issues and to educate public officials and in the process help eradicate gender bias against fathers in the courts.

WFCF has an information web page--wisconsinfathers.org —with links to other states and information resources on various topics.

WFCF has a brotherly relationship with Legislation for Kids and Dads, whose purpose is to advocate change in divorce and custody issues and monitor legislation in Wisconsin on these issues.

WFCF's 608-ALL-DADS hotline answers more than a thousand calls each year. Its purpose is to give initial direction to any caller who has no idea how to begin coping with a family law crisis in his life. WFCF gives lawyer referrals to its members.

WFCF sells a variety of items, including legal form packets, copies of statutes, tapes on shared custody and gender bias in the courts, pro se forms with instructions, and bumper stickers proclaiming." Kids Need Both Parents."

Special thank to WFCF co-founders, Dr. William Fetzner, Dr. Bennett Stark, and James Novak. They have left a structure and legacy to help fathers into the future.

Contacts:

James Novak

2116 Monroe St.

Madison, WI 53711

608-255-1100

Jan Raz, President
10120 W. Forest Home
Hales Corner, WI 53130
414-425-4866

Jim Perry
7206 Fortune Dr.
Middleton, WI 53562
608-831-8620

Joe Vaughn
6909 N. County Rd. M, Lot 35
Evansville, WI 53535
608-882-2412

Family Action Association (FAA)

FAA is a loose alliance of members who meet irregularly in a number of northern Wisconsin cities. Their goal is to reform family law and remove barriers that prevent fathers from remaining parents after divorce.
Contacts:
In Tempeuleau
Dick Frey
Rt. 2, Box 89
Trempeuleau, WI 54661
606-534-6765

In Onalaska:
Jim Olson
515- 16th Ave. North
Onalaska, WI 54650
608-781-6028

In Friendship
Rich Leistikow
1553 -11th Lane
Friendship, WI 53934
608-339-2659

For Kids Sake

For Kids Sake is the effort of Lynn Kempen to improve the situation for children of divorce. As a second wife to a father who has had custody problems, she has been an advocate for joint-parenting of children, recognizing that in most cases this is in children's best interest. Lynn participated in the tape that WFCF produced on joint custody.
Lynn Kempen
N7933 Town Hall Rd.
Black Creek, WI 53934
608-833-9599

Legislation for Kids and Dads (LKD)

This Madison-area group tracks legislation, proposes laws, and lobbies for legislative changes. LKD seeks to preserve and improve the child-father bond, regardless of marital status.

LKD Works closely with WFCF and summarizes legislative activity in Wisconsin regarding family law issues. For more information, call one of the following contacts.
James Luscher
1401 Beld St.
Madison, WI 53715
608-257-1129

Clair Wiederholt
5746 Weis Rd.
Waunakee, WI 53597
608-849-8438

Clair Wiederholt teaches men's studies at Madison Area Technical College. His courses are male-positive and he introduces hundreds of young people each year to develop a better understanding of what it means to be a male in America. Clair follows legislation that would effect fathers of divorce.

Parents Rights Coalition (PRC)

This Milwaukee-based group fosters education in family law issues. PRC members support each other in dealing with the legal system. They work to change family law for greater fairness and equal treatment of fathers and mothers.

The goals of PRC are as follows:

1. Education of members on family laws in Wisconsin and their constitutional rights as parents.

2. Acting as a source of information on dealing with the legal system to achieve equal treatment in placement and child-support cases.

3. Promoting legislation that provides both parents with equal rights and responsibilities.

4. Promoting legislation that would discourage one parent from interfering with the rights of the children and the other parent in maintaining an ongoing parental relationship.

5. Promote legislation that would consider the incomes of both parents in setting child-support awards.

Contact:

Mark Lowerenz

P.O. Box 1411

Waukesha, WI 53187

414-650-1156

Shared Parenting Responsibility Interest Group (SPRIG)

SPRIG is a Madison-based group composed of men and women committed to shared parenting. They encourage the

involvement of both parents in their children's lives after divorce. SPRIG believes that shared parenting reduces the emotional trauma of divorce for children. They believe that the new roles of men and women in both home and professional work is a model for fathers and mothers of divorce. Theirs is an egalitarian approach.
Contact:
Keith Wessel
123 E. Doty St., Suite 303
Madison, WI 53703
608-256-1480

Wisconsin Children Advocates

This group fosters the presumption of joint custody at divorce. It cooperates closely with the PRC in the development of joint custody legislation. Bob Eisenbart is a great resource for those in southeast Wisconsin. He was one of the authors of the proposals for family law reform that eventually were passed in 1999.
Contact:
Bob Eisenbart
2921 93rd St.
Sturtevant, WI 53177
262-886-4196

Victims of Child Abuse Laws (VOCAL)

This national organization has helped many fathers falsely accused of physical and or sexual abuse of their children. VOCAL is a national organization with chapters in most states and in hundreds of cities throughout the United States and Canada. If accused of child abuse, help from this group could be essential.
Contacts:
National VOCAL Office

1-800-848-6225

National Association of State VOCAL Organizations
7485 E. Kenyon Ave.
Denver, CO 80237
800-745-8778

James Krueger or Lorna Waldron
1722 Highway D
Belgium, WI 53004
414-235-1745

National Coalition for Free Men (NCFM)

The National Coalition for Free Men is one of the oldest men's organizations in the United States. It publishes the newsletter titled *Transitions*, a must-read publication to keep you informed of fathers and men's issues. It is well worth the $20/yr. subscription fee.
Contact:
Tom Williamson, President
P.O. Box 129
Manhasset, NY 11030
516-482-6378
Toll free inquiries and messages: 888-223-1280

Transitions
Gerry Bisset, Editor
transitions@ncfm.org
http://www.ncfm.org

Domestic Abuse Project (DAP)

The domestic abuse project was started as a committee of Wisconsin Fathers for Equal Justice. Through the efforts of Dr. Roy Schenk, it is presently the only organization in Wisconsin that officially recognizes that men are also victims of domestic abuse in America. DAP maintains a hotline in Madison, Wisconsin. Counseling and some lodging is available for abused men.

Contact:
Domestic Abuse Project
Dr. Roy Schenk
1129 Drake St.
Madison, WI 53711
608-233-3317
608-255-4028
Private Counseling Sessions

How to Win Custody

James Novak, the author of this book, provides one-on-one workshops for fathers, mothers, and second wives who are facing crisis in family law matters. This workshop is a two-hour private session that explores the politics of divorce and planning strategy. The workshop is ideal for those just beginning the divorce/custody process. It focuses on the following topics:

1. What does it mean to win custody in a situation where the other parent does not go away?

2. How can you find a competent attorney and how can you control your attorney so that he zealously represents you? How does one develop a partnership with his attorney?

3. What is the process that takes place in custody litigation?

4. What are those things not in the statutes, but are essential to winning a custody fight?

5. What are the educational materials a father should read so that he can become "litigation literate" and can intelligently converse with his attorney? How can a father lower his attorney fees by becoming self-educated?

Those who wish to take this two-hour session are first asked to read this book and write down all their questions. At the session, the facts of one case will be applied to the content of this book. James Novak is not an attorney and these sessions should not be substituted for the legal counsel.

This workshop is open only to those dedicated to continue parenting. Cost of the two-hour workshop is $150. To schedule an appointment, call Jim Novak at (608) 255-1100 or (608) 255-3237

A Bibliography of Useful Writings

The easiest way to become self-educated in family law is to read. If you read at a high school level, you will be able to find and understand materials that can help you along in the process to winning custody. One favorable effect of self-education is that you will spend far fewer hours with an attorney, and the hours you do spend with your attorney will be more fruitful. Moreover, as you become more versed in the legal issues of custody, you will become empowered.

Although there are thousands of sources available, many are a waste of time. The following is a short list of what might be most useful, given that you have only a limited amount of time for self-education while you are litigating.

Books

American Bar Association, *Guide to Family Law*, Times Books, (Random House), New York, 1996.

Amneus, Daniel, *The Garbage Generation*, Primrose Press, 2131 S. Primrose Ave. Alhambra, CA 91803. Covers the effects of children raised in mother-headed families without fathers.

August, Eugene, *The New Men's Studies: A Selected and Annotated Interdisciplinary Bibliography*, Libraries Unlimited, Englewood, CO. Tel (800) 237-6124. A source book for all other books on father's and men's issues.

Brennan, Carleen and Michael, *Custody for Fathers*, 250 E. 17th St., Costa Mesa, CA 92627, Tel. (714) 646-6732. A Practical guide through the combat zone of a brutal custody battle.

Christenson, C.B., *My Mother's House*, My Father's House, Athenum: 1989. The social worker's bible of joint-parenting after divorce.

Farrell, Dr. Warren, *The Myth of Male Power*, Simon and Schuster: New York, 1993. The best book on men's issues. Filled with a massive amount of data and statistics you can use. Presents a theory on why bad things happen to men in divorce court.

Gardner, Richard, *The Parental Alienation Syndrome*, Creative Therapeutics, Inc., 155 County Rd., Creskill, NJ 07626-0522.

Horgan, Timothy J., Winning Your Divorce: A Man's Survival Guide, New York: Dutton, 1994.

Leving, Jefferey, *Fathers' Rights*, Basic Books (Div. Of Harper Collins), New York, 1997.

Major, Dr. Jayne, *Creating a Successful Parenting Plan*, living Media, 11835 W. Olympic, Blvd., Los Angeles, CA 90064-5011 Tel. 310-473-5807.

Nolan, Joseph, and Jacqueline Nolan-Haley, *Black's Legal Dictionary*, West Publishing: St. Paul, MN., 1990. Gives definitions of legal terms and spells out basic concepts of law.

Rog, *Divorce Without Court*, Worldwide Interfaith Peace Mission, 1429 Columbia NE, Albuquerque, NM 87106. Tel. (505) 255-2221.

Steinbreder, John and Kent, Richard, *Fighting for Your Children*, Taylor Publishing Co., Dallas, Texas, 1998

Tong, Dean, Don't Blame Me, Daddy, Hampton Roads Publishing Co: Norfolk, Virginia, 1992. A must for anyone falsely accused of child abuse.

Trafford, Abigail, *Crazy Time*, Bantam Books (Harper and Row): New York, 1984. Helps one cope with the emotional crash of divorce on one's life.

Periodicals

Children's Advocate, Published by New Jersey Council for Children's Rights, Box 316, Pluckemin, NJ 07978. Comes with membership, $65/yr.

Fathers are Parents Too (FAPT) News, Published by FAPT, Keith James, Editor; (404) 496-1616 (H) or (404) 934-9441 (W). Bi-monthly.

Full Time Dads, 193 Shelly Avenue, Elizabeth, New jersey 07208, Tel 908-355-9722. E-mail FTDMag@fathersworld.com. The goal of Full Time Dads is to enhance the role of fathers in family and society.

Liberator, published by Men's Defense Assoc. This monthly is a commonsense perspective on gender issues. The Liberator is national in scope and is the most comprehensive coverage of any men's magazine on issues of importance to fathers. Subscription is $30 a year. To subscribe, mail check to Liberator, 17854 Lyons St., Forest Lake, MN 55025-3760,

Todays Dads, published by Wisconsin Fathers for Children and Families, P.O. Box 1742, Madison, WI 53701. Monthly. Free with $30 membership. A Wisconsin publication with news, stories, advertisements, event notices, and articles on issues important to fathers of Wisconsin. Today's Dads is Wisconsin's only newsletter on issues vital to fathers and custody. Goes to all judges and legislators in the state. A must for Wisconsin fathers!

Transitions, Published by Coalition for Free Men, P.O. Box 129, Manhasset, NY 11030. Bi-monthly, $30/yr.

Resources

The following resources are excellent for anyone involved in a custody dispute. However, for the person without funds for an attorney, they are especially important. Two of these resources are invaluable for the pro se father who lacks funds but has the time and intelligence to pursue his case.

System Book for Family Law: A Forms and Procedures Handbook (Two Volumes), by Leonard L. Loeb, Sharon A. Drew, and Gregg M. Herman, CLE Books: The State Bar of Wisconsin, P. O. Box 7158, Madison, WI 53707. To order, call (800) 728-7788 or (800) 362-8096. Cost $195. This is the book attorneys use to guide them through family law. Includes all necessary forms for a pro se litigant with explanations on how to fill them in. The System Book for Family Law gives every pro se dad the opportunity to pursue his case with little expense. The State Bar never intended for this system book to be put in the hands of pro se fathers in divorce court, but no better handbook exists to guide fathers step-by-step through the litigation process. The manuals are expensive, but at $195 it is equivalent to about 11/2 hours with an attorney. The System Book for Family Law is available at the State Law Library in the Capitol Building in Madison and may be in your county courthouse law library. It is in loose-leaf form so that you may easily photocopy those parts you may need. With the System Book for Family Law, you'll be only a step behind most attorneys, and a step in front of some.

Pro Se Modifications of Child-support Awards through the Courts Pilot Project, Final Report, March 1995, by Eleanor H. Landstreet, Copyright 1994. The American Bar Association. A copy may be obtained free by writing The ABA Center on Children and the Law, 1800 M St., NW, Washington, DC 20036. Tel (202) 331-2250. This report was developed under a grant from the State Justice Institute and the Federal Office of Child-support

Enforcement. It includes forms and instructions for the use of those who cannot afford an attorney and who must file a pro se action. When fathers lose a good-paying job, they may not have the money to hire an attorney. Their child-support oblig-ation, however, continues at the rate based upon their higher former income, and the child-support obligation cannot be for-given. For those who cannot afford an attorney, this is a "Catch 22." Thus, it is imperative that a father file for a reduction in child support the very day he loses his job. A reduction is retroactive only to the date of filing. This project report includes forms for reduction of child support and instructions on how to fill them out. The forms need to be adjusted to a Wis-consin format, but all the basics are there for a pro se action.

Family Court Resource Booklet. This is a collaborative project of the Dane County Bar Association, Family Court Commis-sioners Office, Dane County Law Library, and the Family Court Counseling Service. It may be obtained for $1.00 at the Family Court Counseling Service, 108 City-County Building, 210 Martin Luther King Blvd., Madison, WI 53709. The 48-page booklet covers divorce procedures, legal issues in divorce actions, paternity procedures, restraining orders, departments involved in family court actions, and community agencies. This booklet is jam-packed with good information. While it was written specifically for Dane County, more than half its infor-mation is applicable to any Wisconsin resident. A father involved in litigation should check with the clerk of courts or the family court counseling service in his county to see if they have a booklet specific to his county of jurisdiction. The Dane County Family Counseling Service also publishes "Choices for Parents and Children," a 14-page guide to resolving parenting conflicts. This might be a useful tool for those who are non-adversarial enough to work through to a resolution. It may be obtained at the address above.

The Wisconsin State Law Library

Doubtless, this library is the most underutilized secret in the state of Wisconsin. It has some of the best-trained personnel, and they are customer friendly. The staff will take the time to teach you to use this research facility. Most counties also have law libraries in their courthouses.

Here are some of the services provided by the Wisconsin State Law Library:

1. Reference assistance to anyone—in person, by phone or fax, and by e-mail via their web site.

2. Access via their web site to WISOLL (Wisconsin State Online Law Library), the library's automated catalog, and links to many law related sites.

3. The Legal Resource Index, an automated index to articles published in more than 900 periodicals from 1980 to the present.

4. Computerized Legal Research, using Westlaw and Lexis-Nexis.

5. Requested information mailed or faxed for a nominal fee.

6. Workshops on how to use legal information resources, print and electronic.

Wisconsin State Law Library
1 East Main St., 2nd Fl.
P.O.Box 7881
Madison, WI 53707-7881
Toll Free 800-322-9755
Reference-608-267-2319
Fax 608-267-2319
http://wsll.state.wi.us
Open Hours Mon.-Fri. 8-5

Other Research Libraries:
Milwaukee Legal Resource Center

Courthouse Rm. 307A
901 N. 9th St.
Milwaukee, WI 53233
414-278-4900
Fax 414-223-1818
Hours: Mon.-Fri.-8-5

Dane County Law Library
210 Martin Luther King Blvd., Rm. 315
Madison, WI 53703
608-266-6316
Fax 608-266-5988
Hours: Mon/-Fri.-8:30-4:30

Other Organizations and Internet Sites

Children's Rights Council, 300 "I" Street N.E., Suite 401, Washington, Dc 20002. David Levy, (202) 547-6227. http//www.Gocrc.com/

The motto of the Children Rights Council (CRC) is "The Best Parent is Both Parents." CRC works to assure a child the frequent, meaningful, and continuing contact with two parents and extended family the child would normally have during the marriage. Their legislative link is a must to see the status of joint custody in each state. CRC provides, for a fee, a directory of many fathers organizations around the country. Their catalog link provides numerous resources for parenting and divorce.

American Coalition for Fathers and Children, 1718 M Street, N.W., Suite 187, Washington, DC. 20036. Tel 800-978-DADS. Web site: ht.//www.acfc.org

The ACFC's philosophy is that children need both parents and this group strives for equal rights and laws for everyone affected by divorce. The information on legislation and legal issues is valuable, as are the studies and reports section of their web site which is divided into categories such as divorce statistics and child welfare. The site also contains personal testimonials, articles, and legislative information.

Daddy's Home, Web site: http://daddyshome.com This is an on-line resource for primary-care fathers. It includes practical advice for fathers who are raising children.

Wisconsin Lawyer. This is the magazine of the Wisconsin Bar Association. There are many articles that can be found on family law. It can be found on the internet at: http://wisbar/wislawmag/archive/april100/custody.html. The first article you will find is one on the new custody laws effective for cases filed May 1, 2000.

Free Pro Se Workshops

Time Magazine in its June 12, 2000, edition stated that 71 percent of those who divorce in Orange County, California, are pro se. While this percentage to some degree involves couples agreeing to an undisputed divorce, the vast majority are those with substantial adversarial issues, but who cannot afford an attorney to protect their rights.

Last year, Hon. Mary Beth Keppel, a court commissioner in Dane County, chose starting the Family Law Assistance Center as the goal of her presidency of the Dane County Bar Association. The Center was started with the help of Tess O'Brien of the Courthouse Committee and Matt Dregne of the Delivery of Legal Service Committee.

In an interview, she stated that the idea for the center came from the pro se clinic in Milwaukee and the program, "Family Law Forum," on the Internet, started by Ernesto Romero. Pros se forms may be downloaded on his site at (www.wisconsin-forms.com). Another similar program exists in Richland County, and others may be in the process of starting in other counties. The Family Law Assistance Center of Dane County is sponsored by the local bar association. Forty attorneys and five paralegals volunteer two-hour slots, three times a year. These attorneys and paralegals make it clear that they do not personally represent the people they help. They assist pro se clients in filling out the forms needed for divorces, paternity, restraining orders, placement issues, and other post-judgment motions. They provide the pro se forms and help the clients fill them out.

The volunteer attorneys and paralegals provide assistance in filling out forms, provide information regarding family court procedures, and refer clients to community resources. They do not give legal advice, give an opinion about the case, or recommend a specific lawyer for the client.

In Dane County, the pro se clinic is located in the City-County Building, 210 Martin Luther King Blvd., Room 226, Madison, Wisconsin. The clinic is first-come, first-served basis on Wednesdays from 11:30 a.m.-1:30 p.m. Pro se forms and instructions to use them are also available free from the Dane County Library in the courthouse at the same address.

I praise the commitment of the forty attorneys and five paralegals to provide help to those who are in need of help. These are deeply personal issues that include substantial financial repercussions and the risk of a most basic right of liberty-- access to and continued involvement with one's own children. Check your local county bar association to see if they have a similar program to help pro se clients.

Glossary of Legal Terms

Here are the meanings of some key words and phrases used by the legal profession. Many are Latin-derived, and others are common English words that have specific meanings when used in a legal context.

Administrative rule. Agency statement of general applicability and continuing effect that interprets law or policy or describes agency's requirements; has the effect of law.

Child support. In a dissolution or divorce, money paid by one parent to another toward the expenses of the children of the marriage.

Civil suit (into which most family law issues fall). Actions brought to enforce, redress, or protect private rights. As opposed to a criminal suit.

Community property state. A state in which the property is owned in common by husband and wife, each having undivided one-half interest by reason of their marital status. Wisconsin is a community property state.

Consideration. The inducement to a contract. The cause, motive, price, or impelling influence which induces a contracting party to enter a contract.

Criminal suit (as opposed to civil suit). A suit that declares an action as being against the state, prescribed by law, prosecuted by the state, and with a prescribed punishment.

Custody. An ambiguous term. As used, normally refers to primary physical placement in which one parent has the child more than 50.1 percent of the time.

De novo hearing. Trying the matter anew, the same as if it had not been heard before and as if no decision had previously been rendered. In family law actions, matters heard before a court commissioner can be brought before the circuit judge for a de novo hearing.

Ex parte. On one side only. A judicial proceeding, order, injunction, etc. is said to be ex parte when it is taken or granted at the moment and for the benefit of one party only, and without notice to, or consideration by, any person adversely effected.

Family court commissioner. An attorney appointed to hear initial issues in family law cases who hears the facts, can issue some court orders, and who reports to the court. In most Wisconsin courts, this is a full-time employee of the county.

Family court counselor. A person who works for the family court counselor's office, who tries to mediate settlements to divorce and custody issues without going to trial. There is an office in each county and this office reports to the chief judge.

Family support. Family support is a court-ordered payment that substitutes for child support and maintenance.

Guardian ad litem. A special guardian (attorney), appointed by the court in which a particular litigation is pending, whose duty it is to represent children in family law. The status of the guardian ad litem exists only in the specific litigation in which the appointment occurs.

Joint physical custody (placement). The condition in which both parents have exactly 50/50 placement of their children.

Each party legally owes the other child support. Since 50/50 placement in any year is impossible, since there are 365 overnights in any one year, generally the couple stipulates that placement shall be considered to be 50/50.

Legal custody. The right and responsibility to make major decisions concerning the child, except with respect to unspecified decisions as set forth by the court or the parties. Major decisions include, but are not limited to, those regarding the consent to marry, entering military service, obtaining a driver's license, authorization for non-emergency health care, and permission to attend school events. Contrary to the definition given in the statute, in practice and effect the parent with primary placement makes the decisions of which school the child shall attend, the child's religious education, and medical care. Legal custody has little effect in the daily life of a child. Joint legal custody indicates that both parties share custody and neither party's rights are superior to the other's.

Maintenance. The furnishing of financial support by one person to another for living expenses—food, clothing, shelter, etc.—particularly where the legal relationship of the parties is such that one is legally bound to support the other, as between husband and wife.

Mediation. A cooperative process involving the parties and a mediator, the purpose of which is to help the parties by applying communication and dispute skills, and defining and resolving their disagreements, with the best interest of the child as a paramount consideration.

Mixed assets (co-mingled assets). Assets which were exclusively owned by one party before the marriage, but which have been placed under joint control or have been improved or maintained by the other party in a marriage. (Example: A women solely owns a home before her marriage, but after the marriage she and her husband add a room, using common funds, and pay the mortgage out of a joint checking account. This home then becomes a co-mingled asset.)

Overnights. The counting of nights when the children sleep at one parent's house or the other. The significance of the term is that the amount of relief granted from the percentage standard in child support is based upon overnights, not upon time during the day that a child may spend with a parent.

Paternity father. A father who has never married his child's mother. Often, if that father's name is not placed on the birth certificate, he must be declared the father of the child through the court. A paternity child is the child of an unmarried father and mother.

Petitioner. The one who starts an equity proceeding (lawsuit) or the one who initiates an appeal from a judgment.

Physical placement. The condition under which a party has the right to have a child physically placed with that party and has the right and responsibility to make, during placement, routine daily decisions regarding the child's care, consistent with major decisions made by a person having legal custody.

Prenuptial agreement. An agreement entered into by prospective spouses prior to marriage but in contemplation and in consideration of marriage. By it, the property or other financial rights of one or both of the prospective spouses are determined or are secured to one or both of them or their children.

Prenuptial property. Property owned by one party prior to a marriage. This documented property remains in that person's name and is maintained separately apart from the funds or involvement of the other spouse. This may also be property defined under a prenuptial agreement as prenuptial property.

Presumption of joint custody. The state in which it is presumed that each parent will maintain the same rights and responsibilities that they enjoyed with their children during the marriage. Generally, this phrase in effect means that, at divorce, the court shall give joint physical placement to both parents, unless one parent shows cause why joint physical placement will be harmful to the child. The challenging parent must over-come the presumption of the law. The presumption of joint legal custody exists in Wisconsin, but not that of joint physical placement.

Primary physical placement. The person having the child more than 50.1% of the time. Under WDW 40, this person is entitled to receive child support, can determine where the child goes to school and where the child lives, can determine the child's religion, has control over the child, and effectively has control over the other parent's access to the child.

Pro bono. Used to describe work or services done or per-formed free of charge. Most lawyers will not do pro bono work in family law because the length of commitment in a family law case is extensive and more than they wish to donate.

Pro se. Appearing for and representing oneself, as in the case of one who does not retain a lawyer and appears for himself in court.

Reasonable visitation. This phrase often appears in orders regarding physical placement. The phrase is ambiguous be-cause it does not guarantee any specific placement time. In practice, reasonable visitation is the time the parent, who has primary physical placement, thinks is reasonable. This phrase is, in essence, a 24-hour injunction, 365 days a year, that prohibits the non-custodial parent from seeing the child. If you are divorced and do not have specific placement time spelled out in your court order, then you are entitled to no time with your children.

Respondent. In equity practice, the party who makes an answer to a bill or other proceeding in equity. The person who is served papers in a lawsuit.

Restraining order (temporary restraining order; TRO). An order in the nature of an injunction which may be issued upon filing of an application for an injunction forbidding the defendant from carrying out a specified act until a hearing on the application can be held. In the practice of family law, this is often associated with domestic abuse.

Stipulation. Voluntary agreement/contract between opposing parties concerning disposition for some relevant point, so as to obviate need for proof or to narrow the range of litigable issues. A husband and wife may voluntarily agree, or stipulate, on divorce and custody issues without a trial.

Summons. The notification to a defendant that an action has been instituted against him, and that he (the defendant or respondent) is required to answer it at a time and place named. A party upon signing the delivered summons acknowledges that the court has jurisdiction of a legal matter.

Temporary order. An initial order normally issued by a family court commissioner that includes matters such as placement of minor children, restraining orders, legislative instructions, who pays which bills, and child-support orders. This is one of the most deceptive phrases in family law, since the orders put into place in temporary hearings will, in about 80 percent of all contested cases, become the final orders at the end of the litigation process. In family law, one should recognize a temporary order as difficult to change later on.

WDW 40. The administrative rule that interprets the child-support law in Wisconsin. This rule details the percentage standards, provides tables, and includes a worksheet to help determine the extent of child support required.

Model Joint Physical Placement Schedule

Tis appendix presumes that both parties are fit and wish to have maximum time raising their children after divorce. Those who need this appendix will believe that "the best parent is both parents." This representative divorced family will have two working parents with similar incomes, and have two children. Each parent lives within fifteen miles of the children's school district. Each parent is still angry with the other, but each believes that while they have ended the marriage, their children have a right to continuing contact with the other parent.

This model joint parenting schedule is meant to be a useful starting point for parents seeking a fair placement schedule. Each parent will have special needs, and parts of this agreement may have to be changed to accommodate specific situations.

PLACEMENT SCHEDULE

I. Regular Schedule: Each parent will have the child every other week. The parent who has placement during the week will be responsible for all the children's needs, but will consult the other parent if a major decision-making situation arises during that parent's week. The next week the other parent will have the children under the same circumstances. This arrangement will rotate in alternate weeks throughout the year.

II. School Vacation Schedule: There are three major holidays during the school year. They are Thanksgiving, which extends from after school on Wednesday before Thanksgiving to the following Sunday evening at 8:00 p.m. Thanksgiving is a four-day vacation.

Christmas is the most popular national holiday, one during which all parents want to spend time with their children. It starts the Friday after school before Christmas and extends to the first Sunday after New Year's day. Generally there is a break of about 15 days. For this discussion we will be calling the first day of Christmas break December 19 and the day the children go back to school, January 3. Christmas will be divided into two periods. The first period will be from after school on Dec. 19 through 10 a.m. on Christmas morning. The second period will extend from Christmas morning at 10 a.m. through Jan. 3 at 8:00 p.m.

The last vacation period is at Easter and is often called "spring break." It starts after school on the Thursday before Easter and extends to the Sunday night after Easter.

So that each parent can have the children during some of the holidays each year, there will be a rotating, alternate-year schedule of A and B as follows:

Schedule A   1. Thanksgiving. All days (4)
              2. Dec. 25, 10:00 a.m. through Jan. 3 at 8:00 p.m. (10 days)
Schedule B   1. Easter. All days (10 days)
              2. Dec. 19, after school, through Dec. 25 at 0:00 a.m. (5 days)

This schedule allows each parent over a two-year period to celebrate each holiday with their children with the children having access to each set of grandparents on holidays. The holiday time spent with each parent will be about equal.

III. Summer Schedule: The summer schedule will follow the every-other-week routine with one exception. Each parent will have the option of getting one of the other parent's weeks during the summer. This effectively gives each parent a three-week period in which to take a major out-of-town vacation with their children. When they return, they pick up on an every-other-week rotational schedule.

IV. Special Days: Special days take precedence over the other schedules, but in the event they occur during holiday schedules, some negotiations may be necessary.

A. Each parent will have the children on that parent's birthday.

B. Each parent will have one child each year on the child's birthday. Both children will be with each other on birthdays. The child will spend the next year's birthday with the other parent. Each parent will have one child on its birthday each year. In a two-year period, each child will be able to celebrate its birthday once with each parent.

C. The mother will have both children on Mother's Day, and the father will have both children on Father's Day, each from 10:00 a.m. until 8:00 p.m. Many of the above special days will not be a problem, since the days will fall within that parent's regular weekly schedule.

V. Telephone Access. Each child will have daily telephone access to the other parent during the week the child is not placed with that parent.

VI. Internet Access. Parents and children can communicate for next to nothing over the internet. This includes personal letters and a Hotmail site with a personal identification to keep a vengeful parent from intercepting or reading the other parent's or child's mail. Documents such as school art, poetry, and report cards may be scanned and sent by e-mail.

Last, there are some general guidelines in order for this placement schedule to work. It is important that the changeover time be at the same time throughout the year so that children, especially younger ones, can keep track of where they are supposed to be. I suggest a changeover time on Fridays at 3:00 p.m. so that the children can be picked up at school, thus avoiding potential pickup and drop-off confrontations with some parents. Moreover, a Friday after-school changeover allows more flexibility for 3-4 day holiday weekends than a Sunday change that would be in the middle of a long weekend. A criticism of joint-placement schedules made by some professionals is that there are too many changeovers for the children. You should respond by saying that this schedule has far fewer changeovers than the default schedule of every-other-weekend with one overnight on Tuesday or Wednesday of each week.

Remember, this is a template model for the parties in setting up a joint physical placement schedule. There are other ways for setting up joint custody schedules. Adjust this model to fit your personal circumstances so that each parent can continue to have maximum parenting time with their children.

A Model Prenuptial Agreement

L est a man repeat the same mistakes, he should have a premarital agreement in his next marriage. Approximately eighty percent of divorced people remarry within five years. It would be easy to fall into the same traps as in a past marriage. This template agreement will make it easy to personalize your own agreement.

One has a choice in marital agreements in Wisconsin. The state has hundreds of pages of statutes and tens of thousands of pages of case history covering marriage and family. Moreover, every new statute or case of record is part of your marriage contract, even if enacted or decided after your marriage. All of these constitute your premarital agreement if you marry in Wisconsin. The other option is for the two parties to write their own marital agreement. It will be shorter and less complicated than the state's agreement, which consists of all appropriate statutes and case history. Your agreement will be personal and binding on the court. Should you divorce, most litigation following the divorce will be less stressful, since both of the parties voluntarily entered into the agreement.

One major problem in writing a prenuptial agreement is that it feels as if one is planning and writing a divorce. Writing an agreement can bring up many of the painful issues all parties face when they divorce, and this brings about uncomfortable feelings, incompatible with the hopes and aspirations we all feel when going into a relationship and marriage. The prenuptial agreement should be done at least two months before the marriage, since one might find some difficult issues which take time to resolve.

The following is a sample agreement that can serve as a starting point for writing your own. Change and personalize this agreement as you see fit. Both you and your future spouse should work out its terms before either of you consults with an attorney. Attorneys will only make it more difficult to reach an agreement. However, after both parties have reached an agreement, they should consult their own attorneys. When both parties have legal counsel before signing a premarital agreement, it less likely that any possible challenge to the agreement will be successful.

There should be a separate list for each party's assets and liabilities, and these lists should be attached as an appendix to the prenuptial agreement. The declaration of each party's assets and liabilities is an essential part of a prenuptial agreement. It would be wise for each party also to execute a will before the marriage, but this is not an essential part of the prenuptial agreement.

Template Marital Property Agreement

THIS AGREEMENT is between (Name) ("Husband") of (City) , Wisconsin and (Name) of (City), Wisconsin ("Wife"), alternatively referred to as the "Parties" to this Agreement.

RECITALS

WHEREAS, the Parties to this Agreement intend to marry one another and are making this Agreement in contemplation of becoming Husband and Wife; and

WHEREAS, the Parties desire to contract with each other concerning owner-ship and management of their incomes, assets, expenses and liabilities during their marriage; and

WHEREAS, the Parties desire to contract with one another concerning mat-ters of the disposition of their assets and liabilities during their marriage and at the termination of their marriage by dissolution or the death of either of them; and

WHEREAS, Husband has previously been married to another and has a child by that previous marriage who is his presumptive heir-at-law; and (Optional)

WHEREAS, the Parties intend that the terms and provisions of this Agreement shall apply to property and/or property interests currently owned by either of them, and also to property and/or property interests which they or either of them may hereafter acquire; and

WHEREAS, each Party fully understands that in the absence of this Agreement, the law would confer upon him/her certain property rights in the present or future property of the other, and, except as expressly set forth in this Agree-ment, it is the intent of each Party by this Agreement to completely relinquish all rights in such property; and

WHEREAS, except as expressly provided herein, the Parties intend to alter the applicability of the Wisconsin Marital Property Act, 1983 Wisconsin Act 186, 1985 Wisconsin Act 37, and the 1987 Wisconsin Act 393, as amended to date and from time to time hereafter ("Act"), together with any other marital property law or community property law which may at any time be applied to property of the Parties, with respect to various property rights, obligations, remedies and economic incidents which have arisen or will arise during their marriage;

NOW, THEREFORE, with the express intention that this Agreement be legally binding, the Parties revoke all prior agreements and hereby agree as follows:

1. Effective Date

This agreement shall take effect as of the date of the marriage of the Par ties, and shall continue in effect until final disposition of all property sub ject to this Agreement upon termination of the marriage of the Parties by death or dissolution.

2. Intent of Parties

Except as expressly set forth in this Agreement, it is the intent of the Parties to alter the effect of the Act as amended at any time hereafter, together with any marital property law or community property law which may at any time be applied to property of the Parties, with respect to various property rights, obligations, remedies, and economic incidents which have arisen or will arise during their marriage.

3. Consideration

The sole consideration for this Agreement shall be the mutual promises and covenants contained in this Agreement.

4. Financial Disclosure

Both Parties affirm that they have, in negotiating this Agreement, fairly and reasonably disclosed to the other their respective incomes, assets, expenses, and liabilities, and each further represents that he/she is satisfied that fair and reasonable disclosure has been made. Each Party further waives the current right to information about the other's incomes, assets, expenses and liabilities beyond that already provided, and agrees that he/she enters into this Agreement with sufficient knowledge of the financial affairs of the other. However, neither Party waives the right to future information about the other's incomes, assets, expenses and liabilities, all of which the Parties agree to exchange upon reasonable request in the future.

The Parties have exchanged financial statements depicting their assets and liabilities and the approximate values thereof. While neither Party represents his/her respective financial statement to be a precise statement of his/her assets and liabilities, it constitutes a fair and reasonable approximation of such assets and liabilities.

5. Classification and Ownership of Assets

(a) General Rule. The Parties agree that all of their assets now owned or hereafter acquired, shall be classified in accordance with the manner in which such assets are "titled." Assets or interests in assets titled or deemed to be titled in the name of one Party shall be classified as the individual property of that Party under the rules described in sub-paragraph (b) below. Assets titled in the names of both Parties and property defined as "household property" shall be classified and owned according to paragraph 6. Earned income shall be classified and owned according to paragraph 7. The interest of either Party in property titled in the name of that Party and at least one other title holder other than the other Party shall be the individual property of that Party.

(b) The Parties agree that assets shall be "titled" and therefore, classified, in accordance with the following general conventions:

(1) *Real Estate*, including improvements thereon, shall be titled to the Party named as owner on the Deed, Land Contract, or other instrument of conveyance.

(2) *Bank Accounts* (including Certificates of Deposit) shall be titled to the Party named as owner on the passbook or records of the entity holding the account.

(3) *Stocks and Bonds* shall be titled to the Party named as owner on the certificate.

(4) *Tangible Personal Property* for which a certificate of title is issued shall be titled to the Party named as owner on the certificate of title. Except as provided in paragraph 6, relating to household furniture and furnishings and antiques, collections and personal effects, tangible personal property for which a certificate of title is not issued, shall be deemed titled to the Party who would be the owner of the asset as determined by the common law system of property ownership in effect in the State of Wisconsin on (Date).

(5) All assets acquired by device, bequests, or trust distribution regardless of date of acquisition shall be deemed a separate property of the recipient.

(6) Retirement accounts and IRAs will remain individual property.

6. Property Titled in Both Names; Household Property

(a) *Property Titled in Both Names.* The Parties may acquire property with joint funds held, owned, or titled in both their names with or without further designation as to status or classification. In the event that the Parties designate the form of ownership of such property in writing, such designation shall control the classification of, and rights with respect to, such property, including but not limited to, rights defined under common law forms of property ownership. In the event that no designation is made in writing, such property shall be owned by the Parties as survivorship marital property.

(b) Any untitled household furniture and furnishings and antiques, collections and personal effects owned by either Party shall be classified and owned as follows:

(1) *Untitled Household Furniture and Furnishings.* Any untitled household furniture and furnishings owned by either Husband or Wife before the date of their marriage shall be classified as his/her individual property; any untitled household furniture and furnishings acquired by either Husband or Wife on or after the date of their marriage shall be classified and owned as survivorship marital property unless such property is acquired by either Party alone as a gift or inheritance from a third party, in which event such gifted or inherited property shall be classified and owned as individual property

of the acquiring Party. As used herein, the term "untitled household furniture and furnishings: shall include household furniture, furnishings, silverware, equipment, supplies, china, books and other similar property of household use or decoration, provided, however, that such household furniture and furnishings are not antiques, collections, or personal effects, all of which are classified pursuant to (2) below.

(2) *Antiques, Collections and Personal Effects.* The antiques, collections and personal effects of either Party, whether acquired before or after the marriage of the Parties, shall at all times be classified and owned as individual property of the Party who originally furnished monetary consideration in money or moneys worth for the property unless such antiques, collections and personal effects are acquired by either Party as a gift or inheritance from a third party or as a gift from the other Party, in which event such gifted property shall be classified and owned as the individual property of the Party receiving such gift or inheritance. As used herein, the term "antiques, collections and personal effects" shall include all antiques, all collections (coin, stamp, art, etc.), clothing, jewelry, family memorabilia and other similar property of personal use or decoration.

(c) In the event that the classification of property as survivorship marital property in this section is invalid or ineffective for any reason, such property shall be classified and owned as marital property.

(d) If the homestead is in the name of only one party, the other grants a waiver to the titled party to sell the homestead without signature from the other party.

7. Classification of Earned Income

The earned income of either Party shall be classified and owned as his/her individual property. As used herein, the term earned income includes all wages, salaries, commissions, bonuses, gratuities or payments in kind generated by a Party through the application of services, labor, effort, inventiveness, physical or intellectual skill, creativity or managerial activity.

8. Income, Additions, Mixing, Appreciation

The classification and ownership of property as the individual property of a Party shall extend:

(a) To income from the property;

(b) To additions to the property, regardless of the source of the funds or property used to make or acquire the addition;

(c) To property of the other classifications mixed or commingled with the property;

(d) To realized or unrealized appreciation in the value of the property, regardless of whether that appreciation occurred through general market conditions, or through the application of labor, effort, inventiveness, physical or intellectual skill, creativity or managerial activity to the property by either of the Parties without receiving reasonable compensation therefor; and

(e) To property received in exchange for or with the proceeds of sale or financing of such property.

9. Management and Control of Individual Property

Each Party shall have the absolute and unrestricted right of management and control of his/her individual property, free from any claim that might otherwise be made by reason of their marriage, and the other Party hereby ratifies and consents on his/her part to any such management and control and waives any right he/she may otherwise have to pursue any remedy, statutory or otherwise, with respect to such management and control. As used herein, the term "management and control" shall include all common law rights of management and control including, without limitation, the right to buy, sell, use, transfer (with or without consideration), exchange, abandon, lease, consume, expend, assign, create a security interest in, mortgage, encumber, dispose of, institute or defend a civil action regarding or otherwise dealing with property as if it were property of an unmarried person. Each party grants the other a waiver for the other to sell a homestead titled in only one party's name.

10. Individual Liabilities and Obligations

With respect to all liabilities and obligations of either or both Parties, the Parties agree as follows:

(a) Except as provided otherwise in this Agreement, each Party agrees to bear and pay out of his/her individual property and his/her interest in any marital property or survivorship marital property all of his/her individual liabilities and obligations, including, without limitation, the following:

   (1) All of the liabilities and obligations which either Party has incurred or may hereafter incur in his/her sole name, including, without limitation, liabilities arising from tort, obligations arising from contract, punitive damages, penalties, fines and forfeitures.

   (2) Each Party's respective share of all liabilities and obligations which have been or may be incurred jointly, either with the other Party or with third persons.

   (3) All expenditures for his/her gifts and contributions to third persons.

(b) Except with respect to any liability or obligation which may be incurred by both Parties jointly, all obligations of a Party shall be satisfied from property in the following order:

   (1) From the incurring Party's interest in his/her individual property.

(2) When such individual property has been exhausted, from the incurring Party's interest in property which is owned by the Parties as marital property or as survivorship marital property.

(c) Each party agrees to give notice and a copy of this Agreement to all of his/her creditors prior to incurring, renewing, extending or modifying any liability or obligation to such creditor. Such notice shall be in writing and shall be delivered to the creditor by personal delivery or mail.

(d) If either Party fails to provide effective notice to any creditor as required pursuant to (c) above, and if the said creditor thereby acquires and exercises rights in any property of the non-obligated Party, then the non-obligated Party shall be entitled to recover from the obligated Party, in addition to all other rights and remedies provided by law, an amount equal in value to the loss suffered by the non-obligated Party in satisfying the liability or obligation of the obligated Party, together with all reasonable attorney's fees and costs incurred by the non-obligated Party in pursuing a recovery for such loss.

(e) Notwithstanding the foregoing paragraphs, either Party may, at his/her sole option, voluntarily contribute toward the payment of any liability and obligation of the other Party. However, such payment shall not constitute an assumption of such liability and obligation by the contributing Party, nor shall such payment constitute an admission of liability therefor by the contributing Party.

11. Preparation and Filing of Income Tax Returns

The Parties may file a joint income tax return for any calendar year in which they so agree. The United States income tax liability and any state income tax liability due with respect to any such joint returns shall be allocated between the Parties and paid by each of them out of his or her individual property or out of their joint account. The ratio between the amount payable by a Party and the total payable by the Parties filing jointly shall be the same as the ratio between the amount payable by that Party and the total payable by the Parties filing separately. Neither Party shall have, and each Party waives and releases, any claim against the other Party for any reimbursement if the filing of a joint return and the application of the foregoing formula results in no tax due from one Party and a tax savings to the other Party. If an item of income, a deduction, an exemption, or a credit is not clearly allocable to one Party or the other, it shall be divided equally between the Parties. Any additional assessments or costs of taxation by audit or other adjustments, including interest, shall be allocated between the Parties as provided in this paragraph. Any tax refunds from jointly filed tax returns shall become marital property. A Party shall not be responsible for any tax, interest, or penalty liabilities occurring as a result of an audit with regards to past tax years of the other Party prior to the marriage. Such premarital liabilities would be paid from the individual property of the incurring Party. The Parties' election to file joint rather than separate federal or state income tax returns shall not create any marital property interests or reclassification of interests in property.

12. Common Household Expenses

The Parties agree to establish a common checking account to pay common household expenses such as food, joint travel expenses, and joint entertainment. The Parties will contribute to this common checking account in such amounts as they agree from time to time hereafter. The Parties will each receive a monthly allocation from the joint account for their personal expenses.

13. Dissolution of Marriage—Property Division

In the event of the divorce, annulment, or legal separation of the Parties, the Parties agree as follows:

(a) It is the express intention of both Parties that this Agreement shall be binding on the issue of property division. The Parties acknowledge that this Agreement constitutes a written Agreement which is binding upon the court under Wis. Stat. s. 767.255(11). The Parties further acknowledge that this Agreement is equitable to both Parties.

(b) Any property which is classified as marital property or survivorship marital property shall be divided equally between the Parties.

(c) Any property which is classified as individual property shall be retained by that Party.

(d) At the time this Agreement is executed, the Parties acknowledge that they are aware of the decision of the Wisconsin Courts in Button v. Button and Warren v. Warren. In reliance thereon, the Parties agree that the property division set forth above is equitable to both of them. The Parties expressly acknowledge and agree that the value of Husband's and Wife's individual property may significantly increase or decrease in the future and that such increase/decrease standing alone shall not be sufficient to affect the equitableness of this Agreement. The Parties further expressly acknowledge that such increase or decrease has been foreseen by them and considered by them in the negotiation and preparation of this Agreement.

(e) If for any reason the Court having jurisdiction of the action for dissolution determines not to enforce the terms of this Agreement with regard to property division, the Parties agree that the Court shall nonetheless accord this Agreement substantial weight in determining a division of the property of the Parties and, to the fullest extent possible, shall follow the terms of this Agreement with regards to such property division.

(f) Neither Party shall have any obligation to the other for property division except as provided herein.

(g) Spousal maintenance remains open as to both parties.

14. Death—Disposition of Property

(a) *Survivorship Marital Property.* Upon the death of either Party, with the other Party surviving, any property which is classified and owned by the Parties as survivorship marital property or joint property shall pass outright to the surviving Party, by right of survivorship.

(b) Upon death of either Party, with the other party surviving, any property which is classified as individual or personal shall follow the terms of their Last Will and Testament.

15. Interspousal Transfers

Notwithstanding any other provision of this Agreement, either Party may, by appropriate written instrument, transfer, give, convey, devise or bequeath any property to the other. Neither Party intends by this Agreement to limit or restrict the right to receive any such transfer, gift, conveyance, devise or bequest from the other.

16. Social Security Benefits

Notwithstanding anything to the contrary contained herein, neither Party intends to limit or in any other way restrict the right of either Party to receive Social Security benefits after the death of either Party. The surviving Party shall be entitled to apply for and receive all such benefits to the maximum extent provided by law.

17. Prenuptial Custody Agreement

We have entered into marriage out of love and consequently may bring forth children as a celebration of our love; but if our union would unfortunately result in divorce, we agree that section 16 with its conditions will govern any custody settlement so as to avoid conflict and further pain to ourselves and to our children. We believe that this will be in the best interest of our children. We recognize that not all of this section is legally binding on the court, but it represents our wishes while in a state of good will. For this reason we exhort the court to accept this agreement, and also ask the court to state reasons why this stipulation should not be binding as agreed.

(a) We agree that it is the *best interest of children* to continue to have a substantial, continual, and loving relationship with their mother and father. We believe that not to have substantial involvement of both a mother and a father in a child's life would be detrimental to healthy psychological and spiritual growth in the child. We recognize that while divorce may terminate the marriage relationship for the parents, it does not diminish a mother's or a father's parental relationship or responsibilities. Consequently, we stipulate the following:

(1) We stipulate to joint legal custody and to each parent having physical placement of the children 50 percent of the time.

(2) Each parent will, thus, be paying one-half the child support costs since the children would be spending one-half of their time with their mother and father.

(3) Each parent will be responsible for one-half of all medical and dental costs. Each parent will have the right to authorize medical care. Major medical decisions will be made mutually. Both parents must agree to psychological counseling for the children.

(4) Each parent will be responsible for one-half of all child care responsibilities in time spent (parental child care), duties (taking to lessons, doctors, school, etc.), and financial (daycare costs, clothes, etc.).

(5) Both parents will have access to school, medical, and legal records.

(6) Each parent agrees to live within a sufficiently close distance so that 50/50 physical placement is possible.

(b) In the event of a custody disagreement each party will be responsible for its own legal fees, and 50 percent of any other legal fees (court, filing, GAL, etc.)

(c) Neither party will leave the state to live, disrupting the other parent's right to the child, and the children's right to the other parent. If both parents are deemed fit and one parent insists on moving, it shall be presumed that the parent moving so that physical placement is not possible or leaving the state will have diminished physical placement.

(d) In the event that the court would order child support, the parties agree that those funds will be spent exclusively for the children, and that the receiving parent would provide a quarterly financial report for the paying parent accounting for the use of the paying parent's child support.

(e) This stipulation has been entered into voluntarily and without coercion. Each parent recognizes that voluntary stipulation is preferable to extended litigation, and that extended litigation usually harms the children, and is deemed not in their best interests. Neither party considers this stipulation unconscionable.

(f) If a disagreement over the terms of this stipulation arises, we agree that a third party agreeable to both of us be chosen to arbitrate the difference. However, the conclusions of a mediator should attempt to stay as close to the terms of this agreement as possible.

(g) The parties declare that we are at a state of good will toward each other, and that the terms of this stipulation are most likely to conform to our view of the legal standard of "best interests of the children."

18. Governing Law

At the time of the execution of this Agreement, the Parties are domiciled in the State of Wisconsin. The Parties agree that this Agreement shall at all times be construed in accordance with the laws of the State of Wisconsin, notwithstanding the establishment of a domicile elsewhere by either or both of the Parties at any time subsequent to the execution of this Agreement.

Pursuant to Wis. Stat. s. 766.58(3)(g), the Parties agree that the enforceability of this Agreement shall be judged pursuant to the standards set forth in Wis. Stat. s. 766.58. To the extent that Chapter 767 imposes more stringent standards on the issues of property division or custody stipulation, the Parties agree that this said chapter shall be inapplicable in governing the enforceability of this Agreement, and hereby waive their respective rights to make any claim of unenforceability pursuant to Chapter 767.

19. Good Faith Duty

Each of the Parties agrees to act in good faith toward the other pursuant to this Agreement.

20. Binding Effect

It is the express intention of the Parties that they shall be bound by this Agreement regardless of the occurrence of unanticipated events in the future. To the fullest extent permitted by law, the Parties expressly waive all common law contract defenses, and agree to be bound by the standards of enforceability set forth in Wis. Stat. s. 766.58. The Parties believe that each of them is more advantaged by the ability to rely absolutely on this Agreement than by the availability of common law contract defenses.

This Agreement shall be binding upon and enure to the benefit of the Parties and their respective heirs, executors, Personal Representatives, successors and assigns.

21. Voluntariness

Each of the Parties acknowledges that he/she has voluntarily executed this Agreement, with full knowledge and information, and that no coercion or undue influence has been used by or against either Party in making this Agreement.

22. Amendment

This Agreement may be amended or revoked only by a written Agreement signed by both Parties.

23. Entire Agreement

This Agreement represents the entire Agreement of the Parties with respect to the subject matter hereof. All agreements, covenants, representations and warranties, express or implied, oral or written, of the Parties with regard to the subject matter hereof are contained herein. No other agreements, covenants, representations or warranties, express or implied, oral or written, have been made by either Party to the other with respect to the subject matter of this Agreement. All prior and contemporaneous conversations, negotiations, possible and alleged agreements and representations, covenants and warranties with respect to the subject matter hereof are waived, merged herein and superseded hereby.

24. Construction of Agreement

The Parties assume joint responsibility for the form and composition of this Agreement. No provision of this Agreement shall be construed for or against either Party because that Party or that Party's legal representative drafted this Agreement.

25. Severability

In the event any of the provisions of this Agreement are deemed to be invalid, inequitable or unconscionable, the same shall be severed from this Agreement and shall not affect the enforceability of the remainder of this Agreement. If such provision shall be deemed invalid, inequitable or unconscionable due to its scope or breadth, such provision shall be deemed valid to the extent of the scope or breadth permitted by law.

26. Execution of Documents

Each Party shall, upon the request of the other or of the other's personal representative, execute, acknowledge, and deliver any instruments appropriate or necessary to effectuate the intent and provisions of this Agreement.

In particular, if required by this Agreement, a Party shall execute any spousal waivers and consents or take any other action necessary under the provisions of the Employee Retirement Income Security Act of 1974, the Retirement Equity Act of 1984, or any similar law to relinquish any right, claim, or property interest existing under or created by such law in any deferred employment benefit which is classified and owned as the individual property of the other Party, and shall allow such Party to name any beneficiary and to elect any settlement of payment option under such deferred employment benefit and otherwise freely dispose of the same as if the Parties were unmarried persons.

27. Consultation with Attorney

Prior to signing this Agreement, each Party consulted with an attorney of his/her choice. Each Party has received from such attorney an explanation of the terms and legal significance of this Agreement and the effect which it has upon any interest which each Party might acquire in the property of the other and legal rights existing in the absence of this Agreement. Each Party acknowledges that he/she understands the Agreement and its legal effect, and he/she is signing the same freely and voluntarily. Neither Party has any reason to believe that the other did not understand the terms and effects of the Agreement or that he/she did not freely and voluntarily execute said Agreement.

IN WITNESS WHEREOF, this Agreement is signed on the ___ day of 19___
.

_____ (HUSBAND)   _____ (WIFE)

Financial disclosure statements, dated (Date) for both parties are attached.

Children's Bill of Rights

The following is excerpted from the Divorce Resource Booklet produced as a joint project of the Dane County Bar Association, the Dane County Court Commissioners Office, and the Dane County Family Court Counseling Service.

Some fathers are inserting the Children's Bill of Rights into their stipulated settlements. The principles in the Children's Bill of Rights stands as a set of moral principles for both parents and may be used as a guideline for post-divorce litigation when it is part of the custody agreement. I have included this appendix so that fathers can insert it into their custody agreements.

Children's Bill of Rights

1. The right to be treated as important human beings, with unique feelings, ideas, and desires and not as a source of argument between parents.
2. The right to a continuing relationship with both parents and the freedom to receive love and express love for both.
3. The right to express love and affection for each parent without having to stifle that love because of fear of disap-

proval by the other parent.

4. The right to know that their parents' decision to separate is not their responsibility and that they will have contact with both parents.

5. The right to continuing care and guidance from both parents.

6. The right to honest answers to questions about the changing family relationships.

7. The right to know and appreciate what is good in each parent without one parent degrading the other

8. The right to have a relaxed, secure relationship with both parents without being placed in a position to manipulate one parent against the other parent.\

9. The right not to be the source of argument between the parents or to be threatened with not seeing the other parent.

10. The right to be able to experience regular and consistent contact with both parents and to know that the reason for cancellation of time or change of plans.

APPENDIX EIGHT

WISCONSIN ADMINISTRATIVE CODE
Department of Health and Social Services
Effective March 1, 1995
Chapter HSS 80
CHILD SUPPORT PERCENTAGE
OF INCOME STANDARD

WDW 40.01   Introduction.
WDW 40.02   Definitions.
WDW 40.03   Support orders.
WDW 40.04   Determining the child support obligation in special circumstances.
  Serial-family payer (a payer with an existing legal obligation for child support who incurs an additional legal obligation for child support in a subsequent family as a result of a court order.)
  Shared-time payer (a payer who provides overnight child care or equivalent care beyond the threshold and assumes all variable child care costs in proportion to the number of days he or she cares for the child under the shared-time arrangement.)
  Split-custody payer (a payer who has 2 or more children and who has physical placement of one or more but not all of the children.)

WDW 40.05   Determining imputed income for child support.
  Tables
  Worksheet
  Wisconsin Statutes

PREFACE

Section 46.25 (9) (a), Stats., requires the department to adopt and publish a standard to be used by courts in determining child-support obligations. The standard is to be based on a percentage of the gross income and assets of either or both parents.

The percentage standard established in this chapter is based on an analysis of national studies, including a study done by Jacques Van der Gaag as part of the Child-support Project of the Institute for Research on Poverty, University of Wisconsin, Madison, entitled, "On Measuring the Cost of Children," which discloses the amount of income and disposable assets that parents use to raise their children. The standard is based on the principle that a child's standard of living should, to the degree possible, not be adversely affected because his or her parents are not living together. It determines the percentage of a parent's income and potential income from assets that parents should contribute toward the support of children if the family does not remain together. The standard determines the minimum amount each parent is ex-pected to contribute to the support of their children. It expects that the custodial parent shares his or her income directly with their children. It also presumes that the basic needs of the children are being met. This latter presumption may be rebutted by clear and convincing evidence that the needs of the children are not being met.

The rules also prescribe procedures for determining equitable child-support obligations under a variety of financial and family circumstances.

WDW 40.01 Introduction.

(1) Authority and purpose. This chapter is promulgated under the authority of s. 46.25 (9) (a), Stats., for the purpose of establishing a standard to be used in determining child support under ss. 767.02, 767.08, 767.10, 767.23, 767.25, 767.32 and 767.51, Stats.

(2) Applicability. This chapter applies to any petition for a temporary or final order for child support of a marital or nonmarital child in an action affecting a family under s. 767.02, Stats., any stipulated child-support settlement under s. 767.10, Stats., or any revision of judgment under s. 767.32, Stats.

History: Cr. Register, January, 1987, No. 373, eff. 2-1-87; r. (2) (b) to (d), Register, August, 1987, No. 380, eff. 9-1-87; am. (1), r. and recr. (2), Register, February, 1995, No. 470, eff. 3-1-95.

WDW 40.02 Definitions. In this chapter:

(1) "Acknowledgement of paternity" means both the mother and the father voluntarily signed and filed a form under s. 69.15 (3) (b) 1. or 3., Stats., with the state registrar.

(2) "Adjusted base" means the monthly income at which the child-support

obligation is determined for serial family payers, which is the payer's base less the amount of any existing legal obligation for child support.

(3) "Assets available for imputing income" means all real or personal property over which a payer can exercise ownership or control, including but not limited to, life insurance, cash and deposit accounts, stocks and bonds, business interests, net proceeds resulting from worker's compensation or other personal injury awards not intended to replace income, and cash and corporate income in a corporation in which the payer has an ownership interest sufficient to individually exercise control and when the cash or corporate income is not included as gross income under s. WDW 40.02 (13).

(4) "Base" means the monthly income at which the child-support obligation is determined, which is calculated by adding together the payer's gross income and the payer's imputed income for child support, and dividing by 12.

(5) "Child" means the natural or adopted child of the payer.

(6) "Child support" or "child-support obligation" means an obligation to support a marital child either in an intact family or as a result of a court order, an obligation to support the payer's nonmarital child as a result of a court order, or an obligation to support the payer's nonmarital child in an intact family as a result of adoption, maternity or an acknowledgement of paternity.

(7) "Court" means a circuit court judge or family court commissioner.

(8) "Current 6-month treasury bill rate" means the yield of a U.S. government security with a term of 6 months.

(9) "Department" means the Wisconsin Department of Workforce Development.

(10) "Dependent household member" means a person for whom a taxpayer is entitled to an exemption for the taxable year under 26 USC 151.

(11) "Family support" means an amount which a person is legally obligated to pay pursuant to an order under s. 767.261, Stats., as a substitute for child support under s. 767.25, Stats., and maintenance payments under s. 767.26, Stats.

(12) "Federal dependency exemption" means the deduction allowed in computing taxable income pursuant to 26 USC 151 for a child of the taxpayer who has not attained the age of 19 or who is a student.

(13) "Gross income" means:
   (a)   All income considered federal gross income under 26 CFR 1.61-1;
   (b)   Net proceeds resulting from worker's compensation or other personal injury awards intended to replace income;
   (c)   Unemployment compensation;
   (d)   Income continuation benefits;
   (e)   Voluntary deferred compensation, employee contributions to any employee benefit plan or profit- sharing, and voluntary employee contributions to any pension or retirement account whether or not the account provides for tax deferral or avoidance;

(f)   Military allowances and veterans benefits;

(g)   Undistributed income of a corporation, including a closely-held corporation, or any partnership, including a limited or limited liability partnership, in which the payer has an ownership interest sufficient to individually exercise control or to access the earnings of the business, unless the income included is an asset under sub. (3); Note: Income considered under this subsection is subject to the adjustments under s. WDW 40.03 (2).

(h)   Any income imputed to the payer under s. WDW 40.05; and

(i)   All other income, whether taxable or not, except that gross income does not include public assistance or child support received from previous marriages or from paternity adjudications.

(14) "Gross income available for child support" means the amount of gross income after adding wages paid to dependent household members and subtracting business expenses which the court determines are reasonably necessary for the production of that income or operation of the business and which may differ from the determination of allowable business expenses for tax purposes.

(15) "Imputed income for child support" means the amount of income ascribed to assets which are unproductive or to which income has been diverted to avoid paying child support or from which income is necessary to maintain the child or children at the economic level they would enjoy if they were living with both parents, and which exceeds the actual earnings of the assets.

(16) "Intact family" means a family in which the child or children and the payer reside in the same household and the payer shares his or her income directly with the child or children and has a legal obligation to support the child or children.

(17) "Legal obligation for child support" has the meaning prescribed for "child support" or "child-support obligation" in sub. (6).

(18) "Marital child" means a child determined to be a marital child under s. 767.60, Stats.

(19) "Parent" means the natural or adoptive parent of the child.

(20) "Parent with less time" means the parent having physical placement of the child less than 182 days a year.

(21) "Parent with more time" means the parent having physical placement of the child more than 183 days a year.

(22) "Payee" means the parent who is the recipient of child support as a result of a court order.

(23) "Payer" means the parent who incurs a legal obligation for child support as a result of a court order.

(24) "Serial family payer" means a payer with an existing legal obligation for child support who incurs an additional legal obligation for child support in a subsequent family as a result of a court order.

(25) "Shared-time payer" means a payer who provides overnight child care or equivalent care beyond the threshold and assumes all variable child care costs in proportion to the number of days he or she cares for the child under the shared-time arrangement. Note: There are physical placement arrangements in which the payer provides child care beyond the threshold and incurs additional cost in proportion to the time he or she provides care, but because of the physical placement arrangement he or she does not provide overnight care (e.g., payer provides day care while the payee is working). Upon request of one of the parties the court may determine that the physical placement arrangement other than overnight care is the equivalent of overnight care.

(26) "Split custody payer" means a payer who has 2 or more children and who has physical placement of one or more but not all of the children.

(27) "Standard" or "percentage standard" means the percentage of income standard under s. WDW 40.03 (1) which, multiplied by the payer's base or adjusted base, results in the payer's child-support obligation. Note: The standard is based on national studies of the percentage of income used to support a child or children, with adjustment downward of those percentages to reflect costs incurred by the payer for what used to be called visitation under Wisconsin law and is now called physical placement and to maintain health insurance for the child or children.

(28) "Threshold" means 30% of a year or 109.5 out of every 365 days. Note: The threshold was derived by taking 30% of a 365 day year.

(29) "Total annual income for child support" means gross income available for child support plus imputed income for child support.

(30) "Variable costs" means costs that include but are not limited to payment for food, clothing, school, extracurricular activities, recreation and day care.

(31) "Worksheet" means the department's percentage standard worksheet.

History: Cr. Register, January, 1987, No. 373, eff. 2-1-87; r. (2) (b) to (d), r. and recr. (12) to (14), renum. (26) to (28) to be (27) to (29) and am. (29), cr. (26), Register, August, 1987, No. 380, eff. 9-1-87; r. and recr., Register, February, 1995, No. 470, eff. 3-1-95.

WDW 40.03 Support orders.

(1) Determining child support using the percentage standard. The payer's base shall be determined by adding together the payer's gross income available for child support under sub. (2), if appropriate, and the payer's imputed income for child support and dividing by 12. This may be done by completing the worksheet, although use of the worksheet for this purpose is

not required. The percentage of the payer's base or adjusted base that constitutes the child-support obligation shall be:
- (a)   17% for one child;
- (b)   25% for 2 children;
- (c)   29% for 3 children;
- (d)   31% for 4 children; and
- (e)   34% for 5 or more children.

Note: See Tables which indicates the amount of child support at various levels of income using the percentage standard.

(2) Gross income available for child support. In determining the payer's base under sub. (1), the court may adjust the gross income by adding wages paid to dependent household members and by reducing gross income by the business expenses which the court determines are reasonably necessary for the production of that income or operation of the business and which may differ from the determination of allowable business expenses for tax purposes.

(3) Support obligation based on earning capacity. In situations where the income of the parent obligated to pay child support in accordance with the standard under sub. (1) is less than that parent's earning capacity, or in situations where both parents incomes are considered under s. WDW 40.04 (2) (c) and the income of one parent is less than that parent's earning capacity, the court may establish support by applying the percentage standard to:
- (a)   An amount determined by the court to represent the payer's ability to earn, based on the payer's education, training and work experience, and the availability of work in or near the payer's community; or
- (b)   The income a person would earn by working 40 hours per week fo the federal minimum hourly wage under 29 USC 206 (a) (1).

(4 Calculation of family support. When the standard under sub. (1) is used to calculate support under s. 767.261, Stats., the amount determined shall be increased by the amount necessary to provide a net family support payment, after state and federal income taxes are paid, of at least the amount of a child-support payment under the standard.

(5) Expression of ordered support. In temporary, final or revised support orders, the ordered support may be expressed either as a percentage of the base or adjusted base, or as a fixed sum, or as a combination of both as permitted under ss. 767.23 (1), 767.25 (1), 767.32 and 767.51 (4), Stats.

(6) Dependency exemption. The court may order the payee to waive the federal dependency exemption provided that the payee's execution of the exemption waiver is made contingent on the receipt of child-support payments.

(7) Deviation from the percentage standard.
- (a)   Upon request by a party, the court may modify the amount of child-

support payments determined under sub. (1) if, after considering the factors in s. 767.25 (1m) or 767.51 (5), Stats., as applicable, the court finds by the greater weight of the credible evidence that use of the percentage standard is unfair to the child or to any of the parties.

(b)   If the court under par. (a) modifies the amount of child-support pay ment determined under sub. (1), the   court shall state in writing or on the record the amount of support that would be required by using the percentage standard under sub. (1), the amount by which the court's order deviates from that amount, its reasons for finding that use of the percentage standard is unfair to the child or the party, its reasons for the amount of the modification and the basis for the mod- ification as provided under ss. 767.25 (1n) (b) and 767.51 (5d) (b), Stats.

History: Cr. Register, January, 1987, No. 373, eff. 2-1-87; am. (1) (intro.), Register, August, 1987, No. 380, eff. 9-1-87; (1) (intro.), renum. (2) to (4) to be (4) to (6) and am. (5), cr. (2), (3), (7), Register, February, 1995, No. 470, eff. 3-1-95.

WDW 40.04 Determining the child support obligation in special cir-cumstances. Child support may be determined under special circum-stances as follows:

(1) Determining the child-support obligation of a serial-family payer.

(a)   Applicability. This subsection applies only if the additional child-su-port obligation incurred by a payer is the result of a court order and the support obligation being calculated is for children from a subse-quent family or subsequent paternity judgment or acknowledgment. A payer may not use the provisions of this subsection as a basis for seeking modification of an existing order based on a subsequently incurred legal obligation for child support.

(b)   Determination. For a serial-family payer the child-support obligation incurred for a marital or nonmarital child in a subsequent family as a result of a court order may be determined as follows:

1. Determine the payer's base under s. WDW 40.03 (1) (intro.);

2. Determine the order of the payer's legal obligations for child sup port by listing them according to the date each obligation is incurred. For a marital child, the legal obligation for child support is incurred on the child's date of birth. For a nonmarital child, the legal obligation for child support is incurred on the date of the court order. For a nonmarital child in an intact family, it is incurred on the date of adoption or the date of the filing of an acknowledgement of paternity. For a nonmarital maternal child in an intact family, it is incurred on the child's date of birth;

3. Determine the first child-support obligation as follows:
   a. If the payer is subject to an existing support order for that lega obligation, the support for that obligation is the monthly amount of that order; or
   b. If the payer is not subject to an existing support order for th legal obligation, the support is determined by multiplying the appropriate percentage under s. HSS 80.03 (1) for that number of children by the payer's base;
4. Adjust the base by subtracting the support for the first legal obliga tion under subd. 3. from the payer's base under subd. 1;
5. Determine the second child-support obligation as follows:
   a. If the payer is subject to an existing support order for that legal obligation, the support for that obligation is the monthly amount of that order; or
   b. If the payer is not subject to an existing support order for that legal obligation, the support is determined by multiplying the appropriate percentage under s. HSS 80.03 (1) for that number of children by the payer's base;
6. Adjust the base a second time by subtracting the support for the second legal obligation determined under subd. 5. from the first adjusted base determined under subd. 4;
7. Repeat the procedure under subds. 5. and 6. for each additional legal obligation for child support the serial family payer has incurred;
8. Multiply the appropriate percentage under s. WDW 40.03 (1) for the number of children subject to the new order by the final adjusted base determined in either subd. 6. or 7. to determine the new child-support obligation.

Note: The following example shows how the child-support obligation is deter-mined for a serial-family payer whose additional child-support obligation has been incurred for a subsequent family.

Assumptions:
   Parent A's current base is $3000.
   Parent A and Parent B were married, had a child in 1980 and divorced in 1989. Parent A is subject to an existing support order of $450 per month.
   Parent A remarries and has two children, one born in 1991 and the other in 1992, and remains an intact family.
   Parent A was adjudicated the father in 1993 for a child born in 1990. Child support needs to be established for this child.
   Order of parent A's legal obligation for child support.

First legal obligation: one child (1980) (divorce)
Second legal obligation: 2 children (1991 and 1992) (intact family)

Third legal obligation: one child (1993) (paternity)

Calculation:

Parent A's current base	$3000.00
The first legal obligation is subject to an existing monthly support order (divorce)	$ 450.00
Adjust the base	$3000.00 −450.00
First adjusted base	$2550.00
Determine support for the second legal obligation (intact family)	$2550.00 X .25
	$ 637.50
Adjust the first adjusted base	$2550.00 −637.50
Second adjusted base	$1912.50
Determine support for the third legal obligation (paternity)	$1912.50 X .17
	$ 325.12

(2) Determining the child-support obligation of a shared-time payer. The child-support obligation in cases where both parents provide overnight child care beyond the threshold may be determined as follows:

(a) Determine the number of overnights, or the equivalent as determined by the court in accordance with s. WDW 40.02 (25), each parent has the child per year. If the parent with less time has the child at least 110 overnights but not more than 146 overnights, follow the procedure in par. (b). If each parent has the child for at least 147 overnights but for not more than 218 overnights, follow the procedure in par. (c).

(b) In cases where the parent with less time has the child for at least 110 overnights, or the equivalent as determined by the court in accordance with s. WDW 40.02 (25), per year but not more than 146 per year, determine the child support as follows:

1. Determine the child-support obligation under s. WDW 40.03 (1) of the parent with less time;
2. Divide by 365 the number of overnights the parent with less time has physical placement of the child to determine the percentage of the year that the parent with less time provides overnight care;

3. If the percentage under subd. 2. is over 30% but not more than 40%, reduce the child-support obligation under subd. 1. in accordance with Table 80.04 (2) (b);

TABLE 80.04(2)(b)
REDUCTION OF SUPPORT OBLIGATION
FOR 31% TO 40% TIME WITH CHILD

COLUMN A	COLUMN B
% of time with child	*% of original child support obligation*
30	100%
31	96.67%
32	93.34%
33	90.01%
34	86.68%
35	83.35%
36	80.02%
37	76.69%
38	73.36%
39	70.03%
40	66.70%

4. Multiply the child support obligation under subd. 1 by the appropriate percentage from Column B of Table 80.04(2)(b) to determine the amount of child support due; and
5. Express the amount of child support due identified in subd. 4 either as a percentage or as a fixed sum.

Note: The following example shows how to calculate the amount of child support for a shared-time payer who has physical placement of the child more than 30% of the year but not more than 40% of the year.

Assumptions:
Number of children: One

Parent with less time: $2,000 gross income/month
    Assumes child-caring responsibility for 138 days

Parent with more time: $1,500 gross income/month
    Assumes child-caring responsibility for 227 days

Calculation:
The child support obligations of the parent with less time
    $2,000 \times 17\% = \$340$/month.

Percentage of the year that the parent with less time provides
    overnight care = 138 days ÷ 365 days = .378 or 38%.

The percentage of the original child support obligation for the parent with less time using Table 80.04(2)(b) = 73.36%.

The child support owed by the parent with less time = $340 × 73.36% = $249.42.

The percentage of income of the parent with less time = $249.42 ÷ $2,000 = .1247 or 12.5%.

(c) In cases where each parent has the child for at least 147 overnights per year, or the equivalent as determined by the court in accordance with HSS 80.02(25), but not more than 218 overnights per year, determine the child support as follows:

1. Determine the child support obligation under s. HSS 80.03(1) of each parent as if a payer;
2. For each parent, divide the number of overnights that the parent has physical placement of the child by 365 to determine the percentage of the year that the parent provides overnight care;
3. If for a parent the percentage under subd. 2 is over 40% but not more than 59%, reduce the child support obligation for that parent in accordance with Table 80.04(2)(c), and then do the same for the other parent:

TABLE 80.04(2)(c)
REDUCTION OF SUPPORT OBLIGATION
FOR 41% TO 59% TIME WITH CHILD

COLUMN A % of time with child	COLUMN B % of original child support obligation
41	63.37%
42	60.04%
43	56.71%
44	53.38%
45	50.05%
46	46.72%
47	43.39%
48	40.06%
49	36.73%
50	33.40%
51	30.07%
52	26.74%
53	23.41%
54	20.08%
55	16.75%
56	13.42%
57	10.09%

58	6.76%
59	3.43%
60	0.00%

4. For each parent, multiply the child support obligation for that parent under subd. 1 by the appropriate percentage from Column B of Table 80.04(2)(c) to determine the amount of child support due from that parent;
5. Subtract the lesser child support obligation under subd. 4 from the greater child support obligation under subd. 4 to determine the final amount of child support due, and the payer. The resulting payer may be either parent.
6. Express the amount of child support due either as a percentage or as a fixed sum.

Note: The following example shows how to calculate the amount of child support for a shared-time payer who has physical placement of the child for more than 40% but less than 60% of the year.

Assumptions:
Number of children: One

Parent A:$2,000 gross income/month
Assumes child-caring responsibility for 160 days

Parent B: $1,500 gross income/month
Assumes child-caring responsibility for 205 days

Calculation:
Parent A's child support obligation = $2,000 × 17% = $340/month.

Parent B's child support obligation = $1,500 × 17% = $255/month.

The percentage of the year that parent A provides overnight care = 160 days ÷ 365 days = .438 or 44%.

The percentage of the year that parent B provides overnight care = 205 days ÷ 365 days =.561 or 56%.

Using Table 80.04(2)(c): Parent A's percentage of the original child support obligation = 53.38%.

Using Table 80.04(2)(c): Parent B's percentage of the original child support obligation = 13.42%.

The amount of child support parent A owes = $340 × 53.38% = $181.49.

The amount of child support parent B owes = $255 × 13.42% = $34.22.

The payer and the final amount of child support owed
$181.49 ÷ $34.22 = $147.27 owed by parent A.

The percentage of parent A's income owed as child support =
$147.27 ÷ $2,000 = .0736 or 7.36%.

(3) DETERMINING THE CHILD SUPPORT OBLIGATION OF A SPLIT-CUSTODY
PAYER. (intro.) For a split-custody payer, the child support obligation may
be determined as follows:
  (a) Determine the payer's base in accordance with s. HSS 80.03 (1) (intro.)
  for calculating the amount of child support.
  (b) Multiply the payer's base established under par. (a) by the appropriate percentage under s. HSS 80.03 (1) for the number of children in
  the payee's custody to determine the payer's child support obligation
  in dollars.
  (c) Determine the payee's base in accordance with s. HSS 80.03 (1)
  (intro.) for calculating the amount of child support.
  (d) Multiply the payee's base established under par. (e) by the appropriate percentage under s. HSS 80.03 (1) for the number of children in
  the payer's custody to determine the payee's child support obligation.
  (e) Subtract the smaller child support obligation from the larger to determine the reduced amount of child support owed by the parent with
  the larger child support obligation.

Note: The following example shows how to calculate the amount of child
support for a split-custody payer.

Assumptions:
The payer is divorced and has 3 children;
The payer has custody of one child;
The payer's monthly gross income is $3,000;
The payee has custody of 2 children; and
The payee's monthly gross income is $1500.

Calculation:

The payer's base	$3,000
The payer's original child support obligation (25% x $3,000)	750
The payee's base	1,500
The payee's original child support obligation (17% x $1500)	255
The payer owes the payee (750–255)	$495

History: Cr. Register, January, 1987, No. 373, eff. 2-1-87; am. (1) (a), (b)
(intro.) and 1., (3) (intro.), (a) and (c), r. And recr. (2), Register, August,

1987, No. 380, eff. 9-1-87; r. and recr. (1), (2), Register, February, 1995, No. 470, eff. 3-1-95.

WDW 40.05 Determining imputed income for child support. For a payer with assets, a reasonable earning potential may be attributed to the assets as follows:

(1) Determine the payer's gross income;

(2) If the court finds that the payer has underproductive assets or has diverted income into assets to avoid paying child support or that income from the payer's assets is necessary to maintain the child or children at the economic level they would have enjoyed if they and their parents had been living together, identify those assets and then impute income to them by multiplying the total net value of the assets by the current 6-month treasury bill rate or any other rate that the court determines is reasonable; and

(3) Subtract the actual earnings of the assets from the imputed income from the assets to determine the imputed income for child support.

History: Cr. Register, January, 1987, No. 373, eff. 2-1-87; r. and recr. Register, August, 1987, No. 380, eff. 9-1-87; am. (2), Register, February, 1995, eff. 3-1-95.

APPENDIX A
CHILD SUPPORT PERCENTAGE CONVERSION TABLE

BASE	*ONE CHILD*	*TWO CHILDREN*	*THREE CHILDREN*	*FOUR CHILDREN*	*FIVE OR MORE CHILDREN*
	0.17	**0.25**	**0.29**	**0.31**	**0.34**
50.00	8.50	12.50	14.50	15.50	17.00
100.00	17.00	25.00	29.00	31.00	34.00
150.00	25.50	37.50	43.50	46.50	51.00
200.00	34.00	50.00	58.00	62.00	68.00
250.00	42.50	62.50	72.50	77.50	85.00
300.00	51.00	75.00	87.00	93.00	102.00
350.00	59.50	87.50	101.50	108.50	119.00
400.00	68.00	100.00	116.00	124.00	136.00
450.00	76.50	112.50	130.50	139.50	153.00
500.00	85.00	125.00	145.00	155.00	170.00
550.00	93.50	137.50	159.50	170.50	187.00
600.00	102.00	150.00	174.00	186.00	204.00
650.00	110.50	162.50	188.50	201.50	221.00
700.00	119.00	175.00	203.00	217.00	238.00
750.00	127.50	187.50	217.50	232.50	255.00
800.00	136.00	200.00	232.00	248.00	272.00
850.00	144.50	212.50	246.50	263.50	289.00
900.00	153.00	225.00	261.00	279.00	306.00
950.00	161.50	237.50	275.50	294.50	323.00

BASE	ONE CHILD 0.17	TWO CHILDREN 0.25	THREE CHILDREN 0.29	FOUR CHILDREN 0.31	FIVE OR MORE CHILDREN 0.34
1,000.00	170.00	250.00	290.00	310.00	340.00
1,050.00	178.50	262.50	304.50	325.50	357.00
1,100.00	187.00	275.00	319.00	341.00	374.00
1,150.00	195.50	287.50	333.50	356.50	391.00
1,200.00	204.00	300.00	348.00	372.00	408.00
1,250.00	212.50	312.50	362.50	387.50	425.00
1,300.00	221.00	325.00	377.00	403.00	442.00
1,350.00	229.50	337.50	391.50	418.50	459.00
1,400.00	238.00	350.00	406.00	434.00	476.00
1,450.00	246.50	362.50	420.50	449.50	493.00
1,500.00	255.00	375.00	435.00	465.00	510.00
1,550.00	263.50	387.50	449.50	480.50	527.00
1,600.00	272.00	400.00	464.00	496.00	544.00
1,650.00	280.50	412.50	478.50	511.50	561.00
1,700.00	289.00	425.00	493.00	527.00	578.00
1,750.00	297.50	437.50	507.50	542.50	595.00
1,800.00	306.00	450.00	522.00	558.00	612.00
1,850.00	314.50	462.50	536.50	573.50	629.00

BASE	ONE CHILD 0.17	TWO CHILDREN 0.25	THREE CHILDREN 0.29	FOUR CHILDREN 0.31	FIVE OR MORE CHILDREN 0.34
1,900.00	323.00	475.00	551.00	589.00	646.00
1,950.00	331.50	487.50	565.50	604.50	663.00
2,000.00	340.00	500.00	580.00	620.00	680.00
2,050.00	348.50	512.50	594.50	635.50	697.00
2,100.00	357.00	525.00	609.00	651.00	714.00
2,150.00	365.50	537.50	623.50	666.50	731.00
2,200.00	374.00	550.00	638.00	682.00	748.00
2,250.00	382.50	562.50	652.50	697.50	765.00
2,300.00	391.00	575.00	667.00	713.00	782.00
2,350.00	399.50	587.50	681.50	728.50	799.00
2,400.00	408.00	600.00	696.00	744.00	816.00
2,450.00	416.50	612.50	710.50	759.50	833.00
2,500.00	425.00	625.00	725.00	775.00	850.00
2,550.00	433.50	637.50	739.50	790.50	867.00
2,600.00	442.00	650.00	754.00	806.00	884.00
2,650.00	450.50	662.50	768.50	821.50	901.00
2,700.00	459.00	675.00	783.00	837.00	918.00
2,750.00	467.50	687.50	797.50	852.50	935.00
2,800.00	476.00	700.00	812.00	868.00	952.00
2,850.00	484.50	712.50	826.50	883.50	969.00
2,900.00	493.00	725.00	841.00	899.00	986.00

2,950.00	501.50	737.50	855.50	914.50	1,003.00
3,000.00	510.00	750.00	870.00	930.00	1,020.00
3,050.00	518.50	762.50	884.50	945.50	1,037.00
3,100.00	527.00	775.00	899.00	961.00	1,054.00
3,150.00	535.50	787.50	913.50	976.50	1,071.00
3,200.00	544.00	800.00	928.00	992.00	1,088.00
3,250.00	552.50	812.50	942.50	1,007.50	1,105.00
3,300.00	561.00	825.00	957.00	1,023.00	1,122.00
3,350.00	569.50	837.50	971.50	1,038.50	1,139.00
3,400.00	578.00	850.00	986.00	1,054.00	1,156.00
3,450.00	586.50	862.50	1,000.50	1,069.50	1,173.00
3,500.00	595.00	875.00	1,015.00	1,085.00	1,190.00
3,550.00	603.50	887.50	1,029.50	1,100.50	1,207.00
3,600.00	612.00	900.00	1,044.00	1,116.00	1,224.00
3,650.00	620.50	912.50	1,058.50	1,131.50	1,241.00
3,700.00	629.00	925.00	1,073.00	1,147.00	1,258.00
3,750.00	637.50	937.50	1,087.50	1,162.50	1,275.00
3,800.00	646.00	950.00	1,102.00	1,178.00	1,292.00

	ONE CHILD	TWO CHILDREN	THREE CHILDREN	FOUR CHILDREN	FIVE OR MORE CHILDREN
BASE	0.17	0.25	0.29	0.31	0.34
3,850.00	654.50	962.50	1,116.50	1,193.50	1,309.00
3,900.00	663.00	975.00	1,131.00	1,209.00	1,326.00
3,950.00	671.50	987.50	1,145.50	1,224.50	1,343.00
4,000.00	680.00	1,000.00	1,160.00	1,240.00	1,360.00
4,050.00	688.50	1,012.50	1,174.50	1,255.50	1,377.00
4,100.00	697.00	1,025.00	1,189.00	1,271.00	1,394.00
4,150.00	705.50	1,037.50	1,203.50	1,286.50	1,411.00
4,200.00	714.00	1,050.00	1,218.00	1,302.00	1,428.00
4,250.00	722.50	1,062.50	1,232.50	1,317.50	1,445.00
4,300.00	731.00	1,075.00	1,247.00	1,333.00	1,462.00
4,350.00	739.50	1,087.50	1,261.50	1,348.50	1,479.00
4,400.00	748.00	1,100.00	1,276.00	1,364.00	1,496.00
4,450.00	756.50	1,112.50	1,290.50	1,379.50	1,513.00
4,500.00	765.00	1,125.00	1,305.00	1,395.00	1,530.00
4,550.00	773.50	1,137.50	1,319.50	1,410.50	1,547.00
4,600.00	782.00	1,150.00	1,334.00	1,426.00	1,564.00
4,650.00	790.50	1,162.50	1,348.50	1,441.50	1,581.00
4,700.00	799.00	1,175.00	1,363.00	1,457.00	1,598.00
4,750.00	807.50	1,187.50	1,377.50	1,472.50	1,615.00
4,800.00	816.00	1,200.00	1,392.00	1,488.00	1,632.00
4,850.00	824.50	1,212.50	1,406.50	1,503.50	1,649.00

	ONE CHILD	TWO CHILDREN	THREE CHILDREN	FOUR CHILDREN	FIVE OR MORE CHILDREN
4,900.00	833.00	1,225.00	1,421.00	1,519.00	1,666.00
4,950.00	841.50	1,237.50	1,435.50	1,534.50	1,683.00
5,000.00	850.00	1,250.00	1,450.00	1,550.00	1,700.00
5,050.00	858.50	1,262.50	1,464.50	1,565.50	1,717.00
5,100.00	867.00	1,275.00	1,479.00	1,581.00	1,734.00
5,150.00	875.50	1,287.50	1,493.50	1,596.50	1,751.00
5,200.00	884.00	1,300.00	1,508.00	1,612.00	1,768.00
5,250.00	892.50	1,312.50	1,522.50	1,627.50	1,785.00
5,300.00	901.00	1,325.00	1,537.00	1,643.00	1,802.00
5,350.00	909.50	1,337.50	1,551.50	1,658.50	1,819.00
5,400.00	918.00	1,350.00	1,566.00	1,674.00	1,836.00
5,450.00	926.50	1,362.50	1,580.50	1,689.50	1,853.00
5,500.00	935.00	1,375.00	1,595.00	1,705.00	1,870.00
5,550.00	943.50	1,387.50	1,609.50	1,720.50	1,887.00
5,600.00	952.00	1,400.00	1,624.00	1,736.00	1,904.00
5,650.00	960.50	1,412.50	1,638.50	1,751.50	1,921.00
5,700.00	969.00	1,425.00	1,653.00	1,767.00	1,938.00
5,750.00	977.50	1,437.50	1,667.50	1,782.50	1,955.00

	ONE CHILD	TWO CHILDREN	THREE CHILDREN	FOUR CHILDREN	FIVE OR MORE CHILDREN
BASE	**0.17**	**0.25**	**0.29**	**0.31**	**0.34**
5,800.00	986.00	1,450.00	1,682.00	1,798.00	1,972.00
5,850.00	994.50	1,462.50	1,696.50	1,813.50	1,989.00
5,900.00	1,003.00	1,475.00	1,711.00	1,829.00	2,006.00
5,950.00	1,011.50	1,487.50	1,725.50	1,844.50	2,023.00
6,000.00	1,020.00	1,500.00	1,740.00	1,860.00	2,040.00
6,050.00	1,028.50	1,512.50	1,754.50	1,875.50	2,057.00
6,100.00	1,037.00	1,525.00	1,769.00	1,891.00	2,074.00
6,150.00	1,045.50	1,537.50	1,783.50	1,906.50	2,091.00
6,200.00	1,054.00	1,550.00	1,798.00	1,922.00	2,108.00
6,250.00	1,062.50	1,562.50	1,812.50	1,937.50	2,125.00
6,300.00	1,071.00	1,575.00	1,827.00	1,953.00	2,142.00
6,350.00	1,079.50	1,587.50	1,841.50	1,968.50	2,159.00
6,400.00	1,088.00	1,600.00	1,856.00	1,984.00	2,176.00
6,450.00	1,096.50	1,612.50	1,870.50	1,999.50	2,193.00
6,500.00	1,105.00	1,625.00	1,885.00	2,015.00	2,210.00
6,550.00	1,113.50	1,637.50	1,899.50	2,030.50	2,227.00
6,600.00	1,122.00	1,650.00	1,914.00	2,046.00	2,244.00
6,650.00	1,130.50	1,662.50	1,928.50	2,061.50	2,261.00
6,700.00	1,139.00	1,675.00	1,943.00	2,077.00	2,278.00
6,750.00	1,147.50	1,687.50	1,957.50	2,092.50	2,295.00
6,800.00	1,156.00	1,700.00	1,972.00	2,108.00	2,312.00

BASE	ONE CHILD	TWO CHILDREN	THREE CHILDREN	FOUR CHILDREN	FIVE OR MORE CHILDREN
6,850.00	1,164.50	1,712.50	1,986.50	2,123.50	2,329.00
6,900.00	1,173.00	1,725.00	2,001.00	2,139.00	2,346.00
6,950.00	1,181.50	1,737.50	2,015.50	2,154.50	2,363.00
7,000.00	1,190.00	1,750.00	2,030.00	2,170.00	2,380.00
7,050.00	1,198.50	1,762.50	2,044.50	2,185.50	2,397.00
7,100.00	1,207.00	1,775.00	2,059.00	2,201.00	2,414.00
7,150.00	1,215.50	1,787.50	2,073.50	2,216.50	2,431.00
7,200.00	1,224.00	1,800.00	2,088.00	2,232.00	2,448.00
7,250.00	1,232.50	1,812.50	2,102.50	2,247.50	2,465.00
7,300.00	1,241.00	1,825.00	2,117.00	2,263.00	2,482.00
7,350.00	1,249.50	1,837.50	2,131.50	2,278.50	2,499.00
7,400.00	1,258.00	1,850.00	2,146.00	2,294.00	2,516.00
7,450.00	1,266.50	1,862.50	2,160.50	2,309.50	2,533.00
7,500.00	1,275.00	1,875.00	2,175.00	2,325.00	2,550.00
7,550.00	1,283.50	1,887.50	2,189.50	2,340.50	2,567.00
7,600.00	1,292.00	1,900.00	2,204.00	2,356.00	2,584.00
7,650.00	1,300.50	1,912.50	2,218.50	2,371.50	2,601.00
7,700.00	1,309.00	1,925.00	2,233.00	2,387.00	2,618.00

BASE	ONE CHILD	TWO CHILDREN	THREE CHILDREN	FOUR CHILDREN	FIVE OR MORE CHILDREN
	0.17	0.25	0.29	0.31	0.34
7,750.00	1,317.50	1,937.50	2,247.50	2,402.50	2,635.00
7,800.00	1,326.00	1,950.00	2,262.00	2,418.00	2,652.00
7,850.00	1,334.50	1,962.50	2,276.50	2,433.50	2,669.00
7,900.00	1,343.00	1,975.00	2,291.00	2,449.00	2,686.00
7,950.00	1,351.50	1,987.50	2,305.50	2,464.50	2,703.00
8,000.00	1,360.00	2,000.00	2,320.00	2,480.00	2,720.00
8,050.00	1,368.50	2,012.50	2,334.50	2,495.50	2,737.00
8,100.00	1,377.00	2,025.00	2,349.00	2,511.00	2,754.00
8,150.00	1,385.50	2,037.50	2,363.50	2,526.50	2,771.00
8,200.00	1,394.00	2,050.00	2,378.00	2,542.00	2,788.00
8,250.00	1,402.50	2,062.50	2,392.50	2,557.50	2,805.00
8,300.00	1,411.00	2,075.00	2,407.00	2,573.00	2,822.00
8,350.00	1,419.50	2,087.50	2,421.50	2,588.50	2,839.00

APPENDIX B

WISCONSIN DEPARTMENT OF HEALTH AND SOCIAL SERVICES   Check one
Division of Economic Support   ☐ Temporary
DES-3144 (Revised 9/94)   ☐ Final
Judge

CHILD SUPPORT PERCENTAGE WORKSHEET

This form may be used to calculate a child support obligation in accordance with Chapter HSS 80, Branch Wisconsin Administrative Code.
USE OF THIS FORM BY THE COURT IS OPTIONAL.

This worksheet makes use of the financial information provided to the court under Wisconsin Statutes, S. 767.27. Calculation of child support on this form requires, at a minimum, knowing the payer's gross income. Show the net value of any assets which are underproductive or to which income has been diverted to avoid paying child support, or from which income is necessary to maintain the child or children at the economic level they would have enjoyed if they or their parents were living together in order to impute income to those assets. The amount by which the imputed income from assets exceeds the actual earnings of those assets is added to the gross income. Imputation of income to assets is done at the temporary hearing only to the extent that information is available to the court or family court commissioner.

SECTION I—COMPUTATION OF THE BASE AMOUNT
FOR CALCULATING SUPPORT
A.   Calculation of gross income:
INSTRUCTIONS: Determine the payer's annual gross income using the total disclosed to the court on the standard financial disclosure form and reported on the taxpayer's individual income tax as total income.
1.   Annual income from all sources   _____
2.   Enter the amount of public assistance received   _____
3.   Enter the amount of child support received
      from previous marriages or paternity adjudications   _____
4.   Add the amounts in line 2 and 3. This is a subtotal   _____
5.   Subtract Line 4 from line 1.
      This is the payer's gross income   _____
ADJUSTMENTS TO GROSS INCOME:
6.   Enter the amount of wages paid to
      dependent household members (if applicable)   _____
7.   Add line 6 to line 5. This is a subtotal   _____
8.   Enter the amount of business expenses which
      are directly necessary to the production of income
      or operation of the business   _____

    9. Subtract line 8 from line 7. This is the payer's
        gross income available for child support   _____

B.   Calculation of imputed income for child support:

INSTRUCTIONS: Indicate the net value and actual earnings of each asset from the financial disclosure form (Wisconsin Statutes, S. 767.27) which is underproductive or to which income has been diverted to avoid paying child support, or from which income is necessary to maintain the child or children at the economic level they would enjoy if they and their parents were all living together.

Property description	*Net Value*	*Actual earning*
1. _____	$_____	$_____
2. _____	_____	_____
3. _____	_____	_____
4. _____	_____	_____
5. _____	_____	_____
6. _____	_____	_____
7. _____	_____	_____
8. _____	_____	_____
9. _____	_____	_____
10. TOTAL	_____	_____

INSTRUCTIONS: Multiply the total net value of assets listed above by the current six month treasury bill rate or by any other rate the court considers to be reasonable to determine the imputed income from assets.

11. _____ x _____ = _____
    (total net value of assets)   (rate)   (imputed income from assets)

INSTRUCTIONS: Subtract the actual earnings of the assets from the imputed income from assets to determine the imputed income for child support.

12. _____ x _____ = _____
    (imputed income   (actual income   (imputed income
      from assets)   from assets)   for child support)

C.   Determination of total monthly support obligation:
    1. Enter the amount from Part A, line 9
        (gross income available for child support)   _____
    2. Enter the amount from Part B, line 12
        (imputed income for child support)   _____
    3. Add line 1 and line 2. This is the total
        annual income for computing child support.   _____
    4. Enter the amount from line 3
        (total annual income for child support)   _____

5. Divide the amount in line 4 by 12. This is the base. _____
6. Enter the amount from line 5 (base) _____
7. Enter the appropriate percentage
   from the following table _____
   a. One child   17%
   b. Two children   25%
   c. Three children   29%
   d. Four children   31%
   e. Five or more children   34%
8. Multiply line 6 by line 7. This is the
   TOTAL MONTHLY SUPPORT OBLIGATION. _____

SECTION II—COMPUTATION OF THE ADJUSTED
MONTHLY SUPPORT OBLIGATION FOR SERIAL-FAMILY PAYERS
1. Determine the BASE under SECTION I, C.1 through
   C.5 and enter that amount here _____
2. Determine the order of the payer's legal obligations for child support by
   listing them according to the date each obligation is incurred. For marital
   child(ren), the legal obligation for child support is incurred on the child's
   date of birth. For nonmarital child(ren), the legal obligation for child support is incurred on the date of the court order. For nonmarital child(ren)
   in an intact family, it is incurred on the date of adoption or the date of the
   filing of an acknowledgement of paternity. For a nonmarital maternal
   child(ren) in an intact family, it is incurred on the child's date of birth.
   Date of the first legal obligation   _____
   Date of the second legal obligation   _____
   Date of the third legal obligation   _____
   Date of the fourth legal obligation   _____
3. Determine the monthly support for the first legal obligation:
   a) If the payer is subject to an existing support
      order for that legal obligation, the support is
      the monthly amount of that order.
      Enter that amount here _____
   b) If the payer is not subject to an existing
      support order for that legal obligation, the
      support is determined by multiplying the BASE
      (line 1) by the percentage for the appropriate
      family size (I, C. 7). Enter that amount here _____
4. Subtract either line 3(a) or 3(b) from line 1 (BASE).
   This is the First Adjusted Base _____

5. Determine the monthly support for the second legal obligation:
    a) If the payer is subject to an existing support order
    for that legal obligation, the support is the monthly
    amount of that order. Enter that amount here   _____
    b) If the payer is not subject to an existing support
    order for that legal obligation, the support is
    determined by multiplying the FIRST ADJUSTED
    BASE (line 4) by the appropriate percentage for
    the number of children (I, C. 7).
    Enter that amount here   _____
6. Subtract either line 5(a) or 5(b) from line 4
   (First Adjusted Base).
   This is the Second Adjusted Base   _____
7. Determine the monthly support for the third legal obligation:
    a) If the payer is subject to an existing support order
    for that legal obligation, the support for that
    obligation is the monthly amount of that order.
    Enter that amount here   _____
    b) If the payer is not subject to an existing support
    order for that legal obligation, the support is
    determined by multiplying the SECOND ADJUSTED
    BASE (line 6) by the appropriate percentage for
    the number of children (I, C. 7).
    Enter that amount here   _____
8. Subtract either line 7(a) or 7(b) from line 6
   (Second Adjusted Base).
   This is the Third Adjusted Base   _____
9. Continue this process for each additional legal
   obligation for child support the serial-family
   payer has incurred.
10. Multiply the appropriate percentage for the number
    of children subject to the new order by the final
    adjusted base to determine the child support obligation. _____

Note: In cases where a court order needs to be determined for marital children
and the date of an adjudicated paternity falls between the birth dates of the
first and last child in the family with marital children, the legal obligation for
child support to this family is determined as follows:
1. Determine the support for the number of children in
   this family whose birth dates are prior to the date of
   the paternity adjudication (Follow Section II. par. 1
   through 3)   _____

2. Determine the support for the number of children
   in this family whose birth dates fall after the date of
   the paternity adjudication by first doing the following:
   a) Enter the appropriate percentage from I. C. 7 for
       the number of all the children in the marital family   _____
   b) Enter the percentage used for the number of
       children from line 10(1)   _____
   c) Subtract line 10(2)(b) from line 10(2)(a)   _____
   d) Use the percentage in 10(2)(c) to determine the
       support for the remaining children in the marital
       family (follow Section II par. 4 through 7).
       Enter that amount here   _____
3. Determine the appropriate support order for the
   marital family by adding the amounts in line 10(1)
   and line 10(2)(d)   _____

APPENDIX NINE

Chapter 767—
Actions Affecting the Family

767.001 Definitions. In this chapter:

(1d) "Department" means the department of workforce development.

(1m) "Genetic test" means a test that examines genetic markers present on blood cells, skin cells, tissue cells, bodily fluid cells or cells of another body material for the purpose of determining the statistical probability of an alleged father's paternity.

(1s) "Joint legal custody" means the condition under which both parties share legal custody and neither party's legal custody rights are superior, except with respect to specified decisions as set forth by the court or the parties in the final judgment or order.

(2) "Legal custody" means:
   (a)   With respect to any person granted legal custody of a child, other than a county agency or a licensed child welfare agency under par. (b), the right and responsibility to make major decisions concerning the child, except with respect to specified decisions as set forth by the court or the parties in the final judgment or order.
   (b)   With respect to the department of health and family services or a county agency specified in s. 48.56 (1) or a licensed child wel fare agency granted legal custody of a child, the rights and responsibilities specified under s. 48.02 (12).

(2m) "Major decisions" includes, but is not limited to, decisions regarding consent to marry, consent to enter military service, consent to obtain a motor vehicle operator's license, authorization for nonemergency health care and choice of school and religion.

(3) "Mediation" means a cooperative process involving the parties and a mediator, the purpose of which is to help the parties, by applying communication and dispute resolution skills, define and resolve their own disagreements, with the best interest of the child as the paramount consideration.

(4) "Mediator" means a person with special skills and training in dispute resolution.

(5) "Physical placement" means the condition under which a party has the right to have a child physically placed with that party and has the right I and responsibility to make, during that placement, routine daily decisions regarding the child's care, consistent with major decisions made by a person having legal custody.

(6)   "Sole legal custody" means the condition under which one party has legal
       custody.
History: 1987 a. 355; 1995 a. 100, 279, 404; 1997 a. 3, 27, 35.
**NOTE: 1987 Wis. Act 355, which created this section, contains explana-
tory notes.** Sub. (2m) confers the right to choose a child's religion on the
custodial parent. Lange v. Lange, 175 Wis. 2d 373, N.W.2d (Ct. App. 1993).
A custodial parent's right to make major decisions for the children does
not give that parent the right to decide whether the actions of the non-
custodial parent are consistent with those decisions. Wood v. DeHahn, 214
Wis. 2d 221, 571 N.W.2d 186 (Ct. App. 1997).

767.01 Jurisdiction.

(1) The circuit courts have jurisdiction of all actions affecting the family and
    have authority to do all acts and things necessary and proper in such
    actions and to carry their orders and judgments into execution as pre-
    scribed in this chapter. All actions affecting the family shall be com-
    menced and conducted and the orders and judgments enforced accord-
    ing to these statutes in respect to actions in circuit court, as far as applic-
    able, except as provided in this chapter.
(2) In an action to establish paternity or to establish or enforce a child-sup
    port obligation, in regard to a child who is the subject of the action, a l
    person is subject to the jurisdiction of the courts of this state as pro-
    vided in s. 769.201 or 801.05.
(3) An action under s. 767.45 may be brought in the county in which the child
    or the alleged father resides or is found or, if the father is deceased,
    in which proceedings for probate of his estate have been or could be
    commenced.

767.015 Child custody jurisdiction. All proceedings relating to the custody
of children shall comply with the requirements of ch. 822.
History: 1975 c. 283; 1979 c. 32 s. 50; Stats. 1979 s. 767.015.

767.02 Actions affecting the family.

(1) Actions affecting the family are:
    (a)   To affirm marriage.
    (b)   Annulment.
    (c)   Divorce.
    (d)   Legal separation (formerly divorce from bed and board).
    (e)   Custody.
    (f)   For child support.
    (g)   For maintenance payments.
    (h)   For property division.
    (i)   To enforce or modify a judgment or order in an action affecting

the family granted in this state or elsewhere.

(j)   For periodic family support payments.

(k)   Concerning periods of physical placement or visitation rights to children, including an action to prohibit a move with or the removal of a child under s. 767.327 (3) (c).

(l)   To determine paternity.

(m)   To enforce or revise an order for support entered under s. 48.355 (2) (b) 4., 48.357 (5m) (a), 48.363 (2), 938.183 (4), 938.355(2) (b) 4., 938.357 (5m) (a) or 938.363 (2).

(2) Divorce" means divorce from the bonds of matrimony or absolute divorce, when used in this chapter.

767.025 Filing procedures and orders for enforcement or modification of judgments or orders in actions affecting the family. The following filing procedures shall apply to all enforcement or modification petitions, motions or orders to show cause filed for actions affecting the family under s. 767.02 (1)(i):

(1) Except as provided in sub. (2), if a petition, motion or order to show cause requesting enforcement or modification of a judgment or order in an action affecting the family which was granted by a court of this state is filed in a county other than the county in which the judgment was rendered, the petitioner or party bringing the motion or order to show cause shall send a copy of the petition, motion or order to show cause and summons to the clerk of the court in which the judgment was rendered. If a question arises as to which court should exercise jurisdiction, a conference involving both judges, all counsel and guardians ad litem may be convened under s. 807.13 (3)   to resolve the question. The petitioner shall send a copy of any order rendered pursuant to this petition, motion or order to showcause to the clerk of the court in which the original judgment or order was rendered.

(2)(a)   Except as provided in ch. 769, if the petition, motion or order to show cause is for enforcement or modification of a child support, family support or maintenance order, the petition, motion or order to show cause shall be filed in the county in which the original judgment or order was rendered or in the county where the minor children reside unless any of the following applies:

1. All parties, including the state or its delegate if support, support arrearages, costs or expenses are assigned under ch. 49, stip ulate to filing in another county.

2. The court in the county which rendered the original judgment or order orders, upon good cause shown, the enforcement or mod ification petition, motion or order to show cause to be filed in another county.

(b) If the parties have stipulated to filing in another county under par. (a) 1., the petitioner or party bringing the motion or order to show cause shall send a copy of the petition, motion or order to show cause and the summons to the clerk of court in the county in which the original judgment or order was rendered.

(c) If the court in the county which rendered the original judgment or order orders the petition, motion or order to show cause to be filed in another county under par. (a) 2., the petitioner or party bringing the motion or order to show cause shall attach a copy of the order when filing the petition, motion or order to show cause in the other county.

(4) If a petition, motion or order to show cause for enforcement or modification of a child support, family support or maintenance order is filed and heard, regardless of whether it is filed and heard in a county other than the county in which the original judgment or order was rendered, any judgment or order enforcing or modifying the original judgment or order shall specify that payments of support or maintenance, and payments of arrearages in support or maintenance, if any, are payable to the department or its designee, whichever is appropriate.

History: 1989 a. 212; 1993 a. 326, 481; 1995 a. 279; 1997 a. 27. Venue for a petition to modify or enforce an out–of–state custody decree is the county where the judgment is filed even though the judgment may be filed in any county. Sharp v. Sharp, 185 Wis. 2d 416, 518 N.W.2d 254 (Ct. App. 1994).

767.045 Guardian ad litem for minor children.

(1) APPOINTMENT.

(a) The court shall appoint a guardian ad litem for a minor child in any action affecting the family if any of the following conditions exists:

1. The court has reason for special concern as to the welfare of a minor child.

2. The legal custody or physical placement of the child is contested.

(b) The court may appoint a guardian ad litem for a minor child in any action affecting the family if the child's legal custody or physical placement is stipulated to be with any person or agency other than a parent of the child or, if at the time of the action, the child is in the legal custody of, or physically placed with, any person or agency other than the child's parent by prior order or by stipulation in this or any other action.

(c) The attorney responsible for support enforcement under s. 59.458 (1) may request that the court or family court commissioner appoint a guardian ad litem to bring an action or motion on behalf of a minor who is a nonmarital child whose paternity has not been adjudicated for the purpose of determining the paternity of the child, and the court or family court commissioner shall appoint a guardian ad litem, if any of the following applies:

(2) TIME FOR APPOINTMENT. The court shall appoint a guardian ad litem under sub. (1) (a) 1. or (b) whenever the court deems it appropriate. The court shall appoint a guardian ad litem under sub. (1) (a) 2. at the time specified in s. 767.11 (12) (b), unless upon motion by a party or its own motion, the court determines that earlier appointment is necessary.

(3) QUALIFICATIONS. The guardian ad litem shall be an attorney admitted to practice in this state. No person who is an interested party in a proceeding, appears as counsel in a proceeding on behalf of any party or is a relative or representative of an interested party may be appointed guardian ad litem in that proceeding.

(4) RESPONSIBILITIES. The guardian ad litem shall be an advocate for the best interests of a minor child as to paternity, legal custody, physical placement and support. The guardian ad litem shall function independently, in the same manner as an attorney for a party to the action, and shall consider, but shall not be bound by, the wishes of the minor child or the positions of others as to the best interests of the minor child. The guardian ad litem shall consider the factors under s. 767.24 (5) and custody studies under s. 767.11 (14). The guardian ad litem shall review and comment to the court on any mediation agreement and stipulation made under s. 767.11 (12). Unless the child otherwise requests, the guardian ad litem shall communicate to the court the wishes of the child as to the child's legal custody or physical placement under s. 767.24 (5)(b). The guardian ad litem has none of the rights or duties of a general guardian.

(4m) STATUS HEARING. (a) Subject to par. (b), at any time after 120 days after a guardian ad litem is appointed under this section, a party may request that the court schedule a status hearing related to the actions taken and work performed by the guardian ad litem in the matter. (b) A party may, not sooner than 120 days after a status hearing under this subsection is held, request that the court schedule another status hear-ing on the actions taken and work performed by the guardian ad litem in the matter.

(5) TERMINATION AND EXTENSION OF APPOINTMENT. The appointment of a guardian ad litem under sub. (1) terminates upon the entry of the court's final order or upon the termination of any appeal in which the guardian ad litem participates. The guardian ad litem may appeal, may participate in an appeal or may do neither. If an appeal is taken by any party and the guardian ad litem chooses not to participate in that appeal, he or she shall file with the appellate court a statement of reasons for not participating. Irrespective of the guardian ad litem's decision not to participate in an appeal, the appellate court may order the guardian ad litem to participate in the appeal. At any time, the guardian ad litem, any party or the person for whom the appointment is made may requestin writing that the court extend or ter-

WISCONSIN FATHER'S GUIDE TO DIVORCE

minate the appointment or reap-pointment. The court may extend that appointment, or reapoint a guardian ad litem appointed under this section, after the final order or after the termination of the appeal, but the court shall specifically state the scope of the responsibilities of the guardian ad litem during the period of that extension or reappointment.

(6) COMPENSATION. The guardian ad litem shall be compensated at a rate that the court determines is reasonable. The court shall order either or both parties to pay all or any part of the compensation of the guardian ad litem. In addition, upon motion by the guardian ad litem, the court shall order either or both parties to pay the fee for an expert witness used by the guardian ad litem, if the guardian ad litem shows that the use of the expert is necessary to assist the guardian ad litem in per-forming his or her functions or duties under this chapter. If both par-ties are indigent, the court may direct that the county of venue pay the compensation and fees. If the court orders a county to pay the com-pensation of the guardian ad litem, the amount ordered may not exceed the compensation paid to private attorneys under s. 977.08 (4m) (b). The court may order a separate judgment for the amount of the reim-bursement in favor of the county and against the party or parties respon-sible for the reimbursement. The court may enforce its orders under this subsection by means of its contempt power.

Trial court direction that the husband pay the entire fee of the guardian ad litem is held to be an abuse of discretion, requiring modification, so as to charge the wife with 50%. Tesch v. Tesch, 63 W (2d) 320, 217 NW (2d) 647.

Where guardian ad litem's report was timely disclosed to both parties, trial court did not err in failing to introduce report during custody hearing. Allen v. Allen, 78 W (2d) 263, 254 NW (2d) 244.

A guardian ad litem may not be called as a witness in a custody proceeding. The G.A.L. is to communicate with the court as a lawyer for a party and to present information by presenting evidence. Marriage of Hollister v. Hollister, 173 W (2d) 413, 496 NW (2d) 642 (Ct. App. 1992).

767.05 Procedures

(1) JURISDICTION. A court of this state having jurisdiction to hear actions affecting the family may exercise jurisdiction as provided under ch. 769 or 801.

(1m) RESIDENCE. No action under s. 767.02 (1) (a) or (b) may be brought unless at least one of the parties has been a bona fide resident of the county in which the action is brought for not less than 30 days next preceding the commencement of the action, or unless the marriage has been contracted within this state within one year prior to the com-mencement of the action. No action under s. 767.02 (1) (c) or (d) may be brought unless at least one of the parties has been a bona fide resident of the county in which the action is brought for not less than 30 days next preceding the commencement of the action. No action under s. 767.02 (1) (c) may be brought unless at least one of the parties has been a bona fide resident of this state for not less than 6 months next preceding the commencement of the action.

767.077

(2) ACTIONS FOR CUSTODY OF CHILDREN. Subject to ch. 822, the question of a child's custody may be determined as an incident of any action affecting the family or in an independent action for custody. The effect of any determination of a child's custody shall not be binding personally against any parent or guardian unless the parent or guardian has been made personally subject to the jurisdiction of the court in the action as provided under ch. 801 or has been notified under s. 822.05 as provided in s. 822.12. Nothing in this section may be construed to foreclose a person other than a parent who has physical custody of a child from proceeding under ch. 822.

(3) PARTIES. The party initiating an action affecting the family shall be denominated the petitioner. The party responding to the action shall be denominated the respondent. All references to "plaintiff" in chs. 801 to 807 shall apply to the petitioner, and all references to "defendant" in chs. 801 to 807 shall apply to the respondent. Both parties together may initiate the petition by signing and filing a joint petition. The parties to a joint petition shall be called joint petitioners. The parties to a joint petition shall state within the joint petition that both parties consent to per-sonal jurisdiction and waive service of summons.

(4) PETITION. All references to a "complaint" in chs. 801 to 807 shall applyto petitions under s. 767.085.

(5) TITLE OF ACTIONS. An action affecting the family under s. 767.02 (1) (a) to (d) or (g) to (k) shall be entitled "In re the marriage of A.B. and C.D.", except that an independent action for visitation under s.767.245 (3) shall be entitled "In re visitation with A. B.". An action affecting the family under s. 767.02 (1) (f) or (m) shall be entitled "In re the support of A.B.". A child custody action shall be entitled "In re the custody of A.B.". In all other respects, the general provisions of chs. 801 and 802 re-specting the content and form of the summons and pleadings shall apply.

(6) DISMISSAL. An action affecting the family may not be dismissed under s. 805.04 (1) unless all the parties who have appeared in the action have been served with a copy of the notice of dismissal and have had an opportunity to file a responsive pleading or motion.

(7) ACTIONS FOR CERTAIN INTERSPOUSAL REMEDIES. If a spouse has begun an action against the other spouse under s. 766.70 and either or both spouses subsequently bring an action under this chapter for divorce,

annulment or legal separation, the actions may be consolidated by the court exercising jurisdiction under this chapter. If the actions are consolidated, to the extent the procedural and substantive requirements of this chapter conflict with the requirements under s. 766.70, this chaptter controls. No action under s. 766.70 may be brought by a spouse against the other spouse while an action for divorce, annulment or legal separation is pending under this chapter.

767.07 Judgment of divorce or legal separation. A court of competent jurisdiction shall grant a judgment of divorce or legal separation if:
(1) The requirements of this chapter as to residence and marriage assessment counseling have been complied with;
(2) (a) In connection with a judgment of divorce or legal separation, the court finds that the marriage is irretrievably broken under s. 767.12 (2), unless par. (b) applies. (b) In connection with a judgment of legal sep-aration, the court finds that the marital relationship is broken under s. 767.12 (3); and
(3) To the extent it has jurisdiction to do so, the court has considered, approved or made provision for legal custody, the support of any child of the marriage entitled to support, the maintenance of either spouse, the support of the family under s. 767.261 and the disposition of property.
History: 1971 c. 220; 1977 c. 105; 1979 c. 32 ss. 50, 92 (4); Stats. 1979 s. 767.07; 1987 a. 355; 1989 a. 132. A divorce judgment did not bar a wife's action against her former husband for torts allegedly committed during the marriage. Stuart v. Stuart, 143 Wis. 2d 347, 421 N.W.2d 505 (1988).

767.075 State is real party in interest.
(1) The state is a real party in interest within the meaning of s. 803.01 for purposes of establishing paternity, securing reimbursement of aid paid, future support and costs as appropriate in an action affecting the family in any of the following circumstances:
(a) An action to establish paternity whenever there is a completed application for legal services filed with the child support program under s. 49.22 or whenever s. 767.45 (6m) or (6r) applies.
(b) An action to establish or enforce a child support or maintenance obligation whenever there is a completed application for legal ser vices filed with the child-support program under s. 49.22.
(c) Whenever aid under s. 46.261, 48.57 (3m) or (3n), 49.19 or 49.45 is provided on behalf of a dependent child or benefits are provided to the child's custodial parent under ss. 49.141 to 49.161. (cm) Whenever aid under s. 46.261, 48.57 (3m) or (3n), 49.19 or 49.45 has, in the past, been provided on behalf of a dependent child, or benefits have, in the past, been provided to the child's custodial

parent under ss. 49.141 to 49.161, and the child's family is eligible for continuing child-support services under 45 CFR 302.33.

(2)(a)   Except as provided in par. (b), in any action affecting the family under a child-support enforcement program, an attorney acting under s. 49.22 or 59.53 (5), including any district attorney or corporation counsel, represents only the state. Child support services provided by an attorney as specified in sub. (1) do not create an attorney–client relationship with any other party. (b) Paragraph (a) does not apply to an attorney who is employed by the department under s. 49.22 or a county under s. 59.53 (5) or (6) (a) to act as the guardian ad litem of the minor child for the purpose of establishing paternity.

767.077 Support for dependent child. The state or its delegate under s. 49.22 (7) shall bring an action for support of a minor child under s. 767.02 (1) (f) or, if appropriate, for paternity determination and child support under s. 767.45 whenever the child's

767.077
right to support is assigned to the state under s. 46.261, 48.57 (3m) (b) 2. or (3n) (b) 2., 49.145 (2) (s), 49.19 (4) (h) 1. b. or 49.775 (2) (bm) if all of the following apply:
(1) The child has been deprived of parental support by reason of the continued absence of a parent from the home.
(2) A court has not issued an order under s. 767.25 requiring the parent who is absent from the home to support the child.
History: 1987 a. 27; 1995 a. 289, 404; 1997 a. 27, 105.

767.078 Order in case involving dependent child.
(1)(a)   In this subsection, "case involving a dependent child" means an action which meets all of the following criteria:
    1. Is an action for modification of a child-support order under s 767.32 or an action in which an order for child support is required under s. 767.25 (1), 767.51 (3) or 767.62 (4).
    2 The child's right to support is assigned to the state under s. 48.57 (3m) (b) 2. or (3n) (b) 2. or 49.19 (4) (h) 1. b.
    3. The child has been deprived of parental support by reason of the continued absence of a parent from the home.
(b)   Except as provided in par. (c), in a case involving a dependent child, if the child's parent who is absent from the home is not employed, the court shall order that parent to do one or more of the following:
    1. Register for work at a public employment office established under s. 106.09.

2. Apply for jobs.
3. Participate in a job training program.
(c) An order is not required under par. (b) if the court makes written findings that there is good cause for not issuing the order.
(2) Subsection (1) does not limit the authority of a court to issue an order, other than an order under sub. (1), regarding employment of a parent in an action for modification of a child support order under s. 767.32 or an action in which an order for child support is required under s. 767.25 (1), 767.51 (3) or 767.62 (4).

History: 1987 a. 27; 1991 a. 39; 1993 a. 16; 1995 a. 27 ss. 7098, 7098e, 9130 (4); 1995 a. 289, 404; 1997 a. 105, 191; 1999 a. 9. A divorce action terminates on the death of a spouse. After the death an order prohibiting an act in regard to marital property entered in the divorce may not be enforced under ch. 767. As the parties are legally married at the time of death, the sole remedy for resolving for resolving disputes over marital property lies under s. 766.70. Socha v. Socha, 204 Wis. 2d 474, 555 N.W.2d 152 (Ct. App. 1996).

767.08 Actions to compel support.

(1) In this section:
  (a) "Nonlegally responsible relative" means a relative who assumes responsibility for the care of a child without legal custody, but is not in violation of a court order. "Nonlegally responsible relative" does not include a relative who has physical custody of a child during a court–ordered visitation period.
  (b) "Relative" means any person connected with a child by consanguinity or direct affinity.
(2)(a) If a person fails or refuses to provide for the support and maintenance of his or her spouse or minor child, any of the following may commence an action in any court having jurisdiction in actions affecting the family to compel the person to provide any legally required support and maintenance:
  1. The person's spouse.
  2. The minor child.
  3. The person with legal custody of the child.
  4. A nonlegally responsible relative.
  (b) The court in the action shall, as provided under s. 767.25 or 767.26, determine and adjudge the amount, if any, the person should reasonably contribute to the support and maintenance of the spouse or child and how the sum should be paid. This amount may be expressed as a percentage of the person's income or as a fixed sum, or as a combination of both in the alternative by requiring payment of the greater or lesser of either a percentage of the person's income

or a fixed sum. The amount so ordered to be paid may be changed or modified by the court upon notice of motion or order to show cause by either party upon sufficient evidence.

(c)   The determination may be enforced by contempt proceedings, an account transfer under s. 767.267 or other enforcement mechanisms as provided under s. 767.30.

(d)   In any such support action there shall be no filing fee or other costs taxable to the person's spouse, the minor child, the person with legal custody or the nonlegally responsible relative, but after the action has been commenced and filed the court may direct that any part of or all fees and costs incurred shall be paid by either party.

(3) If the state or any subdivision thereof furnishes public aid to a spouse or dependent child for support and maintenance and the spouse, person with legal custody or nonlegally responsible relative fails or refuses to institute an appropriate court action under this chapter to provide for the same, the person in charge of county welfare activities, the county child-support agency under s. 59.53 (5) or the department is a real party in interest under s. 767.075 and shall initiate an action under this section, for the purpose of obtaining support and maintenance. Any attorney employed by the state or any subdivision thereof may initiate an action under this section. The title of the action shall be "In re the support or maintenance of A.B. (Child)".

History: 1971 c. 220; 1971 c. 307 s. 116; 1973 c. 237; 1975 c. 82; 1977 c. 105, 271; 1979 c. 32 ss. 50, 92 (4); Stats. 1979 s. 767.08; 1981 c. 317; 1983 a. 27; 1985 a. 29, 176; 1987 a. 413; 1989 a. 212; 1993 a. 481; 1995 a. 27 s. 9126 (19); 1995 a. 201, 404; 1997 a. 27, 35.

Discussion of factors required to find a party estopped from seeking a revision of an order. Nichols v. Nichols, 162 Wis. 2d 96, 469 N.W.2d 619 (1991). County child-support agencies can initiate actions to compel support under this section without payment of filing fee. 72 Atty. Gen. 72.

767.081 Information from family court commissioner.

(1) Upon the filing of an action affecting the family, the family court commissioner shall inform the parties of any services, including referral services, offered by the family court commis-sioner and by the director of family court counseling services under s. 767.11.

(2) Upon request of a party to an action affecting the family, including a revision of judgment or order under s. 767.32 or 767.325:

(a)   The family court commissioner shall, with or without charge, pro vide the party with written information on the follow-ing, as appropriate to the action commenced:

1. The procedure for obtaining a judgment or order in the action.

2. The major issues usually addressed in such an action.

3. Community resources and family court counseling services available to assist the parties.

4. The procedure for setting, modifying and enforcing child support awards or modifying and enforcing legal custody or physical place ment judgments or orders. (b) The family court commissioner shall provide a party, for inspection or purchase, with a copy of the statu tory provisions in this chapter generally pertinent to the action.

History: 1977 c. 105, 271, 447, 449; 1979 c. 32 s. 50; 1987 a. 355.

767.082 Suspension of proceedings to effect reconciliation.

During the pendency of any action for divorce or legal separation, the court may, upon written stipulation of both parties that they desire to attempt a reconciliation, enter an order suspending any and all orders and proceedings for such period, not exceeding 90 days, as the court determines advisable so as to permit the parties to attempt a reconciliation without prejudice to their respective rights. During the period of suspension the parties may resume living together as husband and wife and their acts and conduct shall not constitute an admission that the marriage is not irretrievably broken or a waiver of the ground that the parties have voluntarily lived apart continuously for 12 months or more immediately prior to the commencement of the action if such is the case. Suspension may be revoked upon motion of either party by order of the court. If the parties become reconciled, the court shall dismiss the action. If the parties are not reconciled after the period.

767.087 Prohibited acts during pendency of action.

(1) In an action affecting the family, the petitioner upon filing the petition, the joint petitioners upon filing the joint petition and the respondent upon service of the petition are prohibited from doing any of the following:

(a) Harassing, intimidating, physically abusing or imposing any restraint on the personal liberty of the other party or a minor child of either of the parties.

(b) If the action is one under s. 767.02 (1) (a), (b), (c), (d), (h) or (i), encumbering, concealing, damaging, destroying, transferring or otherwise disposing of property owned by either or both of the parties, without the consent of the other party or an order of the court or family court commissioner, except in the usual course of busi ness, in order to secure necessities or in order to pay reasonable costs and expenses of the action, including attorney fees.

(c) Unless the action is one under s. 767.02 (1) (g) or (h), without the consent of the other party or an order of the court or family court commissioner, establishing a residence with a minor child of the parties outside the state or more than 150 miles from the residence of the other party within the state, removing a minor child of the par ties from the state for more than 90 consecutive days or concealing a minor child of the parties from the other party.

(2) The prohibitions under sub. (1) shall apply until the action is dismissed, until a final judgment in the action is entered or until the court or family court commissioner orders otherwise.

(3)(a) Except as provided in par. (b), a party who violates any provision of sub. (1) may be proceeded against under ch. 785 for contempt of court.

(b) An act in violation of sub. (1) (c) is not a contempt of court if the court finds that the action was taken to protect a party or a minor child of the parties from physical abuse by the other party and that there was no reasonable opportunity under the circum-stances for the party to obtain an order under sub. (2) authorizing the action.

History: 1993 a. 78.

767.09 Power of court in divorce and legal separation actions.

(1) When a party requests a legal separation rather than a decree of divorce, the court shall grant the decree in that form unless the other party requests a divorce, in which case the court shall hear and determine which decree shall be granted. A decree of separation shall provide that in case of a rec-onciliation at any time thereafter, the parties may apply for a revocation of the judgment. Upon such application the court shall make such orders as may be just and reasonable.

(2) By stipulation of both parties, or upon motion of either party not earlier than one year after entry of a decree of legal separation, the court shall convert the decree to a decree of divorce.

History: 1977 c. 105; 1979 c. 32 s. 50; Stats. 1979 s. 767.09. Factors to be considered in ordering a divorce where the plaintiff has asked for only a sep-aration are discussed. Husting v. Husting, 54 Wis. 2d 87, 194 N.W.2d 801. If the requirements of sub. (2) are met, conversion to a divorce decree is mandatory. Bartz v. Bartz, 153 Wis. 2d 756, 452 N.W.2d 160 (Ct. App. 1989).

767.10 Stipulation and property division.

(1) The parties in an action for an annulment, divorce or legal separation may, subject to the approval of the court, stipulate for a division of property, for maintenance payments, for the support of children, for periodic family sup-port payments under s. 767.261 or for legal custody and physical place-ment, in case a divorce or legal separa-tion is granted or a marriage annulled.

(2)(a) A court may not approve a stipulation for child support or family sup-port unless the stipulation provides for payment of child support, determined in a manner consistent with s. 767.25 or 767.51.

(b)   A court may not approve a stipulation for a division of property that assigns substantially all of the property to one of the parties in the action if the other party in the action is in the process of applying for medical assistance under subch. IV of ch. 49 or if the court determines that it can be reasonably anticipated that the other party in the action will apply for medical assistance under subch. IV of ch. 49 within 30 months of the stipulation.

767.11 Family court counseling services.

(1) DIRECTOR.

(a)   Except as provided in par. (b) and subject to approval by the chief judge of the judicial administrative district, the circuit judge or judges in each county shall designate a person meeting the qualifications under sub. (4) as the director of family court counseling services in that county.

(b)   If 2 or more contiguous counties enter into a cooperative agreement under sub. (3) (b), the circuit judges for the counties involved shall, subject to approval by the chief judge of the judicial administrative district, designate a person meeting the qualifications under sub. (4) as the director of family court counseling services for those counties.

(c)   A county or counties may designate a family court commissioner as the director under par. (a) or (b).

(2) DUTIES. A director of family court counseling services designated under sub. (1) shall administer a family court counseling office if such an office is established under sub. (3) (a) or (b). Regardless of whether such an office is established, the director shall:

(a)   Employ staff to perform mediation and to perform any legal custody and physical placement study services authorized under sub. (14), arrange and monitor staff training, and assign and monitor staff case load.

(b)   Contract under sub. (3) (c) with a person or public or private entity to perform mediation and to perform any legal custody and physical placement study services authorized under sub. (14).

(c)   Supervise and perform mediation and any legal custody and physical placement study services authorized under sub. (14), and evaluate the quality of any such mediation or study services.

(d)   Administer and manage funding for family court counseling services.

(3) MEDIATION PROVIDED. Mediation shall be provided in every county in this state by any of the following means:

(a)   A county may establish a family court counseling office to provide mediation in that county.

(b)   Two or more contiguous counties may enter into a cooperative agree
ment to establish one family court counseling office to provide mediation in those counties.

(c)   A director of family court counseling services designated under sub.
(1) may contract with any person or public or private entity, located
in a county in which the director administers family court counseling services or in a contiguous county, to provide mediation
in such a county.

(4) MEDIATOR QUALIFICATIONS. Every mediator assigned under sub. (6)
shall have not less than 25 hours of mediation training or not less than 3
years of professional experience in dispute resolution.

(5) MEDIATION REFERRALS.

(a)   In any action affecting the family, including a revision of judgment
or order under s. 767.32 or 767.325, in which it appears that legal
custody or physical placement is contested, the court or family court
commissioner shall refer the parties to the director of family court
counseling services for possible mediation of those contested
issues. The court or the family court commissioner shall inform the
parties that the confidentiality of communications in mediation is
waived if the parties stipulate under sub. (14) (c) that the person who
provided mediation to the parties may also conduct the legal cus
tody or physical placement study under sub. (14).

(b)   If both parties to any action affecting the family wish to have joint
legal custody of a child, either party may request the court or family
court commissioner to refer the parties to the diretor of family court
counseling services for assistance in resolving any problem relating
to joint legal custody and physical placement of the child. Upon
request, the court shall so refer the parties.

(c)   A person who is awarded periods of physical placement, a child of
such a person, a person with visitation rights or a person with phys
ical custody of a child may notify the family court commissioner of
any problem he or she has relating to any of these matters. Upon
notification, the family court commissioner may refer any person
involved in the matter to the director of family court counseling ser
vices for assistance in resolving the problem.

(6) ACTION UPON REFERRAL. Whenever a court or family court commissioner
refers a party to the director of family court counseling services for possible mediation, the director shall assign a mediator to the case. The mediator shall provide mediation if he or she determines it is appropriate. If the
mediator determines mediation is not appropriate, he or she shall so notify
the court. Whenever a court or family court commissioner refers a party
to the director of family court counseling services for any other family court

counseling service, the director shall take appropriate action to provide the service.

(7) PRIVATE MEDIATOR. The parties to any action affecting the family may, at their own expense, receive mediation services from a mediator other than one who provides services under sub. (3). Parties who receive services from such a mediator shall sign and file with the director of family court counseling services and with the court or family court commissioner a written notice stating the mediator's name and the date of the first meeting with the mediator.

(8) INITIAL SESSION OF MEDIATION REQUIRED.

(a)   Except as provided in par. (b), in any action affecting the family, including an action for revision of judgment or order under s. 767.32 or 767.325, in which it appears that legal custody or physical place ment is contested, the parties shall attend at least one session with a mediator assigned under sub. (6) or contracted with under sub. (7) and, if the parties and the mediator determine that continued mediation is appropriate, no court may hold a trial of or a final hear ing on legal custody or physical placement until after mediation is completed or terminated.

(b)   A court may, in its discretion, hold a trial or hearing without requir ing attendance at the session under par. (a) if the court finds that attending the session will cause undue hardship or would endanger the health or safety of one of the parties. In making its determina tion of whether attendance at the session would endanger the health or safety of one of the parties, the court shall consider evidence of the following:

1.   That a party engaged in abuse, as defined in s. 813.122 (1) (a), of the child, as defined in s. 48.02 (2).

2.   Interspousal battery as described under s. 940.19 or 940.20 (1m) or domestic abuse as defined in s. 813.12 (1) (a).

3.   That either party has a significant problem with alcohol or drug abuse.

4.   Any other evidence indicating that a party's health or safety will be endangered by attending the session. (c) The initial session under par. (a) shall be a screening and evaluation mediation ses sion to determine whether mediation is appropriate and whether both parties wish to continue in mediation.

(9) PROHIBITED ISSUES IN MEDIATION. If mediation is provided by a medi ator assigned under sub. (6), no issue relating to property division, main tenance or child support may be considered during the mediation unless all of the following apply:

(a)   The property division, maintenance or child-support issue is directly related to the legal custody or physical placement issue.

(b)   The parties agree in writing to consider the property division, maintenance or child-support issue.

(10) POWERS AND DUTIES OF MEDIATOR. A mediator assigned under sub. (6) shall be guided by the best interest of the child and may do any of the following, at his or her discretion:

(a)   Include the counsel of any party or any appointed guardian ad litem in the mediation.

(b)   Interview any child of the parties, with or without a party present.

(c)   Require a party to provide written disclosure of facts relating to any legal custody or physical placement issue addressed in mediation, including any financial issue permitted to be considered.

(d)   Suspend mediation when necessary to enable a party to obtain an appropriate court order or appropriate therapy.

(e)   Terminate mediation if a party does not cooperate or if mediation is not appropriate or if any of the following facts exist:
   1. There is evidence that a party engaged in abuse, as defined in s. 813.122 (1) (a), of the child, as defined in s. 48.02 (2).
   2. There is evidence of interspousal battery as described under s. 940.19 or 940.20 (1m) or domestic abuse as defined in s. 813.12 (1) (a).
   3. Either party has a significant problem with alcohol or drug abuse.
   4. Other evidence which indicates one of the parties' health or safety will be endangered if mediation is not terminated.

(12) MEDIATION AGREEMENT.

(a)   Any agreement which resolves issues of legal custody or periods of physical placement between the parties reached as a result of media tion under this section shall be prepared in writing, reviewed by the attorney, if any, for each party and by any appointed guardian ad litem, and submitted to the court to be included in the court order as a stipulation. Any reviewing attorney or guardian ad litem shall certify on the mediation agreement that he or she reviewed it and the guardian ad litem, if any, shall comment on the agreement based on the best interest of the child. The mediator shall certify that the written mediation agreement is in the best interest of the child based on the information presented to the mediator and accurately reflects the agreement made between the parties. The court may approve or reject the agreement, based on the best interest of the child. The court shall state in writing its reasons for rejecting an agreement.

(b)   If after mediation under this section the parties do not reach agreement on legal custody or periods of physical placement, the parties or the mediator shall so notify the court. Except as provided in s. 767.045 (1) (am), the court shall promptly appoint a guardian ad litem under s. 767.045. Regardless of whether the court appoints a guardian ad litem, the court shall, if appropriate, refer the matter for a legal custody or physical placement study under sub. (14). If the parties come to agreement on legal custody or physical placement after the matter has been referred for a study, the study shall be terminated. The parties may return to mediation at any time before any trial of or final hearing on legal custody or periods of physical place ment. If the parties return to mediation, the county shall collect any applicable fee under s. 814.615.

(13) POWERS OF COURT OR FAMILY COURT COMMISSIONER. Except as provided in sub. (8), referring parties to mediation under this section does not affect the power of the court or family court commissioner to make any necessary order relating to the parties during the course of the mediation.

(14) LEGAL CUSTODY AND PHYSICAL PLACEMENT STUDY.

(a)   A county or 2 or more contiguous counties shall provide legal cus tody and physical placement study services. The county or coun ties may elect to provide these services by any of the means set forth in sub. (3) with respect to mediation. Regardless of whether a county so elects, whenever legal custody or physical placement of a minor child is contested and mediation under this section is not used or does not result in agreement between the parties, or at any other time the court considers it appropriate, the court may order a person or entity designated by the county tinvestigate the following matters relating to the parties:

1. The conditions of the child's home.

2. Each party's performance of parental duties and responsibilitiies relating to the child.

3. Any other matter relevant to the best interest of the child. (b) The person or entity investigating the parties under par. (a) shall complete the investigation and submit the results to the court. The court shall make the results available to both parties. The report shall be a part of the record in the action unless the court orders otherwise.

(c)   No person who provided mediation to the parties under this section may investigate the parties under this subsection unless each party personally so consents by written stipulation after mediation has ended and after receiving notice from the person who provided mediation that consent waives the inadmissibility of communications in mediation under s. 904.085.

(15) APPLICABILITY. This section applies to each county on the date established by that county, or on June 1, 1989, whichever is earlier.

History: 1987 a. 355; 1989 a. 56; 1991 a. 269; Sup. Ct. Order No. 93–03, 179 Wis. 2d xv; 1995 a. 275, 343; 1999 a. 9.

NOTE: 1987 Wis. Act 355, which created this section, contains explanatory notes. Judicial Council Note, 1993. Subsections (5) (a) and (14) (c) are amended because the rule of inadmissibility under s. 904.085 is not a privilege; it is waivable only if the parties stipulate that the mediator may conduct the custody investigation.

767.115 Educational programs and classes in actions affecting the family.
(1) (a)   At any time during the pendency of an action affecting the family in which a minor child is involved and in which the court or family court commissioner determines that it is appropriate and in the best interest of the child, the court or family court commissioner, on its own motion, may order the parties to attend a program specified by the court or family court commissioner concerning the effects on a child of a dissolution of the marriage.

(b)   At any time during the pendency of an action to determine the paternity of a child, or an action affecting the family for which the under lying action was an action to determine the paternity of a child, if the court or family court commissioner determines that it is appropriate and in the best interest of the child, the court or family court com missioner, on its own motion, may order eitheror both of the parties to attend a program specified by the court or family court commissioner providing training in parenting or coparenting skills, or both.

(1m)   A program under sub. (1) shall be educational rather thantherapeu tic in nature and may not exceed a total of 4 hours in length. The parties shall be responsible for the cost, if any, of attendance at the program. The court of family court commissioner may specifically assign responsibility for payment of any cost. No facts or informa tion obtained in the course of the program, and no report resulting from the program, is admissible in any action or proceeding.

(2) Notwithstanding s. 767.07, the court or family court commissioner may require the parties to attend a program under sub. (1) as a condition to the granting of a final judgment or order in the action affecting the family that is pending before the court or family court commissioner.

(3) A party who fails to attend a program ordered under sub. (1) or pay costs specifically ordered under sub. (1m) may be pro-ceeded against under ch. 785 for contempt of court.

(4) (a)   At any time during the pendency of a divorce or paternity action, the court or family court commissioner may order the parties to attend a class that is approved by the court or family court commissioner and that addresses such issues as child development, family dynamics, how parental separation affects a child's development and what

parents can do to make raising a child in a separated situation less stressful for the child.

(b) The court or family court commissioner may not require the parties to attend a class under this subsection as a condition to the grant ing of the final judgment or order in the divorce or pater-nity action, however, the court or family court commissioner may refuse to hear a custody or physical placement motion of a party who refuses to attend a class ordered under this subsection.

(c) 1. Except as provided in subd. 2., the parties shall be responsible for any cost of attending the class.

2. If the court or family court commissioner finds that a party is indi gent, any costs that would be the responsibility of that party shall be paid by the county.

History: 1993 a. 225; 1997 a. 45; 1999 a. 9.

767.23 Temporary orders for support of spouse and children; suit money; attorney fees.

(1) Except as provided in ch. 822, in every action affecting the family, the court or family court commissioner may, during the pendency thereof, make just and reasonable temporary orders concerning the fol-lowing matters:

(a) Upon request of one party, granting legal custody of the minor chil dren to the parties jointly, to one party solely or to a relative or agency specified under s. 767.24 (3), in a manner consistent with s. 767.24, except that the court or family court commissioner may l order sole legal custody without the agreement of the other party and without the findings required under s. 767.24 (2) (b) 2. This order may not have a binding effect on a final custody determination.

(am) Upon the request of a party, granting periods of physical place ment to a party in a manner consistent with s. 767.24. The court or family court commissioner shall make a determination under this paragraph within 30 days after the request for a temporary order regarding periods of physical placement is filed.

(b) Notwithstanding ss. 767.085 (1) (j) and 767.087 (1) (c), prohibiting the removal of minor children from the jurisdiction of the court.

(bm) Allowing a party to move with or remove a child after a notice of

objection has been filed under s. 767.327 (2) (a).

(c) Subject to s. 767.477, requiring either party or both parties to make payments for the support of minor children, which payment amounts may be expressed as a percentage of parental income or as a fixed sum, or as a combination of both in the alternative by requiring payment of the greater or lesser of either a percentage of parental income or a fixed sum.

(d)   Requiring either party to pay for the maintenance of the other party. This maintenance may include the expenses and attorney fees incurred by the other party in bringing or responding to the action affecting the family.

(e)   Requiring either party to pay family support under s. 767.261.

(f)   Requiring either party to execute an assignment of income under s. 767.265 or an authorization for transfer under s. 767.267.

(g)   Requiring either party or both parties to pay debts or perform other actions in relation to the persons or property of the parties.

(h)   Notwithstanding ss. 767.085 (1) (i) and 767.087 (1) (b), prohibiting either party from disposing of assets within the jurisdiction of the court.

(i)   Requiring counseling of either party or both parties.

(k)   Subject to s. 767.477, requiring either party or both parties to maintain minor children as beneficiaries on a health insurance policy or plan.

(l)   Requiring either party or both parties to execute an assignment of income for payment of health care expenses of minor children.

(1g) Notwithstanding 1987 Wisconsin Act 355, section 73, as affected by 1987 Wisconsin Act 364, the parties may agree to the adjudication of a temporary order under this section in an action affecting the family that is pending on May 3, 1988.

(1m) If a family court commissioner believes that a temporary restraining order or injunction under s. 813.12 is appropriate in an action, the court commissioner shall inform the parties of their right to seek the order or injunction and the procedure to follow. On a motion for such a restraining order or injunction, the family court commissioner shall submit the motion to the court within 5 working days.

(1n) Before making any temporary order under sub. (1), the court or family court commissioner shall consider those factors that the court is required by this chapter to consider before entering a final judgment on the same subject matter. In making a determination under sub. (1) (a) or (am), the court or family court commissioner shall consider the factors under s. 767.24 (5). If the court or family court commissioner makes a temporary child support order that deviates from the amount of support that would be required by using the percentage standard established by the department under s. 49.22 (9), the court or family court commissioner shall comply with the requirements of s. 767.25 (1n). A temporary order under sub. (1) may be based upon the written stipulation of the parties, subject to the approval of the court or the family court commissioner. Temporary orders made by the family court commissioner may be reviewed by the court as provided in s. 767.13 (6).

(2) Notice of motion for an order or order to show cause under sub. (1) may

be served at the time the action is commenced or at any time thereafter and shall be accompanied by an affidavit stat-ing the basis for the request for relief.

(3) (a)   Upon making any order for dismissal of an action affecting the family or for substitution of attorneys in an action affecting the family or for vacation of a judgment theretofore granted in any such action, the court shall prior to or in its order render and grant separate judg-ment in favor of any attorney who has appeared for a party to the action and in favor of any guardian ad litem for a party or a child for the amount of fees and disburse-ments to which the attorney or guardian ad litem is, in the court's judgment, entitled and against the party responsible therefor.

(b)   Upon making any order for dismissal of an action affecting the family or for vacation of a judgment granted in any such order, the court shall, prior to or in its order of dismissal or vacation, also preserve the right of the state or a political subdivision of the state to collect any arrearages, by an action under this chapter or under ch. 785, owed to the state if either party in the case was a recipient of aid under ch. 49.

767.24 Custody and physical placement.

(1) GENERAL PROVISIONS. In rendering a judgment of annulment, divorce, legal separation or paternity, or in rendering a judgment in an action under s. 767.02 (1) (e) or 767.62 (3), the court shall make such provisions as it deems just and reasonable concerning the legal custody and physical place-ment of any minor child of the parties, as provided in this section.

(1m) PARENTING PLAN. In an action for annulment, divorce or legal sepa-ration, an action to determine paternity or an action under s. 767.02 (1) (e) or 767.62 (3) in which legal custody or physical placement is contested, a party seeking sole or joint legal custody or periods of physical placement shall file a parenting plan with the court before any pretrial conference. Except for cause shown, a party required to file a parenting plan under this subsection who does not timely file a parenting plan waives the right to object to the other party's parenting plan. A parenting plan shall provide information about the following questions:

(a)   What legal custody or physical placement the parent is seeking.

(b)   Where the parent lives currently and where the parent intends to live during the next 2 years. If there is evidence that the other parent engaged in interspousal battery, as described under s. 940.19 or 940.20 (1m), or domestic abuse, as defined in s. 813.12 (1) (a), with respect to the parent providing the parenting plan, the parent pro-viding the parenting plan is not required to disclose the specific address but only a general description of where he or she currently lives and intends to live during the next 2 years.

(c)   Where the parent works and the hours of employment. If there is evidence that the other parent engaged in interspousal battery, as described under s. 940.19 or 940.20 (1m), or domestic abuse, as defined in s. 813.12 (1) (a), with respect to the parent providing the parenting plan, the parent providing the parenting plan is not required to disclose the specific address but only a general description of I where he or she works.

(d)   Who will provide any necessary child care when the parent cannot and who will pay for the child care.

(e)   Where the child will go to school.

(f)   What doctor or health care facility will provide medical care for the child.

(g)   How the child's medical expenses will be paid.

(h)   What the child's religious commitment will be, if any.

(i)   Who will make decisions about the child's education, medical care, choice of child care providers and extracurricular activities.

(j)   How the holidays will be divided.

(k)   What the child's summer schedule will be.

(l)   Whether and how the child will be able to contact the other parent when the child has physical placement with the parent providing the parenting plan.

(m)   How the parent proposes to resolve disagreements related to matters over which the court orders joint decision making.

(n)   What child support, family support, maintenance or other income transfer there will be.

(o)   If there is evidence that either party engaged in interspousal battery, as described under s. 940.19 or 940.20 (1m), or domestic abuse, as defined in s. 813.12 (1) (a), with respect to the other party, how the child will be transferred between the parties for the exercise of physical placement to ensure the safety of the child and the parties.

(2) CUSTODY TO PARTY; JOINT OR SOLE.

(a)   Subject to pars. (am), (b) and (c), based on the best interest of the child and after considering the factors under sub. (5), the court may give joint legal custody or sole legal custody of a minor child. (am) The court shall presume that joint legal custody is in the best interest of the child.

(b)   The court may give sole legal custody only if it finds that doing so is in the child's best interest and that either of the following applies:
1. Both parties agree to sole legal custody with the same party.

2. The parties do not agree to sole legal custody with the same party, but at least one party requests sole legal custody and the court specifically finds any of the following:
   a. One party is not capable of performing parental duties and responsibilities or does not wish to have an active role in raising the child.
   b. One or more conditions exist at that time that would substantially interfere with the exercise of joint legal custody.
   c. The parties will not be able to cooperate in the future decision making required under an award of joint legal custody. In making this finding the court shall consider, along with any other pertinent items, any reasons offered by a party objecting to joint legal custody. Evidence that either party engaged in abuse, as defined in s. 813.122 (1) (a), of the child, as defined in s. 48.02 (2), or evidence of interspousal battery, as described under s. 940.19 or 940.20 (1m), or domestic abuse, as defined in s. 813.12 (1) (a), creates a rebuttable presumption that the parties will not be able to cooperate in the future decision making required.

(c) The court may not give sole legal custody to a parent who refuses to cooperate with the other parent if the court finds that the refusal to cooperate is unreasonable.

(3) CUSTODY TO AGENCY OR RELATIVE.

(a) If the interest of any child demands it, and if the court finds that neither parent is able to care for the child adequately or that neither parent is fit and proper to have the care and custody of the child, the court may declare the child to be in need of protection or services and transfer legal custody of the child to a relative of the child, as defined in s. 48.02 (15), to a county department, as defined under s. 48.02 (2g), or to a licensed child welfare agency. If the court transfers legal custody of a child under this subsection, in its order the court shall notify the parents of any applicable grounds for termination of parental rights under s. 48.415.

(b) If the legal custodian appointed under par. (a) is an agency, the agency shall report to the court on the status of the child at least once each year until the child reaches 18 years of age, is returned to the custody of a parent or is placed under the guardianship of an agency. The agency shall file an annual report no less than 30 days before the anniversary of the date of the order. An agency may file an additional report at any time if it determines that more frequent reporting is appropriate. A report shall summarize the child's permanency plan and the recommendations of the review panel under s. 48.38 (5), if any.

(c)   The court shall hold a hearing to review the permanency plan within 30 days after receiving a report under par. (b). At least 10 days before the date of the hearing, the court shall provide notice of the time, date and purpose of the hearing to the agency that prepared the report, the child's parents, the child, if he or she is 12 years of age or over, and the child's foster parent, treatment foster parent or the operator of the facility in which the child is living.

(d)   Following the hearing, the court shall make all of the determinations specified under s. 48.38 (5) (c) and, if it determines that an alter native placement is in the child's best interest, may amend the order to transfer legal custody of the child to another relative, other than a parent, or to another agency specified under par. (a).

(e)   The charges for care furnished to a child whose custody is trans ferred under this subsection shall be pursuant to the procedure under ls. 48.36 (1) or 938.36 (1) except as provided in s. 767.29 (3).

(4) ALLOCATION OF PHYSICAL PLACEMENT.

(a)   1. Except as provided under par. (b), if the court orders sole or joint legal custody under sub. (2), the court shall allocate periods of physi cal placement between the parties in accordance with this subsec tion. 2. In determining the allocation of periods of physical place ment, the court shall consider each case on the basis of the factors in sub. (5). The court shall set a placement schedule that allows the child to have regularly occurring, meaningful periods of physical placement with each parent and that maximizes the amount of time the child may spend with each parent, taking into account geographic separation and accommodations for different households.

(b)   A child is entitled to periods of physical placement with both par ents unless, after a hearing, the court finds that physical placement with a parent would endanger the child's physical, mental or emo tional health.

(c)   No court may deny periods of physical placement for failure to meet, or grant periods of physical placement for meeting, any financial obligation to the child or, if the parties were married, to the former spouse.

(cm) If a court denies periods of physical placement under this section, the court shall give the parent that was denied periods of physical placement the warning provided under s. 48.356.

(d)   If the court grants periods of physical placement to more than one parent, it shall order a parent with legal custody and physical place ment rights to provide the notice required under s. 767.327 (1).

(5) FACTORS IN CUSTODY AND PHYSICAL PLACEMENT DETERMINATIONS. In determining legal custody and periods of physical placement, the court shall consider all facts relevant to the best interest of the child. The court

may not prefer one parent or potential custodian over the other on the basis of the sex or race of the parent or potential custodian. The court shall consider the following factors in making its determination:

(a) The wishes of the child's parent or parents, as shown by any stipulation between the parties, any proposed parenting plan or any legal custody or physical placement proposal submitted to the court at trial.

(b) The wishes of the child, which may be communicated by the child or through the child's guardian ad litem or other appropriate professional.

(c) The interaction and interrelationship of the child with his or her parent or parents, siblings, and any other person who may significantly affect the child's best interest.

(cm) The amount and quality of time that each parent has spent with the child in the past, any necessary changes to the parents' custodial roles and any reasonable life–style changes that a parent proposes to make to be able to spend time with the child in the future.

(d) The child's adjustment to the home, school, religion and community.

(dm) The age of the child and the child's developmental and educational needs at different ages.

(e) The mental and physical health of the parties, the minor children and other persons living in a proposed custodial household.

(em) The need for regularly occurring and meaningful periods of physical placement to provide predictability and stability for the child.

(f) The availability of public or private child care services.

(fm) The cooperation and communication between the parties and whether either party unreasonably refuses to cooperate or communicate with the other party.

(g) Whether each party can support the other party's relation-ship with the child, including encouraging and facilitating frequent and continuing contact with the child, or whether one party is likely to unreasonably interfere with the child's continuing relationship with the other party.

(h) Whether there is evidence that a party engaged in abuse, as defined in s. 813.122 (1) (a), of the child, as defined in s. 48.02 (2).

(i) Whether there is evidence of interspousal battery as described under s. 940.19 or 940.20 (1m) or domestic abuse as defined in s. 813.12 (1) (a).

(j) Whether either party has or had a significant problem with alcohol or drug abuse.

(jm) The reports of appropriate professionals if admitted into evidence.

(k) Such other factors as the court may in each individual case determine to be relevant.

(6) FINAL ORDER.
  (a)   If legal custody or physical placement is contested, the court shall state in writing why its findings relating to legal custody or physical placement are in the best interest of the child.
  (am)   In making an order of joint legal custody, upon the request of one parent the court shall specify major decisions in addition to those specified under s. 767.001 (2m).
  (b)   Notwithstanding s. 767.001 (1s), in making an order of joint legal custody, the court may give one party sole power to make specified decisions, while both parties retain equal rights and responsibilities for other decisions.
  (c)   In making an order of joint legal custody and periods of physical placement, the court may specify one parent as the primary care-taker of the child and one home as the primary home of the child, for the purpose of determining eligibility for aid under s. 49.19 or benefits under ss. 49.141 to 49.161 or for any other purpose the court considers appropriate.
  (d)   No party awarded joint legal custody may take any action inconsistent with any applicable physical placement order, unless the court expressly authorizes that action.
  (e)   In an order of physical placement, the court shall specify the right of each party to the physical control of the child in sufficient detail to enable a party deprived of that control to implement any law providing relief for interference with custody or parental rights.
(7) ACCESS TO RECORDS.
  (a)   Except under par. (b) or unless otherwise ordered by the court, access to a child's medical, dental and school records is available to a parent regardless of whether the parent has legal custody of the child.
  (b)   A parent who has been denied periods of physical placement with a child under this section is subject to s. 118.125 (2) (m) with respect to that child's school records, s. 51.30 (5) (bm) with respect to the child's court or treatment records, s. 55.07 with respect to the child's records relating to protective services and s. 146.835 with respect to the child's patient health care records.
(7m) MEDICAL AND MEDICAL HISTORY INFORMATION.
  (a)   In making an order of legal custody, the court shall order a parent who is not granted legal custody of a child to provide to the court medical and medical history information that is known to the parent. The court shall send the information to the physician or other health care provider with primary responsibility for the treatment and care of the child, as designated by the parent who is granted legal custody of the child, and advise the physician or other health care

provider of the identity of the child to whom the information relates. The information provided shall include all of the following:

1. The known medical history of the parent providing the information, including specific information about stillbirths or congenital anomalies in the parent's family, and the medical histories, if known, of the parents and siblings of the parent and any sibling I of the child who is a child of the parent, except that medical history information need not be provided for a sibling of the child if the parent or other person who is granted legal custody of the child also has legal custody, including joint legal custody, of that sibling.

2. A report of any medical examination that the parent providing the information had within one year before the date of the order.

(am) The physician or other health care provider designated under par. (a) shall keep the information separate from other records kept by I the physician or other health care provider. The information shall be assigned an identification number and maintained under the name of the parent who provided the information to the court. The patient health care records of the child that are kept by the physician or other health care provider shall include a reference to that name and identification number. If the child's patient health care records are transferred to another physician or other health care provider or another health care facility, the records containing the information provided under par. (a) shall be transferred along with the child's patient health care records. Not-withstanding s. 146.819, the information provided under par. (a) need not be maintained by a physician or other health care provider after the child reaches age 18.

(b) Notwithstanding ss. 146.81 to 146.835, the information shall be kept confidential, except only as follows:

1. The physician or other health care provider with custody of the information, or any other record custodian at the request of the physician or other health care provider, shall have access to the information if, in the professional judgment of the physician or other health care provider, the information may be relevant to the child's medical condition.

2. The physician or other health care provider may release only that portion of the information, and only to a person, that the physician or other health care provider determines is relevant to the child's medical condition.

(8) NOTICE IN JUDGMENT. A judgment which determines the legal custody or physical placement rights of any person to a minor child shall include notification of the contents of s. 948.31.

(9) APPLICABILITY. Notwithstanding 1987 Wisconsin Act 355, section 73, as affected by 1987 Wisconsin Act 364, the parties may agree to the adjudication of a custody or physical placement order under this section in an action affecting the family that is pending on May 3, 1988.

History: 1971 c. 149, 157, 211; 1975 c. 39, 122, 200, 283; 1977 c. 105, 418; 1979 c. 32 ss. 50, 92 (4); 1979 c. 196; Stats. 1979 s. 767.24; 1981 c. 391; 1985 a. 70, 176; 1987 a. 332 s. 64; 1987 a. 355, 364, 383, 403; 1989 a. 56 s. 259; 1989 a. 359; 1991 a. 32; 1993 a. 213, 446, 481; 1995 a. 77, 100, 275, 289, 343, 375; 1997 a. 35, 191; 1999 a. 9.

NOTE: 1987 Wis. Act 355, which made many changes in this section, contains a "legislative declaration" in section 1 and explanatory notes.

Impropriety of the award of custody of a child to the mother cannot be predicated on the guardian ad litem's contrary recommendation. Heiting v. Heiting, 64 Wis. 2d 110, 218 N.W.2d 334.

The award of custody to the father was reversible error where the trial court should have recognized the rule of comity and declined to exercise its jurisdiction. Sheridan v. Sheridan, 65 Wis. 2d 504, 223 N.W.2d 557.

In a child custody dispute between the children's father, who was divorced by his wife, and the wife's parents, subsequent to her death, the trial court erred in concluding that it had no choice but to award custody to the surviving natural parent unless it found him unfit or unable to care for the children. LaChapell v. Mawhinney, 66 Wis. 2d 679, 225 N.W.2d 501.

Res judicata is not to be applied to custody matters with the same strictness as to other matters. Kuesel v. Kuesel, 74 Wis. 2d 636, 247 N.W.2d 72.

Consideration of evidence concerning a mother's attempts to frustrate the father's visitation privileges was proper in awarding custody. Marotz v. Marotz, 80 Wis. 2d 477, 259 N.W.2d 524.

In a post–divorce child custody dispute where the original award was by stipulation, a full–scale hearing was necessary. Haugen v. Haugen, 82 Wis. 2d 411, 262 N.W.2d 769.

The trial court may not order a custodial parent to live in designated part of the state or else lose custody. Groh v. Groh, 110 Wis. 2d 117, 327 N.W.2d 655 (1983).

In a custody dispute between a parent and a third party, unless the court finds that the parent is unfit or unable to care for the child or that there are compelling reasons for denying custody to the parent, the court must grant custody to the parent. Barstad v. Frazier, 118 Wis. 2d 549, 348 N.W.2d 479 (1984).

Custody and visitation are controlled by statute and case law and cannot be contracted away. A co–parenting contract between a parent and a non–parent is unenforceable. In re Interest of Z.J.H. 162 Wis. 2d 1002, 471 N.W.2d 202 (1991).

Revision of s. 767.24to allow joint custody in cases where both parties did not agree was not a "substantial change in circumstances" justifying a change to joint custody.

Licary v. Licary, 168 Wis. 2d 686, 484 N.W.2d 371 (Ct. App. 1992). Section 767.001 (2m) confers the right to choose a child's religion on the custodial parent. Reasonable restrictions on visitation to prevent subversion of this right do not violate the constitution. Lange v. Lange, 175 Wis. 2d 373, N.W.2d (Ct. App. 1993). There is no authority to order a change of custody at an unknown time in the future upon the occurrence of some stated contingency. Koeller v. Koeller, 195 Wis. 2d 660, 536 N.W.2d 216 (Ct. App. 1995).

A custodial parent's right to make major decisions for the children does not give that parent the right to decide whether the actions of the noncustodial parent are consistent with those decisions. Wood v. DeHahn, 214 Wis. 2d 221, 571 N.W.2d 186 (Ct. App. 1997).

Neither sub. (4) (b) nor s. 767.325 (4) permits a prospective order prohibiting a parent from requesting a change of physical placement in the future. Jocius v. Jocius, 218 Wis. 2d 103, 580 N.W.2d 708 (Ct. App. 1998).

Section 813.122 implicitly envisions a change of placement and custody if the trial court issues a child abuse injunction under that section against a parent who has custody or placement of a child under a divorce order or judgment. Scott M.H. v. Kathleen M.H. 218 Wis. 2d 605, 581 N.W.2d 564 (Ct. App. 1998). Sub. (5) (b), while requiring consideration of the child's wishes, leaves to the court's discretion whether to allow the child to testify. That the child is a competent witness under s. 906.01 does not affect the court's discretion. Hughes v. Hughes, 223 Wis. 2d 111, 588 N.W.2d 346 (Ct. App. 1998).

Wisconsin's Custody, Placement and Paternity Reform Legislation. Walther. Wis.Law. April 2000.

Custody—to which parent? Podell, Peck, First, 56 MLR 51. The best interest of the child doctrine in Wisconsin custody cases. 64 MLR 343 (1980).

Debating the Standard in Child Custody Placement Decisions. Molvig. Wis. Law. July 1998.

767.242 Enforcement of physical placement orders.
(1) DEFINITIONS. In this section:
  (a) "Petitioner" means the parent filing a petition under this section, regardless of whether that parent was the petitioner in the action in which periods of physical placement were awarded under s. 767.24.
  (b) "Respondent" means the parent upon whom a petition under this section is served, regardless of whether that parent was the

respondent in the action in which periods of physical placement were awarded under s. 767.24.

(2)   WHO MAY FILE. A parent who has been awarded periods of physical placement under s. 767.24 may file a petition under sub.

(3)   if any of the following applies:

    (a)   The parent has had one or more periods of physical placemen denied by the other parent.

    (b)   The parent has had one or more periods of physical placement substantially interfered with by the other parent.

    (c)   The parent has incurred a financial loss or expenses as a result of the other parent's intentional failure to exercise one or more periods of physical placement under an order allocating specific times for the exercise of periods of physical placement.

(3) PETITION.

    (a)   The petition shall allege facts sufficient toshow the following:

        1. The name of the petitioner and that the petitioner has been awarded periods of physical placement.

        2. The name of the respondent.

        3. That the criteria in sub. (2) apply.

    (b)   The petition shall request the imposition of a remedy or any combination of remedies under sub. (5) (b) and (c). This paragraph does not prohibit a judge or family court commissioner from imposing a remedy under sub. (5) (b) or (c) if the remedy was not requested in the petition.

    (c)   A judge or family court commissioner shall accept any legible petition for an order under this section.

    (d)   The petition shall be filed under the principal action under which the periods of physical placement were awarded.

    (e)   A petition under this section is a motion for remedial sanction for purposes of s. 785.03 (1) (a).

(4) SERVICE ON RESPONDENT; RESPONSE. Upon the filing of a petition under sub. (3), the petitioner shall serve a copy of the petition upon the respondent by personal service in the same manner as a summons is served under s. 801.11. The respondent may respond to the petition either in writing before or at the hearing under sub. (5) (a) or orally at that hearing.

(5) HEARING; REMEDIES.

    (a)   A judge or family court commissioner shall hold a hearing on the petition no later than 30 days after the petition has been served, unless the time is extended by mutual agreement of the parties or upon the motion of a guardian ad litem and the approval of the judge or family court commissioner. The judge or family court commissioner may, on his or her own motion or the motion of any party, order that a guardian ad litem be appointed for the child prior to the hearing.

(b) If, at the conclusion of the hearing, the judge or family court commissioner finds that the respondent has intentionally and unreasonably denied the petitioner one or more periods of physical placement or that the respondent has intentionally and unreasonably interfered with one or more of the petitioner's periods of physical placement, the court or family court commissioner:

1. Shall do all of the following:
   a. Issue an order granting additional periods of physical placement to replace those denied or interfered with.
   b. Award the petitioner a reasonable amount for the cost of maintaining an action under this section and for attorney fees.

2. May do one or more of the following:
   a. If the underlying order or judgment relating to periods of physical placement does not provide for specific times for the exercise of periods of physical placement, issue an order specifying the times for the exercise of periods of physical placement.
   b. Find the respondent in contempt of court under ch. 785.
   c. Grant an injunction ordering the respondent to strictly comply with the judgment or order relating to the award of physical placement. In determining whether to issue an injunction, the judge or family court commissioner shall consider whether alternative remedies requested by the petitioner would be as effective in obtaining compliance with the order or judgment relating to physical placement.

(c) If, at the conclusion of the hearing, the judge or family court commissioner finds that the petitioner has incurred a financial loss or expenses as a result of the respondent's failure, intentionally and unreasonably and without adequate notice to the petitioner, to exercise one or more periods of physical placement under an order allocating specific times for the exercise of periods of physical placement, the judge or family court commissioner may issue an order requiring the respondent to pay to the petitioner a sum of money sufficient to compensate the petitioner for the financial loss or expenses.

(d) Except as provided in par. (b) 1. a. and 2. a., the judge or family court commissioner may not modify an order of legal custody or physical placement in an action under this section.

(e) An injunction issued under par. (b) 2. c. is effective according to its terms, for the period of time that the petitioner requests, but not more than 2 years.

(6) ENFORCEMENT ASSISTANCE.

(a)   If an injunction is issued under sub. (5) (b) 2. c., upon request by the petitioner the judge or family court commissioner shall order the sheriff to assist the petitioner in executing or serving the injunction.

(b)   Within 24 hours after a request by the petitioner, the clerk of the cir cuit court shall send a copy of an injunction issued under sub. (5) (b) 2. c. to the sheriff or to any other local law enforcement agency that is the central repository for orders and that has jurisdiction over the respondent's residence. If the respondent does not reside in this state, the clerk shall send a copy of the injunction to the sheriff of the county in which the circuit court is located.

(c)   The sheriff or other appropriate local law enforcement agency under par. (b) shall make available to other law enforcement agencies, through a verification system, information on the existence and status of any injunction issued under sub. (5) (b) 2. c. The information need not be maintained after the injunction is no longer in effect.

(8) PENALTY. Whoever intentionally violates an injunction issued under sub. (5) (B) 2. c. may be fined not more than $10,000 or inprisoned for not more than 2 years or both.

History: 1999 a. 9. Wisconsin's Custody, Placement and Paternity Reform Leg- islation. Walther. Wis.Law. April 2000.

767.245 Visitation rights of certain persons.

(1) Except as provided in subs. (1m) and (2m), upon petition by a grand parent, great-grandparent, stepparent or person who has maintained a rela- tionship similar to a parent-child relationship with the child, the court may grant reasonable visitation rights to that person if the parents have notice of the hearing and if the court determines that visitation is in the best inter- est of the child.

(1m) (a)   Except as provided in par. (b), the court may not grant visitation rights under sub. (1) to a person who has been convicted under s. 940.01 of the first-degree intentional homicide, orunder s. 940.05 of the 2nd-degree intentional homicide, of a parent of the child, and the conviction has not been reversed, set aside or vacated.

(b)   Paragraph (a) does not apply if the court determines by clear and convincing evidence that the visitation would be in the best inter ests of the child. The court shall consider the wishes of the child in making the determination.

(2)   Whenever possible, in making a determination under sub. (1), the court shall consider the wishes of the child.

(2m) Subsection (3), rather than sub. (1), applies to a grand-parent request-ing visitation rights under this section if sub. (3) (a) to (c) applies to the child.

(3) The court may grant reasonable visitation rights, with respect to a child, to a grandparent of the child if the child's parents have notice of the hearing and the court determines all of the following:

(a)   The child is a non-marital child whose parents have not subse-quently married each other.

(b)   Except as provided in sub. (4), the paternity of the child has been determined under the laws of this state or another jurisdiction if the grandparent filing the petition is a parent of the child's father.

(c)   The child has not been adopted.

(d)   The grandparent has maintained a relationship with the child or has attempted to maintain a relationship with the child but has been prevented from doing so by a parent who has legal custody of the child.

(e)   The grandparent is not likely to act in a manner that is contrary to decisions that are made by a parent who has legal custody of the child and that are related to the child's physical, emotional, educational or spiritual welfare.

(f)   The visitation is in the best interest of the child.

(3c) A grandparent requesting visitation under sub. (3) may file a petition to commence an independent action for visitation under this chapter or may file a petition for visitation in an underlying action affecting the family under this chapter that affects the child.

(3m) (a)   A pretrial hearing shall be held before the court in an action under sub. (3). At the pretrial hearing the parties may present and cross-examine witnesses and present other evidence relevant to the determination of visitation rights. A record or minutes of the pro-ceeding shall be kept.

(b)   On the basis of the information produced at the pretrial hearing, the court shall evaluate the probability of granting visitation rights to a grandparent in a trial and shall so advise the parties. On the basis of the evaluation, the court may make an appropriate rec-ommendation for settlement to the parties.

(c)   If a party or the guardian ad litem refuses to accept a recommen-dation under this subsection, the action shall be set for trial.

(d)   The informal hearing under this subsection may be terminated and the action set for trial if the court finds it unlikely that all parties will accept a recommendation under this subsection.

(4) If the paternity of the child has not yet been determined in an action under sub. (3) that is commenced by a person other than a parent of the child's mother but the person filing the petition under sub. (3) has, in con-

junction with that petition, filed a petition or motion under s. 767.45 (1) (k), the court shall make a determination as to paternity before determining visitation rights under sub. (3).

(5) Any person who interferes with visitation rights granted under sub. (1) or (3) may be proceeded against for contempt of court under ch. 785, except that a court may impose only the remedial sanctions specified in s. 785.04 (1) (a) and (c) against that per-son.

(6)   (a)   If a person granted visitation rights with a child under this sec tion is convicted under s. 940.01 of the first-degree intentional homicide, or under s. 940.05 of the 2nd-degree intentional homicide, of a parent of the child, and the conviction has not been reversed, set aside or vacated, the court shall modify the visitation order by denying visitation with the child upon petition, motion or order to show cause by a parent or guardian of the child, or upon the court's own motion, and upon notice to the person granted visitationrights.

(b)   Paragraph (a) does not apply if the court determines by clear and convincing evidence that the visitation would be in the best interests of the child. The court shall consider the wishes of the child in making that determination.

767.25 Child support.

(1) Whenever the court approves a stipulation for child support under s. 767.10, enters a judgment of annulment, divorce or legal separation, or enters an order or a judgment in a paternity action or in an action under s. 767.02 (1) (f) or (j), 767.08 or 767.62 (3), the court shall do all of the following:

(a)   Order either or both parents to pay an amount reasonable or nec essary to fulfill a duty to support a child. The support amount may be expressed as a percentage of parental income or as a fixed sum, or as a combination of both in the alternative by requiring payment of the greater or lesser of either a percentage of parental income or a fixed sum.

(b)   Ensure that the parties have stipulated which party, if either is eligible, will claim each child as an exemption for federal income tax purposes under 26 USC 151 (c) (1) (B), or as an exemption for state income tax purposes under s. 71.07 (8) (b) or under the laws of another state. If the parties are unable to reach an agreement about the tax exemption for each child, the court shall make the decision in accordance with state and federal tax laws. In making its decision, the court shall consider whether the parent who is assigned responsibility for the child's health care expenses under sub. (4m) is covered under a health insurance policy or plan, including a self-insured plan, that is not subject to s. 632.897 (10) and that conditions coverage of a dependent child on whether the child is claimed by the insured parent as an exemption for purposes of federal or state income taxes.

(1g) In determining child-support payments, the court may consider all relevant financial information or other information relevant to the parent's earning capacity, including information reported under s. 49.22 (2m) to the department or the county child support agency under s. 59.53 (5).

(1j) Except as provided in sub. (1m), the court shall determine child-support payments by using the percentage standard established by the department under s. 49.22 (9).

(1m) Upon request by a party, the court may modify the amount of child-support payments determined under sub. (1j) if, after considering the following factors, the court finds by the greater weight of the credible evidence that use of the percentage standard is unfair to the child or to any of the parties:

(a)   The financial resources of the child.

(b)   The financial resources of both parents.

(bj)   Maintenance received by either party.

(bp)   The needs of each party in order to support himself or herself at a level equal to or greater than that established under 42 USC 9902 (2).

(bz)   The needs of any person, other than the child, whom either party is legally obligated to support.

(c)   If the parties were married, the standard of living the child would have enjoyed had the marriage not ended in annulment, divorce or legal separation.

(d)   The desirability that the custodian remain in the home as a full-time parent.

(e)   The cost of day care if the custodian works outside the home, or the value of custodial services performed by the custodian if the custodian remains in the home.

(ej)   The award of substantial periods of physical placement to both parents.

(em)   Extraordinary travel expenses incurred in exercising the right to periods of physical placement under s. 767.24.

(f)   The physical, mental and emotional health needs of the child, including any costs for health insurance as provided for under sub. (4m).

(g)   The child's educational needs.

(h)   The tax consequences to each party.

(hm)   The best interests of the child.

(hs)   The earning capacity of each parent, based on each parent's education, training and work experience and the availability of work in or near the parent's community.

(i)   Any other factors which the court in each case determines are relevant.

(1n) If the court finds under sub. (1m) that use of the percent-age standard is unfair to the child or the requesting party, the court shall state in writing or on the record the amount of support that would be required by using the percentage standard, the amount by which the court's order deviates from that amount, its reasons for finding that use of the percentage standard is unfair to the child or the party, its reasons for the amount of the modification and the basis for the modification.

(2) The court may protect and promote the best interests of the minor children by setting aside a portion of the child support which either party is ordered to pay in a separate fund or trust for the support, education and welfare of such children.

(3) Violation of physical placement rights by the custodial parent does not constitute reason for failure to meet child-support obligations.

(4) The court shall order either party or both to pay for the sup-port of any child of the parties who is less than 18 years old, or any child of the parties who is less than 19 years old if the child is pur-suing an accredited course of instruction leading to the acquisition of a high school diploma or its equivalent.

(4m)(a) In this subsection, "health insurance" does not include medical assistance provided under subch. IV of ch. 49.

(b)   In addition to ordering child support for a child under sub. (1), the court shall specifically assign responsibility for and direct the manner of payment of the child's health care expenses. In assigning responsibility for a child's health care expenses, the court shall consider whether a child is covered under a parent's health insurance policy or plan at the time the court approves a stipulation for child support under s. 767.10, enters a judgment of annulment, divorce or legal separation, or enters an order or a judgment in a paternity action or in an action under s. 767.02 (1) (f) or (j), 767.08 or 767.62 (3), the availability of health insuranceto each parent through an employer or other organization, the extent of coverage available to a child and the costs to the parent for the coverage of the child. A parent may be required to initiate or continue health care insurance coverage for a child under this subsection. If a parent is required to do so, he or she shall provide copies of necessary program or policy identification to the custodial parent and is liable for any health care costs for which he or she receives direct payment from an insurer. This subsection shall not be construed to limit the authority of the court to enter or modify support orders containing provisions for payment of medical expenses, medical costs, or insurance premiums which are in addition to and not inconsistent with this subsection.

(c) 1. In directing the manner of payment of a child's health care expenses, the court may order that payment, including payment for health insurance premiums, be withheld from income and sent to the appropriate health care insurer, provider or plan, as provided in s. 767.265 (3h), or sent to the department or its designee, whichever is appropriate, for disbursement to the person for whom the payment has been awarded if that person is not a health care insurer, provider or plan. If the court orders income with holding and assignment for the payment of health care expenses, the court shall send notice of assignment in the manner provided under s. 767.265 (2r) and may include the notice of assignment under this subdivision with a notice of assignment under s. 767.265. The department or its designee, whichever is appropriate, shall keep a record of all moneys received and disbursed by the department or its designee for health care expenses that are directed to be paid to the department or its designee.

2. If the court orders a parent to initiate or continue health insurance coverage for a child under a health insurance policy that is available to the parent through an employer or other organization but the court does not specify the manner in which payment of the health insurance premiums shall be made, the clerk of court may provide notice of assignment in the manner provided under s. 767.265 (2r) for the withholding from income of the amount necessary to pay the health insurance premiums. The notice of assignment under this subdivision may be sent with or included as part of any other notice of assignment under s. 767.265, if appropriate. A person who receives notice of assignment under this subdivision shall send the withheld health insurance premiums to the appropriate health care insurer, provider or plan, as provided in s. 767.265 (3h).

(d) If the court orders a parent to provide coverage of the health care expenses of the parent's child and the parent is eligible for family coverage of health care expenses under a health benefit plan that is provided by an employer on an insured or on a self-insured basis, the employer shall do all of the following:

1. Permit the parent to obtain family coverage of health care expenses for the child, if eligible for coverage, without regard to any enrollment period or waiting period restrictions that may apply.

2. Provide family coverage of health care expenses for the child, if eligible for coverage, upon application by the parent, the child's other parent, the department or the county child-support

agency under s. 59.53 (5), or upon receiving a notice under par. (f) 1.

2m. Notify the county child-support agency under s. 59.53 (5) when coverage of the child under the health benefit plan is in effect and, upon request, provide copies of necessary program or policy identification to the child's other parent.

3. After the child has coverage under the employer's health benefit plan, and as long as the parent is eligible for family coverage under the employer's health benefit plan, continue to provide coverage for the child unless the employer receives satisfactory written evidence that the court order is no longer in effect or that the child has coverage of health care expenses under another health insurance policy or health benefit plan that provides comparable coverage of health care expenses.

(e) 1. If a parent who has been ordered by a court to provide coverage of the health care expenses of a child who is eligible for medical assistance under subch. IV of ch. 49 receives payment from a 3rd party for the cost of services provided to the child but does not pay the health care provider for the services or reimburse the department or any other person who paid for the services on behalf of the child, the department may obtain a judgment against the parent for the amount of the 3rd party payment.

2. Section 767.265 (4) applies to a garnishment based on a judgment obtained under subd. 1.

(f) 1. If a parent who provides coverage of the health care expenses of a child under an order under this subsection changes employers and that parent has a court-ordered child-support obligation with respect to the child, the county child-support agency under s. 59.53 (5) shall provide notice of the order to provide coverage of the child's health care expenses to the new employer and to the parent.

2. The notice provided to the parent shall inform the parent that coverage for the child under the new employer's health benefit plan will be in effect upon the employer's receipt of the notice. The notice shall inform the parent that he or she may, within 10 business days after receiving the notice, by motion request a hearing before the court on the issue of whether the order to provide coverage of the child's health care expenses should remain in effect. A motion under this subdivision may be heard by a family court commissioner. If the parent requests a hearing and the court or family court commissioner determines that the order to provide coverage of the child's health

care expenses should not remain in effect, the court shall provide notice to the employer that the order is no longer in effect.

(5) Subject to ss. 767.51 (4) and 767.62 (4m), liability for past support shall be limited to the period after the birth of the child.

(6) A party ordered to pay child support under this section shall pay simple interest at the rate of 1% per month on any amount in arrears that is equal to or greater than the amount of child sup-port due in one month. If the party no longer has a current obligation to pay child support, interest at the rate of 1% per month shall accrue on the total amount of child support in arrears, if any. Interest under this subsection is in lieu of interest computed under s. 807.01 (4), 814.04 (4) or 815.05 (8) and is paid to the department or its designee under s. 767.29. Except as provided in s. 767.29 (1m), the department or its designee, whichever is appropriate, shall apply all payments received for child support as follows:

(a) First, to payment of child support due within the calendar month during which the payment is received.

(b) Second, to payment of unpaid child support due before the payment is received.

(c) Third, to payment of interest accruing on unpaid child support.

(7) An order of joint legal custody under s. 767.24 does not affect the amount of child support ordered.

History: 1971 c. 157; 1977 c. 29, 105, 418; 1979 c. 32 ss. 50, 92 (4); 1979 c. 196; Stats. 1979 s. 767.25; 1981 c. 20; 1983 a. 27; 1985 a. 29; 1987 a. 27, 37, 355, 413; 1989 a. 31, 212; 1991 a. 39; 1993 a. 481; 1995 a. 27 ss. 7101, 7102, 9126 (19); 1995 a. 201, 279, 404; 1997 a. 27, 35, 191; 1999 a. 9, 32.

A provision in a judgment as to the education of children past the age of majority, inserted pursuant to a stipulation of the parties, cannot later be challenged and can be enforced by contempt proceedings. Bliwas v. Bliwas, 47 Wis. 2d 635, 178 N.W.2d 35.

Where parents each own a 1/2 interest in future proceeds of real estate and the state contributes to child support, the court may order the custodial parent to pay child support in the form of an accumulating real estate lien in favor of the state. State ex rel. v. Reible, 91 Wis. 2d 394, 283 N.W.2d 427 (Ct. App. 1979).

The trial court abused its discretion by setting child-support payments without considering the needs of the children or the payor's ability to pay. Edwards v. Edwards, 97 Wis. 2d 111, 293 N.W.2d 160 (1980).

Sub. (4) has retroactive effect. Behnke v. Behnke, 103 Wis. 2d 449, 309 N.W.2d 21 (Ct. App. 1981).

A personal injury damage award to a noncustodial spouse can be considered as a change of circumstances justifying increased support. Sommer v. Sommer, 108 Wis. 2d 586, 323 N.W.2d 144 (Ct. App. 1982). Sub. (6)

imposes interest on arrearages existing on July 2, 1983, as well as on those accruing afterward. Greenwood v. Greenwood, 129 Wis. 2d 388, 385 N.W.2d 213(Ct. App. 1986).

Federal Supplemental Security Income may not be considered an economic resource for purposes of computing a child-support obligation. However, a seek-work order may be appropriate. Langlois v. Langlois, 150 Wis. 2d 101, 441 N.W.2d 286 (Ct. App. 1989).

Educational grants and loans, AFDC, and other child support are not economic resources for purposes of computing a child-support obligation. Thibadeau v. Thibadeau, 150 Wis. 2d 109, 441 N.W.2d 281 (Ct. App. 1989).

Orders assigning health care responsibility pursuant to s. 767.25 (4m) are subject to revision under s. 767.32. Kuchenbecker v. Schultz, 151 Wis. 2d 868, 447 N.W.2d 80 (Ct. App. 1989).

On a request for modification under sub. (1m), it was error for the trial court to consider post-high school educational expenses in setting support. Consideration of expenses incurred by a child as an adult is error. Resong v. Vier, 157 Wis. 2d 382, 459 N.W.2d 591 (Ct. App. 1990).

A divorce stipulation waiving or setting a ceiling on child support and preventing modification is against public policy and will not be enforced. Ondrasek v. Tenneson, 158 Wis. 2d 690, 462 N.W.2d 915 (Ct. App. 1990).

The trial court's use of a computer program to analyze financial evidence was not error. Bisone v. Bisone, 165 Wis. 2d 114, 477 N.W.2d 59 (Ct. App. 1991).

A stepparent has no legal obligation to support a stepchild. Under appropriate circumstances the theory of equitable estoppel may apply to cases involving child support. Ulrich v. Cornell, 168 Wis. 2d 792, 484 N.W.2d 546 (1992).

In a joint custody situation the parent with primary physical custody may be ordered to pay child support. Matz v. Matz, 166 Wis. 2d 326, 479 N.W.2d 245 (Ct. App. 1991).

The absence of a mortgage obligation is relevant to the assessment of a party's economic circumstances, but does not translate into imputed income under the applicable administrative rule. In Marriage of Zimmerman v. Zimmerman, 169 Wis. 2d 516, 485 N.W.2d 294 (Ct. App. 1992).

A support order against actual AFDC grants is prohibited by Thibadeau, but an order against earned income of one who also receives AFDC is not. In Support of B., L., T. & K. 171 Wis. 2d 617, 492 N.W.2d 350 (Ct. App. 1992).

No matter how corporate income is labeled, a family court may pierce the corporate shield if it is convinced the obligor's intent is to avoid financial obligations. Evjen v. Evjen, 171 Wis. 2d 677, 492 N.W.2d 360 (Ct. App. 1992).

The parties' extrajudicial agreement that child-support payments be discontinued was enforceable via the doctrine of equitable estoppel. Harms v. Harms, 174 Wis. 2d 780, 498 N.W.2d 229 (1993).

Discussion of the "serial family payer" rule adopted under the percentage standards referred to in sub. (1). Brown v. Brown, 177 Wis. 2d 512, 503 N.W.2d 280 (Ct. App. 1993).

The mandatory percentage standards for determining support do not allow for deferred payments. Kelly v. Hougham, 178 Wis. 2d 546, 504 N.W.2d 440 (Ct. App. 1993).

An AFDC recipient assigns all rights to child-support payments to the state. As such the payments may not be held in trust for the child under sub. (2). Paternity of Lachelle A.C. 180 Wis. 2d 708, 510 N.W.2d 718 (Ct. App. 1993).

A lump sum separation benefit received upon termination of employment was properly considered income subject to the percentage standards for support. Gohde v. Gohde, 181 Wis. 2d 770, 512 N.W.2d 199 (Ct. App. 1993).

In deciding not to apply the percentage standard, the court erred when it compared the parties available incomes after deducting the percentage amount from the payor's income, but failed to consider the assumed contribution of the same percentage by the payee. Kjelstrum v. Kjelstrum, 181 Wis. 2d 973, 512 N.W.2d 264 (Ct. App. 1994).

A trial court could may not set child support at zero, convert post-divorce income to marital property and order that income to be held in trust to be distributed to the child when AFDC benefits ended. Luna v. Luna, 183 Wis. 2d 20, 515 N.W.2d 480 (Ct. App. 1994).

Parties are free to contract in a settlement agreement that the primary custodian will not have spending discretion over child support if the interests of the children and custodial parent are protected. Jacquart v. Jacquart, 183 Wis. 2d 372, 515 N.W.2d 539 (Ct. App. 1994).

An asset and its income stream may not be counted both as an asset in the property division and as part of the payor's income from which support is paid. Maley v. Maley, 186 Wis. 2d 125, 519 N.W.2d 717 (Ct. App. 1994).

Trust income which is income to the beneficiary under federal tax law is subject to a child-support order regardless of whether a distribution is made to the beneficiary. Grohmann v. Grohmann, 189 Wis. 2d 532, 525 N.W.2d 261 (1995).

A minimum fixed child-support amount, rather than the percentage standard, based on the payor's "potential income" was appropriate where the court found the payor had a substantial potential to manipulate the amount of support. Doerr v. Doerr, 189 Wis. 2d 112, 525 N.W.2d 745 (Ct. App. 1994).

The trial court may consider the amount of time a child is placed with the paying parent and the parent's second family in setting support. Molstad v. Molstad, 193 Wis. 2d 602, 535 N.W.2d 63 (Ct. App. 1995).

The percentage standards may be used to generate future as well as present support. Paternity of Tukker M.O., 199 Wis. 2d 186, 544 N.W.2d 417 (1996).

The percentage standards presumptively apply in the case of a high income payee absent the payer's showing of unfairness by the greater weight of the credible evidence. Luciani v. Montemurro-Luciani, 199 Wis. 2d 280, 544 N.W.2d 561 (1996).

Sub. (6) makes interest on child-support arrearages mandatory. A trial court has no discretion in awarding interest, even if it determines that to do so would be inequitable. Douglas County Child Support v. Fisher, 200 Wis. 2d 807, 547 N.W.2d 801 (Ct. App. 1996).

A court may consider earning capacity rather than actual earnings in determining child support and maintenance if it find's a parent's job choice voluntary and unreasonable. Sellers v. Sellers, 201 Wis. 2d 578, 549 N.W.2d 481 (Ct. App. 1996).

The fact that a party by deliberate conduct frustrates an accurate calculation of the party's income does not prevent the trial court from making the appropriate finding of fact. The court may make its findings based on the available evidence. Lellman v. Mott, 204 Wis. 2d 166, 554 N.W.2d 525 (Ct. App. 1996).

The court did not abuse its discretion in ruling against a request in a high income payer case for an increase in support according to the percentage standards where the court believed the request was really a disguised claim for extra money to support the custodial parent's own lifestyle. Nelsen v. Candee, 205 Wis. 2d 625, 556 N.W.2d 789 (Ct. App. 1996).

In certain cases, such as with military retirement pay, an asset may be divided in the property division and its income stream considered as income in determining child support. Cook v. Cook, 208 Wis. 2d 166, 560 N.W.2d 246 (1997).

When a noncustodial parent seeks to impose a trust on arrearages owed under a pre-August 1, 1987 support order, that parent must demonstrate that the trust is in the child's best interest and, when the custodial parent does not agree to the trust, that the primary custodian was unwilling to or incapable of managing the support money. Cameron v. Cameron, 209 Wis. 2d 88, 562 N.W.2d 126 (1997).

Income disparity resulting from applying the percentage standards is only relevant if the payer can show inability to pay or that the income disparity will adversely affect the children or payer. Equalizing lifestyles between parents is not a support objective.

The amount of discretionary income either parent will have to spend on their children is a secondary consideration. Raz v. Brown, 213 Wis. 2d 296, 570 N.W.2d 605 (Ct. App. 1997).

The repayment to the payer spouse of a loan made by him to a company that he owned was a proper addition to the payer's income available for support. It was properly

found to be deferred compensation which is included within the applicable definition

of income. Raz v. Brown, 213 Wis. 2d 296, 570 N.W.2d 605 (Ct. App. 1997).

A stipulation for child support with no time limit or opportunity for review was against public policy and the payer was not estopped form seeking a modification due to a material change in circumstances. Krieman v. Goldberg, 214 Wis. 2d 163, 571 N.W.2d 425 (1997).

Absent a finding that an individual partner has authority to unilaterally control a partnership asset, partnership assets will be imputed as available income only in accordance with the partnership agreement. Health insurance premiums paid by a partnership are included in the partners income available for child support. Weis v. Weis, 215 Wis. 2d 135, 572 N.W.2d 123 (Ct. App. 1997).

The trial court properly exercised its discretion under sub. (1m) (i) by excluding from the application of the percentage standards the value of non-assignable trips received by the payor spouse as employment bonuses although the trips constituted taxable income. State v. Wall, 215 Wis. 2d 591, 573 N.W.2d 862 (Ct. App. 1997).

In concluding that a deviation from the percentage standards is warranted, all listed factors need not be applied. State v. Alonzo R. 230 Wis. 2d 17, 601 N.W.2d 328 (Ct. App. 1999).

Federal preemption doctrine does not prohibit states from requiring payment of child support out of veterans' disability benefits. Rose v. Rose, 481 U.S. 619 (1987).

No-fault divorce: Tax consequences of support, maintenance and property settlement. Case, 1977 WBB 11.

A practitioner's approach to child support. Bailey. WBB June 1987.

WDW 40: New Rules for Child-support Obligations. Hickey. Wis. Law. April, 1995. Which Came First? The Serial Family Payer Formula. Stansbury. Wis. Law. April, 1995.

See also notes to s. 767.32 for decisions regarding post-judgment modifications. See also Wisconsin Administrative Code Citations published in the Wisconsin Administrative Code for a list of citations to cases citing ch. WDW 40, the percentage standards developed by the Department of Health and Social Services.

767.253 Seek–work orders. In an action for modification of a child-support order under s. 767.32 or an action in which an order for child support is required under s. 767.25 (1), 767.51 (3) or 767.62 (4), the court may order either or both parents of the child to seek employment or participate in an employment or training program.
History: 1989 a. 212; 1997 a. 191; 1999 a. 9.

767.254 Unemployed teenage parent.
(1) In this section, "unemployed teenage parent" means a parent who satisfies all of the following criteria:

    (a)   Is less than 20 years of age.
    (b)   Is unemployed.
    (c)   Is financially unable to pay child support.
    (d)   Would be ordered to make payments for the support of a child but for par. (c).

(2) In an action for revision of a judgment or order providing for child support under s. 767.32 or an action in which an order for child support is required under s. 767.25 (1), 767.51 (3) or 767.62 (4), the court shall order an unemployed teenage parent to do one or more of the following:

    (a)   Register for work at a public employment office established under s. 106.09.
    (b)   Apply for jobs.
    (c)   Participate in a job training program.
    (d)   Pursue or continue to pursue an accredited course of instruction leading to the acquisition of a high school diploma or its equivalent if the unemployed teenage parent has not completed a recognized high school course of study or its equivalent, except that the court may not order the unemployed teenage parent to pursue instruction if the instruction requires the expenditure of funds by the unemployed teenage parent other than normal transportation and personal expenses.

History: 1991 a. 313; 1995 a. 27; 1997 a. 191; 1999 a. 9.

767.255 Property division. (1) Upon every judgment of annulment, divorce or legal separation, or in rendering a judgment in an action under s. 767.02 (1) (h), the court shall divide the property of the parties and divest and transfer the title of any such property accordingly. A certified copy of the portion of the judgment that affects title to real estate shall be recorded in the office of the register of deeds of the county in which the lands so affected are situated. The court may protect and promote the best interests of the children by setting aside a portion of the property of the parties in a separate fund or trust for the support, maintenance, education and general welfare of any minor children of the parties.

(2)   (a)   Except as provided in par.
    (b),   any property shown to have been acquired by either party prior to or during the course of the marriage in any of the following ways shall remain the property of that party and is not subject to a property division under this section:
        1. As a gift from a person other than the other party.
        2. By reason of the death of another, including, but not limited to, life insurance proceeds; payments made under a deferred employment benefit plan, as defined in s. 766.01 (4) (a), or an individual retirement account; and property acquired by

right of survivorship, by a trust distribution, by bequest or inheritance or by a payable on death or a transfer on death arrangement under ch. 705.

3. With funds acquired in a manner provided in subd. 1. or 2. (b) Paragraph (a) does not apply if the court finds that refusal to divide the property will create a hardship on the other party or on the children of the marriage. If the court makes such a finding, the court may divest the party of the property in a fair and equitable manner.

(3) The court shall presume that all property not described in sub. (2) (a) is to be divided equally between the parties, but may alter this distribution without regard to marital misconduct after considering all of the following:

(a) The length of the marriage.

(b) The property brought to the marriage by each party.

(c) Whether one of the parties has substantial assets not subject to division by the court.

(d) The contribution of each party to the marriage, giving appropriate economic value to each party's contribution in homemaking and child-care services.

(e) The age and physical and emotional health of the parties.

(f) The contribution by one party to the education, training or increased earning power of the other.

(g) The earning capacity of each party, including educational background, training, employment skills, work experience, length of absence from the job market, custodial responsibilities for children and the time and expense necessary to acquire sufficient education or training to enable the party to become self-supporting at a standard of living reasonably comparable to that enjoyed during the marriage.

(h) The desirability of awarding the family home or the right to live therein for a reasonable period to the party having physical placement for the greater period of time.

(i) The amount and duration of an order under s. 767.26 granting maintenance payments to either party, any order for periodic family support payments under s. 767.261 and whether the property division is in lieu of such payments.

(j) Other economic circumstances of each party, including pension benefits, vested or unvested, and future interests.

(k) The tax consequences to each party.

(l) Any written agreement made by the parties before or during the marriage concerning any arrangement for property distribution; such agreements shall be binding upon the court except that no such agreement shall be binding where the terms of the agreement are inequitable as to either party. The court shall presume any such agreement to be equitable as to both parties.

(m)   Such other factors as the court may in each individual case determine to be relevant.

767.26 Maintenance payments.

Upon every judgment of annulment, divorce or legal separation, or in rendering a judgment in an action under s. 767.02 (1) (g) or (j), the court may grant an order requiring maintenance payments to either party for a limited or indefinite length of time after considering:

(1) The length of the marriage.

(2) The age and physical and emotional health of the parties.

(3) The division of property made under s. 767.255.

(4) The educational level of each party at the time of marriage and at the time the action is commenced.

(5) The earning capacity of the party seeking maintenance, including educational background, training, employment skills, work experience, length of absence from the job market, custodial responsibilities for children and the time and expense necessary to acquire sufficient education or training to enable the party to find appropriate employment.

(6) The feasibility that the party seeking maintenance can become self–supporting at a standard of living reasonably comparable to that enjoyed during the marriage, and, if so, the length of time necessary to achieve this goal.

(7) The tax consequences to each party.

(8) Any mutual agreement made by the parties before or during the marriage, according to the terms of which one party has made financial or service contributions to the other with the expectation of reciprocation or other compensation in the future, where such repayment has not been made, or any mutual agreement made by the parties before or during the marriage concerning any arrangement for the financial support of the parties.

(9) The contribution by one party to the education, training or increased earning power of the other.

(10) Such other factors as the court may in each individual case determine to be relevant.

History: 1971 c. 220; 1973 c. 12 s. 37; 1977 c. 105; 1979 c. 32 ss. 50, 92 (4); 1979 c. 196; Stats. 1979 s. 767.26.

While arrearages under a temporary order for alimony and attorney fees and costs that the husband is required to pay do not constitute part of a wife's division of the estate, they are, nevertheless, a charge against the entire estate. Tesch v. Tesch, 63 Wis. 2d 320, 217 N.W.2d 647.

An obligation to support children is a factor in determining the amount of maintenance payments. Besaw v. Besaw, 89 Wis. 2d 509, 279 N.W.2d 192 (1979).

The trial court abused its discretion by denying a mother's choice to remain at home to care for small children. Hartung v. Hartung, 102 Wis. 2d 58, 306 N.W.2d 16 (1981).

Trial court abused its discretion by terminating maintenance without sufficiently addressing the factors under this section. Vander Perren v. Vander Perren, 105 Wis. 2d 219, 313 N.W.2d 813 (1982).

Compensation for a person who supports a spouse while the spouse is in school can be achieved through both property division and maintenance payments. Lundberg v. Lundberg, 107 Wis. 2d 1, 318 N.W.2d 918 (1982).

The trial court may begin its maintenance evaluation with the proposition that the dependent partner may be entitled to 50% of the total earnings of both parties. Bahr v. Bahr, 107 Wis. 2d 72, 318 N.W.2d 391 (1982).

The trial court may not consider marital misconduct as a relevant factor in granting maintenance payments. Dixon v. Dixon, 107 Wis. 2d 492, 319 N.W.2d 846 (1982).

Maintenance payments to a former wife were improperly discontinued solely upon the ground of cohabitation with another man. Van Gorder v. Van Gorder, 110 Wis. 2d 188, 327 N.W.2d 674 (1983).

Three formulas were approved for calculating maintenance or property division awards in cases where one spouse has contributed to the other's pursuit of an advanced degree. Haugan v. Haugan, 117 Wis. 2d 200, 343 N.W.2d 796 (1984).

An alcoholic spouse's refusal of treatment is relevant to the trial court's determination regarding a request for permanent maintenance. DeLaMatter v. DeLaMatter, 151 Wis. 2d 576, 445 N.W.2d 676 (Ct. App. 1989).

Military disability payments may be considered in assessing ability to pay maintenance. Weberg v. Weberg, 158 Wis. 2d 540, 463 N.W.2d 382 (Ct. App. 1990).

The trial court's use of a computer program to analyze financial evidence was not error. Bisone v. Bisone, 165 Wis. 2d 114, 477 N.W.2d 59 (Ct. App. 1991).

An award may be based on a percentage of the payer's income in "unusual circumstances."

Unpredictable future income warrants a percentage award. Hefty v. Hefty, 172 Wis. 2d 124, 493 N.W.2d 33 (1992).

Maintenance furthers two objectives: 1) to support the recipient spouse in accordance with the needs and earning capacities of the parties and 2) to ensure a fair and equitable financial agreement between the parties. In the interest of fairness maintenance may exceed the recipient's budget. Hefty v. Hefty, 172 Wis. 2d 124, 493 N.W.2d 33 (1992).

Maintenance is measured by the parties' lifestyle immediately before the divorce and that they could anticipate enjoying if they were to stay married. The award may take into account income increases the parties could reasonably anticipate. Hefty v. Hefty, 172 Wis. 2d 124, 493 N.W.2d 33 (1992).

A maintenance award must account for the recipient's earning capacity and ability to be self–supporting at a level comparable to that during marriage. It is unfair to require one spouse to continue income production levels to maintain the standard of living of the other who chooses a decrease in production. Forester v. Forester, 174 Wis. 2d 78, 497 N.W.2d 78 (Ct. App. 1993).

Consideration of one spouse's solicitation to have the other murdered in denying maintenance did not violate the statutory scheme and was not an improper consideration of "marital misconduct". Brabec v. Brabec, 181 Wis. 2d 270, 510 N.W.2d 762 (Ct. App. 1993).) (Ct. App. 1994).

A maintenance award based on equalization of income is not "self-evidently fair" and does not meet the statutory objectives of support and fairness. Olson v. Olson, 186 Wis. 2d 287, 520 N.W.2d 284 (Ct. App. 1994).

An otherwise short term marriage should not be considered a longer term marriage because there are children. Luciani v. Montemurro–Luciani, 191 Wis. 2d 67, 528 N.W.2d 477 (Ct. App. 1995).

One spouse's contribution of child–rearing services and family support while the other spouse completed an education program was not sufficient grounds for awarding compensatory maintenance. Luciani v. Montemurro–Luciani, 191 Wis. 2d 67, 528 N.W.2d 477 (Ct. App. 1995).

Leaving maintenance open due to potential future health problems of one spouse without expert testimony was proper, but failure to limit the order accordingly was improper. Grace v. Grace, 195 Wis. 2d 153, 536 N.W.2d 109 (Ct. App. 1995).

Post–divorce increases in a pension fund valued in a divorce should be treated as an income stream available for maintenance. Olski v. Olski, 197 Wis. 2d 237, 540 N.W.2d 412 (1995).

A court may consider earning capacity rather than actual earnings in determining child support and maintenance if it find's a spouse's job choice voluntary and unreasonable. Sellers v. Sellers, 201 Wis. 2d 578, 549 N.W.2d 481 (Ct. App. 1996).

When parties have been married to each other more than once, a trial court can look at the total years of marriage when determining maintenance. The trial court is not bound by the terms of maintenance in the first divorce and may look to current conditions in setting maintenance. Wolski v. Wolski, 210 Wis. 2d 184, 565 N.W.2d 196 (Ct. App. 1997).

A stipulation incorporated into a divorce judgment is in the nature of a contract. That a stipulation appears imprudent is not grounds for construction of an unambiguous agreement. Rosplock v. Rosplock, 217 Wis. 2d 22, 577 N.W.2d 32 (Ct. App. 1998).

The purpose of maintenance is, at least in part, to put the recipient in a solid financial position that allows the recipient to become self–supporting by the end of the maintenance period. That the recipient becomes employed and makes productive investments of property division proceeds and maintenance payments is not a substantial change in circumstances, but an expected result of receiving maintenance. Rosplock v. Rosplock, 217 Wis. 2d 22, 577 N.W.2d 32 (Ct. App. 1998).

The trial court's exclusion of pension payments when considering the income available to a maintenance recipient was correct where the pension had been awarded to the recipient as part of the property division and had no value outside of the payments made from it. Seidlitz v. Seidlitz, 217 Wis. 2d 82, 576 N.W.2d 585 (Ct. App. 1998).

The "fairness objective" of equalizing total income does not apply in a post-divorce situation. Modification of maintenance has nothing to do with contributions, economic or noneconomic, made during the marriage. Johnson v. Johnson, 217 Wis. 2d 124, 576 N.W.2d 585 (Ct. App. 1998).

When a reviewing court finds that a trial court erroneously exercised its discretion in awarding maintenance, the case should be remanded for the trial to properly exercise its discretion. It was an abuse of discretion for a trial court to assume that a spouse is legally entitled to maintenance. King v. King, 224 Wis. 2d 235, 590 N.W.2d 480 (1999).

Equal division of income is a reasonable starting point in determining maintenance, but the goal is the standard of living enjoyed during the marriage, not 50% of the total predivorce earnings. Maintenance may surpass 50% of the couple's pre-divorce income, but the payee is not entitled to live a richer lifestyle than that enjoyed during the marriage. Johnson v. Johnson, 225 Wis. 2d 513, 593 N.W.2d 827 (Ct. App. 1999).

In most cases limited-term maintenance provides the recipient with funds for training intended to enable the recipient to be self-supporting by the end of the maintenance period. Another purpose may be to limit the responsibility of the payor to a certain time and to avoid future litigation and, absent a substantial change of circumstances, the parties may rightfully expect no change. The law of change of circumstances should not require a payor spouse to finance unwise financial decisions of therecipient. Maintenance is not intended to provide a permanent annuity. Murray v. Murray, 231 Wis. 2d 71, 604 N.W.2d 912 (Ct. App. 1999).A trial court may not consider premarital contributions in its maintenance and property division determinations. A degree is not an asset for purposes of unjust enrichment and premarital contributions toward the degree of one spouse by the other may not be the basis of a claim therefor. Meyer v. Meyer, 2000 WI 12, 232 Wis. 2d 191, 606 N.W. 184.

The federal tax consequences of divorce. Meldman, Ryan, 57 MLR 229.

No–fault divorce: Tax consequences of support, maintenance and property settlement. Case, 1977 WBB 11.

See also notes to s. 767.32 for decisions regarding post-judgment modifications.

767.261 Family support. The court may make a financial order designated "family support" as a substitute for child-support orders under s. 767.25 and maintenance payment orders under s.

767.26.
A party ordered to pay family support under this section shall pay simple interest at the rate of 1% per month on any amount in arrears that is equal to or greater than the amount of child support due in one month. If the party no longer has a current obliga-tion to pay child support, interest at the rate of 1% per month shall accrue on the total amount of child support in arrears, if any. Interest under this section is in lieu of interest computed under s. 807.01 (4), 814.04 (4) or 815.05 (8) and is paid to the department or its designee under s. 767.29. Except as provided in s. 767.29 (1m), the department or its designee, whichever is appropriate, shall apply all payments received for family support as follows:
(1) First, to payment of family support due within the calendar month during which the payment is received.
(2) Second, to payment of unpaid family support due before the payment is received.
(3) Third, to payment of interest accruing on unpaid family support.
History: 1977 c. 105; 1979 c. 32 ss. 50, 92 (4); Stats. 1979 s. 767.261; 1983 a. 27; 1985 a. 29; 1993 a. 481; 1995 a. 279; 1997 a. 27, 191; 1999 a. 9, 32.
The offset of excess child-support payments against arrears in alimony may be permissible. Anderson v. Anderson, 82 Wis. 2d 115, 261 N.W.2d 817.

767.262 Award of attorney fees.
(1) The court, after considering the financial resources of both parties, may do the following:
    (a)   Order either party to pay a reasonable amount for the cost to the other party of maintaining or responding to an action affecting the family and for attorney fees to either party.
    (b)   If one party receives services under s. 49.22 or services provided by the state or county as a result of an assignment of income under s. 49.19, order the other party to pay any fee chargeable under s. 49.22 (6) or the cost of services rendered by the state or county under s. 49.19.
(2) Any amount ordered under sub. (1) may include sums for legal services rendered and costs incurred prior to the commencement of the proceeding or after entry of judgment.
(3) The court may order that the amount be paid directly to the attorney or to the state or the county providing services under s. 49.22 or 49.19, who may enforce the order in its name.

(4)(a)   Except as provided in par. (b), no court may order payment of costs under this section by the state or any county which may be a party to the action.

(b)   The court may order payment of costs under this section by the department or its designee, whichever is appropriate, in an action in which the court finds that the record of payments and arrearages kept by the department or its designee is substantially incorrect and that the department or its designee has failed to cor-rect the record within 30 days after having received information that the court deter mines is sufficient for making the correction.

History: 1977 c. 105; 1979 c. 32 s. 50; 1979 c. 352 s. 39; Stats. 1979 s. 767.262; 1983 a. 27; 1993 a. 481, 490; 1995 a. 201, 279, 404; 1997 a. 27, 35, 252.

An allowance of $2,300 as a contribution to the wife's attorney's fees incurred in the litigation was not excessive where it was obvious that the trial court reasonably believed that a considerable portion of the attorney fee liabil-ity was attributable to the husband who, represented by 4 successive attor-neys or firms, caused a needlessly protracted trial, made numerous defense motions, and prosecuted a meritless appeal, an element which, together with others, constituted a firm basis for fixing such contribution. Martin v. Martin, 46 Wis. 2d 218, 174 N.W.2d 468.

An allowance of $1,000 attorneys fees on appeal, after the award of a gener-ous property settlement, constituted a penalty for appealing. Molloy v. Molloy, 46 Wis. 2d 682, 176 N.W.2d 292.

Attorney fees on appeal depend on need, ability to pay and whether there is reasonable ground for the appeal. Klipstein v. Klipstein, 47 Wis. 2d 314, 177 N.W.2d 57.

A circuit court does not have subject matter jurisdiction in a divorce action to determine attorney fees between an attorney and client that the attor-ney continues to represent in the divorce action. Stasey v. Stasey, 168 Wis. 2d 37, 483 N.W.2d 221 (1992).

Nonmarital assets may be considered in determining whether to order one party to contribute to the other's fees. Doerr v. Doerr, 189 Wis. 2d 112, 525 N.W.2d 745 (Ct. App. 1994).

767.27 Disclosure of assets required.

(1) In any action affecting the family, except an action to affirm marriage under s. 767.02 (1) (a), the court shall require each party to furnish, on such stan-dard forms as the court may require, full disclosure of all parties jointly. Such disclosure may be made by each party individually or by the parties jointly. Assets required to be disclosedshall include, but shall not be lim-ited to, real estate, savings accounts, stocks and bonds, mortgages and notes, life insurance, interest in a partnership, limited liability company or

corporation, tangible personal property, income from employment, future interests whether vested or nonvested, and any other financial interest or source. The court shall also require each party to furnish,on the same standard form, information pertaining to all debts and liabilities of the parties. The form used shall contain a statement in conspicuous print that complete disclosure of assets and debts is required by law and deliberate failure to provide complete disclosure constitutes perjury. The court may on its own ini-tiative and shall at the request of either party require the parties to furnish copies of all state and federal income tax returns filed by them for the past 2 years, and may require copies of such returns for prior years.

(1m) In any action affecting the family which involves a minor child, the court shall require, in addition to the disclosure under sub. (1), that each party furnish the court with information regarding the types and costs of any health insurance policies or plans which are offered through each party's employer or other organization. This disclosure shall include a copy of any health care policy or plan which names the child as a beneficiary at the time that the disclosure is filed under sub. (2).

(2) Except as provided in sub. (2m), disclosure forms required under this section shall be filed within 90 days after the service of summons or the filing of a joint petition or at such other time as ordered by the court or family court commissioner. Information contained on such forms shall be updated on the record to the date of hearing.

(2m) In every action in which the court has ordered a party to pay child support under s. 767.25, 767.51 or 767.62 (4) or family support under s. 767.261 and the circumstances specified in s. 767.075 (1) apply, the court shall require the party who is ordered to pay the support to annually furnish the disclosure form required under this section and may require that party to annually furnish a copy of his or her most recently filed state and federal income tax returns to the county child-support agency under s. 59.53 (5) for the county in which the order was entered. In any action in which the court has ordered a party to pay child support under s. 767.25, 767.51 or 767.62 (4) or family support under s. 767.261, the court may require the party who is ordered to pay the support to annually furnish the disclosure form required under this section and a copy of his or her most recently filed state and federal income tax returns to the party for whom the support has been awarded. A party who fails to furnish the information as required by the court under this subsection may be proceeded against for contempt of court under ch. 785.

(3)(a)   Except as provided in par. (b), information disclosed under this section shall be confidential and may not be made avail-able to any person for any purpose other than the adjudication, appeal, modification or enforcement of judgment of an action affecting the family of the disclosing parties.

(b) The clerk of circuit court shall provide information from court records to the department under s. 59.40 (2) (p).

(4) Failure by either party timely to file a complete disclosure statement as required by this section shall authorize the court to accept as accurate any information provided in the statement of the other party or obtained under s. 49.22 (2m) by the department or the county child-support agency under s. 59.53 (5).

(5) If any party deliberately or negligently fails to disclose information required by sub. (1) and in consequence thereof any asset or assets with a fair market value of $500 or more is omitted from the final distribution of property, the party aggrieved by such nondisclosure may at any time petition the court granting the annulment, divorce or legal separation to declare the creation of a constructive trust as to all undisclosed assets, for the benefit of the parties and their minor or dependent children, if any, with the party in whose name the assets are held declared the constructive trustee, said trust to include such terms and conditions as the court may determine. The court shall grant the petition upon a finding of a failure to disclose such assets as required under sub. (1).

History: 1977 c. 105; 1979 c. 32 ss. 50, 92 (4); 1979 c. 196; 1979 c. 352 s. 39; Stats. 1979 s. 767.27; 1985 a. 29; 1987 a. 413; 1993 a. 112, 481; 1995 a. 27 s. 9126 (19); 1995 a. 201, 404; 1997 a. 27, 35, 191.

767.275 Disposition of assets prior to action. In any action affecting the family, except an action to affirm marriage under s. 767.02 (1) (a), any asset with a fair market value of $500 or more which would be considered part of the estate of either or both of the parties if owned by either or both of them at the time of the action, but which was transferred for inadequate consideration, wasted, given away or otherwise unaccounted for by one of the parties within one year prior to the filing of the petition or the length of the marriage, whichever is shorter, shall be rebuttably presumed to be part of the estate for the purposes of s. 767.255 and shall be subject to the disclosure requirement of s. 767.27. Transfers which resulted in an exchange of assets of substantially equivalent value need not be specifically disclosed where such assets are otherwise identified in the statement of net worth.

History: 1977 c. 105; 1979 c. 32 ss. 50, 92 (4); 1979 c. 352 s. 39; Stats. 1979 s. 767.275.

767.28 Maintenance, legal custody and support when divorce or separation denied.

In a judgment in an action for divorce or legal separation, although such divorce or legal separation is denied, the court may make such order for the legal custody of and periods of physical placement with any of the minor children and for the maintenance of either spouse and support of such children by either spouse out of property or income, as the nature of the case may render just and reasonable. If the court orders child support under this section, the court shall determine the child support payments in a manner consistent with s. 767.25, regardless of the fact that the court has not entered a judgment of divorce or legal separation.

History: 1971 c. 220; 1979 c. 32 s. 50; Stats. 1979 s. 767.28; 1987 a. 355; 1993 a. 481.

767.29 Maintenance, child support and family support payments, receipt and disbursement; family court commissioner, fees and compensation.

(1) (a)　All orders or judgments providing for temporary or permanent maintenance, child support or family support payments shall direct the payment of all such sums to the department or its designee for the use of the person for whom the same has been awarded. A party securing an order for temporary maintenance, child support or family support payments shall forthwith file the order, together with all pleadings in the action, with the clerk of court.

(b)　Upon request, after the filing of an order or judgment or the receipt of an interim disbursement order, the clerk of court shall advise the county child-support agency under s. 59.53 (5) of the terms of the order or judgment within 2 business days after the fil-ing or receipt. The county child-support agency shall, within the time required by federal law, enter the terms of the order or judg-ment into the statewide support data system, as required by s. 59.53 (5) (b).

(c)　Except as provided in sub. (1m), the department or its designee shall disburse the money received under the judgment or order in the manner required by federal regulations and take receipts therefor, unless the department or its designee is unable to disburse the moneys because they were paid by check or other draft drawn upon an account containing insufficient funds. All moneys received or disbursed under this section shall be entered in a record kept by the department or its designee, whichever is appropriate, which shall be open to inspection by the parties to the action, their attorneys and the family court commissioner.

(d)　For receiving and disbursing maintenance, child support or family support payments, and for maintaining the records required under par. (c), the department or its designee shall collect an annual fee of $25. The court or family court commissioner shall order each party ordered to make payments to pay the annual fee under this paragraph in each year for which payments are ordered. In directing the manner of payment of the annual fee, the court or family court commissioner shall order that the annual fee be withheld from income and sent to the department or its designee, as provided under s. 767.265. All fees collected under this paragraph shall be deposited in the appropriation account under s. 20.445 (3) (ja). At the time of ordering the payment of an annual fee under this paragraph, the court or family court commissioner shall notify each party ordered to make payments of the requirement to pay the annual fee and of the amount of the annual fee. If the annual fee under this paragraph is not paid when due, the department or its designee may not deduct the annual fee from the maintenance or child or family support payment, but may move the court for a remedial sanction under ch. 785.

(dm) 1m.   The department or its designee may collect any unpaid fees under s. 814.61 (12) (b), 1997 stats., that are shown on the department's automated payment and collection system on December 31, 1998, and shall deposit all fees collected under this subdivision in the appropriation account under s. 20.445 (3) (ja). The department or its designee may collect unpaid fees under this subdivision through income withholding under s. 767.265

(2m).   If the department or its designee determines that income with holding is inapplicable, ineffective or insufficient for the collection of any unpaid fees under this subdivision, the department or its designee may move the court for a remedial sanction under ch. 785. The department or its designee may contract with or employ a collection agency or other person for the collection of any unpaid fees under this subdivision and, notwithstanding s. 20.930, may contract with or employ an attorney to appear in any action in state or federal court to enforce the payment obligation. The department or its designee may not deduct the amount of unpaid fees from any maintenance or child or family support payment. 2m. A clerk of court may collect any unpaid fees under s. 814.61 (12) (b), 1997 stats., that are owed to the clerk of court, or to his or her predecessor, and that were not shown on the department's automated payment and collection system on December 31, 1998, through income withholding under s. 767.265 (2m). If the clerk of court determines that income withholding is inapplicable, ineffective or insufficient for the collection of any unpaid fees under this subdivision, the clerk of court may move the court for a remedial sanction under ch. 785.

(e)   If the maintenance, child support or family support payments adjudged or ordered to be paid are not paid to the department or its designee at the time provided in the judgment or order, the county child-support agency under s. 59.53 (5) or the family court commissioner of the county shall take such proceedings as he or she considers advisable to secure the payment of the sum including enforcement by contempt proceedings under ch. 785 or by other means. Copies of any order issued to compel the payment shall be mailed to counsel who represented each party when the maintenance, child support or family support payments were awarded. In case any fees of officers in any of the proceedings, including the compensation of the family court commissioner at the rate of $50 per day unless the commissioner is on a salaried basis, is not collected from the person proceeded against, the fees shall be paid out of the county treasury upon the order of the presiding judge and the certificate of the department.

(f)   If the department determines that the statewide automated support and maintenance receipt and disbursement system will be operational before October 1, 1999, the department shall publish a notice in the Wisconsin Administrative Register that states the date on which the system will begin operating. Before that date or October 1, 1999, whichever is earlier, the circuit courts, county child-support agencies under s. 59.53 (5), clerks of court and employers shall cooperate with the department in any measures taken to ensure an efficient and orderly transition from the county-wide system of support receipt and disbursement to the statewide system.

(1m)   Notwithstanding ss. 767.25 (6) and 767.261, if the department or its designee receives support or maintenance money that exceeds the amount due in the month in which it is received and that the department or its designee determines is for support or maintenance due in a succeeding month, the department or its designee may hold the amount of overpayment that does not exceed the amount due in the next month for disbursement in the next month if any of the following applies:

(a) The payee or the payer requests that the overpayment be held until the month when it is due.

(b) The court or the family court commissioner has ordered that overpayments of child support, family support or maintenance that do not exceed the amount of support or maintenance due in the next month may be held for disbursement in the next month.

(c) The party entitled to the support or maintenance money has applied for or is receiving aid to families with dependent children and there is an assignment to the state under s. 49.19 (4) (h) 1. b. of the party's right to the support or maintenance money.

(cm) A kinship care relative or a long-term kinship care relative of the child who is entitled to the support money has applied for or is receiving kinship care payments or long-term kinship care payments for that child and there is an assignment to the state under s. 48.57 (3m) (b) 2. or (3n) (b) 2. of the child's right to the support money.

(d) The department or its designee determines that the overpayment should be held until the month when it is due.

(2) If any party entitled to maintenance payments or support money, or both, is receiving public assistance under ch. 49, the party may assign the party's right thereto to the county department under s. 46.215, 46.22 or 46.23 granting such assistance. Such assignment shall be approved by order of the court granting the maintenance payments or support money, and may be terminated in like manner; except that it shall not be terminated in cases where there is any delinquency in the amount of maintenance payments and support money previously ordered or adjudged to be paid to the assignee without the written consent of the assignee or upon notice to the assignee and hearing. When an assignment of maintenance payments or support money, or both, has been approved by the order, the assignee shall be deemed a real party in interest within s. 803.01 but solely for the purpose of securing payment of unpaid maintenance payments or support money adjudged or ordered to be paid, by participating in proceedings to secure the payment thereof. Notwithstanding assignment under this subsection, and without further order of the court, the department or its designee, upon receiving notice that a party or a minor child of the parties is receiving public assistance under ch. 49 or that a kinship care relative or long-term kinship care relative of the minor child is receiving kinship care payments or long–term kinship care payments for the minor child, shall forward all support assigned under s. 48.57 (3m) (b) 2. or (3n) (b) 2., 49.19 (4) (h) 1. or 49.45 (19) to the assignee under s. 48.57 (3m) (b) 2. or (3n) (b) 2., 49.19 (4) (h) 1. or 49.45 (19).

(3)(a) If maintenance payments or support money, or both, is ordered to be paid for the benefit of any person, who is com-mitted by court order to an institution or is in confinement, or whose legal custody is vested by court order under ch. 48 or 938 in an agency, department or relative, the court or family court commissioner may order such maintenance payments or support money to be paid to the relative or agency, institution, welfare department or other entity having the legal or actual custody of said person, and to be used for the latter's care and maintenance, without the appointment of a guardian under ch. 880.

(b) If a child who is the beneficiary of support under a judgment or order is placed by court order in a child caring institution, juvenile correctional institution or state mental institution, the right of the child to support during the period of the child's confinement, including any right to unpaid support accruing during that period, is assigned to the state. If the judgment or order providing for the support of a child who is placed in a child caring institution, juvenile correctional institution or state mental institution includes support for one or more other children, the support that is assigned to the state shall be the proportionate share of the child placed in the institution, except as otherwise ordered by the court or family court commissioner on the motion of a party.

(4) If an order or judgment providing for the support of one or more children not receiving aid under s. 48.57 (3m) or (3n) or 49.19 includes support for a minor who is the beneficiary of aid under s. 48.57 (3m) or (3n) or 49.19, any support payment made under the order or judgment is assigned to the state under s. 48.57 (3m) (b) 2. or (3n) (b) 2. or 49.19 (4) (h) 1. b. in the amount that is the proportionate share of the minor receiving aid under s. 48.57 (3m) or (3n) or 49.19, except as otherwise ordered by the court on the motion of a party.

767.325 Revision of legal custody and physical placement orders.

Except for matters under s. 767.327 or 767.329, the following provisions are applicable to modifications of legal custody and physical placement orders:

(1) SUBSTANTIAL MODIFICATIONS.

(a)   Within 2 years after initial order. Except as provided under sub. (2), a court may not modify any of the following orders before 2 years after the initial order is entered under s. 767.24, unless a party seeking the modification, upon petition, motion, or order to show cause shows by substantial evidence that the modification is necessary because the current custodial conditions are physically or emotionally harmful to the best interest of the child:

1. An order of legal custody.

2. An order of physical placement if the modification would substantially alter the time a parent may spend with his or her child.

(b)   After 2–year period.

1. Except as provided under par. (a) and sub. (2), upon petition, motion or order to show cause by a party, a court may modify an order of legal custody or an order of physical placement where the modification would substantially alter the time a parent may spend with his or her child if the court finds all of the following:

a. The modification is in the best interest of the child.

b. There has been a substantial change of circumstances since the entry of the last order affecting legal custody or the last order substantially affecting physical placement.

2. With respect to subd. 1., there is a rebuttable presumption that:
   a. Continuing the current allocation of decision making under a legal custody order is in the best interest of the child. b. Continuing the child's physical placement with the parent with whom the child resides for the greater period of time is in the best interest of the child.

3. A change in the economic circumstances or marital status of either party is not sufficient to meet the standards for modifica-tion under subd. 1.

(2) MODIFICATION OF SUBSTANTIALLY EQUAL PHYSICAL PLACEMENT ORDERS. Notwithstanding sub. (1):

(a) If the parties have substantially equal periods of physical placement pursuant to a court order and circumstances make it impractical for the parties to continue to have substantially equal physical placement, a court, upon petition, motion or order to show cause by a party, may modify such an order if it is in the best interest of the child.

(b) In any case in which par. (a) does not apply and in which the parties have substantially equal periods of physical placement pursuant to a court order, a court, upon petition, motion or order to show cause of a party, may modify such an order based on the appropriate standard under sub. (1). However, under sub. (1) (b) 2., there is a rebuttable presumption that having substantially equal periods of physical placement is in the best interest of the child.

(2m) MODIFICATION OF PERIODS OF PHYSICAL PLACEMENT FOR FAILURE TO EXERCISE PHYSICAL PLACEMENT. Notwithstanding subs. (1) and (2), upon petition, motion or order to show cause by a party, a court may modify an order of physical placement at any time with respect to periods of physical placement if it finds that a parent has repeatedly and unreasonably failed to exercise periods of physical placement awarded under an order of physical placement that allocates specific times for the exercise of periods of physical placement.

(3) MODIFICATION OF OTHER PHYSICAL PLACEMENT ORDERS. Except as provided under subs. (1) and (2), upon petition, motion or order to show cause by a party, a court may modify an order of physical placement which does not substantially alter the amount of time a parent may spend with his or her child if the court finds that the modification is in the best interest of the child.

(4) DENIAL OF PHYSICAL PLACEMENT. Upon petition, motion or order to show cause by a party or on its own motion, a court may deny a parent's physical placement rights at any time if it finds that the physical placement rights would endanger the child's physical, mental or emotional health.

(4m) DENIAL OF PHYSICAL PLACEMENT FOR KILLING OTHER PARENT.

(a)   Notwithstanding subs. (1) to (4), upon petition, motion or order to show cause by a party or on its own motion, a court shall modify a physical placement order by denying a parent physical placement with a child if the parent has been convicted under s. 940.01 of the first-degree intentional homicide, or under s. 940.05 of the 2nd-degree intentional homicide, of the child's other parent, and the conviction has not been reversed, set aside or vacated.

(b)   Paragraph (a) does not apply if the court determines by clear and convincing evidence that physical placement with the parent would be in the best interests of the child. The court shall consider the wishes of the child in making the determination.

(5) REASONS FOR MODIFICATION. If either party opposes modification or termination of a legal custody or physical placement order under this section the court shall state, in writing, its reasons for the modification or termination.

(5m) FACTORS TO CONSIDER. In all actions to modify legal custody or physical placement orders, the court shall consider the factors under s. 767.24 (5) and shall make its determination in a manner consistent with s. 767.24.

(6) NOTICE. No court may enter an order for modification under this section until notice of the petition, motion or order to show cause requesting modification has been given to the child's parents, if they can be found, and to any relative or agency having custody of the child.

(6m) PARENTING PLAN. In any action to modify a legal custody or physical placement order under sub. (1), the court may require the party seeking the modification to file with the court a parenting plan under s. 767.24 (1m) before any hearing is held.

(7) TRANSFER TO DEPARTMENT. The court may order custody transferred to the department of health and family services only if that department agrees to accept custody.

(8) PETITION, MOTION OR ORDER TO SHOW CAUSE. A petition, motion or order to show cause under this section shall include notification of the availability of information under s. 767.081 (2).

(9) APPLICABILITY. Notwithstanding 1987 Wisconsin Act 355, section 73, as affected by 1987 Wisconsin Act 364, the parties may agree to the adjudication of a modification of a legal custody or physical placement order under this section in an action affecting the family that is pending on May 3, 1988.

767.327 Moving the child's residence within or outside the state.

(1) NOTICE TO OTHER PARENT.

(a)   If the court grants periods of physical placement to more than one parent, it shall order a parent with legal custody of and physical place-

ment rights to a child to provide not less than 60 days written notice to the other parent, with a copy to the court, of his or her intent to:
1. Establish his or her legal residence with the child at any location outside the state.
2. Establish his or her legal residence with the child at any location within this state that is at a distance of 150 miles or more from the other parent.
3. Remove the child from this state for more than 90 consecutive days.

(b) The parent shall send the notice under par. (a) by certified mail. The notice shall state the parent's proposed action, including the spe cific date and location of the move or specific beginning and ending dates and location of the removal, and that the other parent may object within the time specified in sub. (2) (a).

(2) OBJECTION; PROHIBITION; MEDIATION.

(a) Within 15 days after receiving the notice under sub. (1), the other parent may send to the parent proposing the move or removal, with a copy to the court, a written notice of objection to the proposed action.

(b) If the parent who is proposing the move or removal receives a notice of objection under par. (a) within 20 days after sending a notice under sub. (1) (a), the parent may not move with or remove the child pending resolution of the dispute, or final order of the court under sub. (3), unless the parent obtains a temporary order to do so under s. 767.23 (1) (bm).

(c) Upon receipt of a copy of a notice of objection under par. (a), the court or family court commissioner shall promptly refer the parents or mediation or other family court counseling services under s. 767.11 and may appoint a guardian ad litem. Unless the parents agree to extend the time period, if mediation or counseling services do not resolve the dispute within 30 days after referral, the matter shall proceed under subs. (3) to (5).

(3) STANDARDS FOR MODIFICATION OR PROHIBITION IF MOVE OR REMOVAL CONTESTED.

(a) 1. Except as provided under par. (b), if the parent proposing the move or removal has sole legal or joint legal custody of the child and the child resides with that parent for the greater period of time, the parent objecting to the move or removal may file a petition, motion or order to show cause for modification of the legal custody or physical placement order affecting the child. The court may modify the legal custody or physical placement order if, after considering the factors under sub. (5), the court finds all of the following:
a. The modification is in the best interest of the child.

   b. The move or removal will result in a substantial change of cir cumstances since the entry of the last order affecting legal custody I or the last order substantially affecting physical placement.
2. With respect to subd. 1.:
   a. There is a rebuttable presumption that continuing the current allo- cation of decision making under a legal custody order or contin- uing the child's physical placement with the parent with whom the child resides for the greater period of time is in the best inter- est of the child. This presumption may be overcome by a show- ing that the move or removal is unreasonable and not in the best interest of the child.
   b. A change in the economic circumstances or marital status of either party is not sufficient to meet the standards for modifica-tion under that subdivision.
3. Under this paragraph, the burden of proof is on the parent object ing to the move or removal. (b) 1. If the parents have joint legal cus- tody and substantially equal periods of physical placement with the child, either parent may file a petition, motion or order to show cause for modification of the legal custody or physical placement order. The court may modify an order of legal custody or physical place ment if, after considering the factors under sub. (5), the court finds all of the following:
   a. Circumstances make it impractical for the parties to con-tinue to have substantially equal periods of physical placement.
   b. The modification is in the best interest of the child.
2. Under this paragraph, the burden of proof is on the parent filing the petition, motion or order to show cause.
(c) 1. If the parent proposing the move or removal has sole legal or joint legal custody of the child and the child resides with that parent for the greater period of time or the parents have substantially equal peri- ods of physical placement with the child, as an alternative to the peti- tion, motion or order to show cause under par. (a) or (b), the parent objecting to the move or removal may file a petition, motion or order to show cause for an order prohibiting the move or removal. The court may prohibit the move or removal if, after considering the fac- tors under sub. (5), the court finds that the prohibition is in the best interest of the child.
2. Under this paragraph, the burden of proof is on the parent object- ing to the move or removal.
(4) GUARDIAN AD LITEM; PROMPT HEARING. After a petition, motion or order to show cause is filed under sub. (3), the court shall appoint a guardian ad litem, unless s. 767.045 (1) (am) applies, and shall hold a hear- ing as soon as possible.

(5) FACTORS IN COURT'S DETERMINATION. In making its determination under sub. (3), the court shall consider all of the following factors:

   (a)   Whether the purpose of the proposed action is reasonable.

   (b)   The nature and extent of the child's relationship with the other parent and the disruption to that relationship which the proposed action may cause.

   (c)   The availability of alternative arrangements to foster and continue the child's relationship with and access to the other parent.

(5m) DISCRETIONARY FACTORS TO CONSIDER. In making a determination under sub. (3), the court may consider the child's adjustment to the home, school, religion and community.

(6) NOTICE REQUIRED FOR OTHER REMOVALS.

   (a)   Unless the parents agree otherwise, a parent with legal custody and physical placement rights shall notify the other parent before removing the child from his or her primary residence for a period of not less than 14 days.

   (b)   Notwithstanding par. (a), if notice is required under sub. (1), a parent shall comply with sub. (1).

   (c)   Except as provided in par. (b), subs. (1) to (5) do not apply to a notice provided under par. (a).

(7) APPLICABILITY. Notwithstanding 1987 Wisconsin Act 355, section 73, as affected by 1987 Wisconsin Act 364, the parties may agree to the adjudication of a modification of a legal custody or physical placement order under this section in an action affecting the family that is pending on May 3, 1988.

History: 1987 a. 355, 364; 1991 a. 32, 269; 1995 a. 70; 1999 a. 9. Discussion of application of sub. (5) factors to the determination of the best interests of the child. Kerkvliet v. Kerkvliet, 166 Wis. 2d 930, 480 N.W.2d 823 (Ct. App. 1992).

Sections 767.325 and 76.327 do not conflict. If one party files a notification of intention to move under s. 767.327, the other parent may file a motion to modify placement under s. 767.325, and the court may consider all relevant circumstances, including, but not limited to, the move. Hughes v. Hughes, 223 Wis. 2d 111, 588 N.W.2d 346 (Ct. App. 1998).

Wisconsin's Child Removal Law. Wis. Law. June 1993.

767.329 Revisions agreed to by stipulation. If after an initial order is entered under s. 767.24, the parties agree to a modification in an order of physical placement or legal custody and file a stipulation with the court that specifies the agreed upon modification, the court shall incorporate the terms of the stipulation into a revised order of physical placement or legal custody.

History: 1987 a. 355. Acceptance of a stipulation is not mandatory. The trial court is not prohibited from examining the best interests of the child. In re Paternity of S.A. 165 Wis. 2d 530, 478 N.W.2d 21 (Ct. App. 1991).

767.33 Annual adjustments in child support order.

(1) An order for child support under s. 767.23 or 767.25 may provide for an adjustment in the amount to be paid based on a change in the obligor's income, as reported on the disclosure form under s. 767.27 (2m) or as disclosed under s. 49.22 (2m) to the department or county child-support agency under s. 59.53 (5). The order may specify the date on which the annual adjustment becomes effective. No adjustment may be made unless the order so provides and the party receiving payments applies for an adjustment as provided in sub. (2). An adjustment under this section may be made only once in any year.

(1m)(a) Except as provided in par. (b), this section applies only to an order under s. 767.23 or 767.25 in which payment is expressed as a fixed sum. It does not apply to such an order in which payment is expressed as a percentage of parental income.

(b) If payment is expressed in an order under s. 767.23 or 767.25 in the alternative as the greater or lesser of either a percent-age of parental income or a fixed sum, this section applies only to the fixed sum alternative under the order. (2) An adjustment under sub. (1) may be made only if the party receiving payments applies to the family court commissioner for the adjustment. If the order specifies the date on which the annual adjustment becomes effective, the application to the family court commissioner must be made at least 20 days before the effective date of the adjustment. The family court commissioner, upon application by the party receiving payments, shall send a notice by certified mail to the last-known address of the obligor. The notice shall be postmarked no later than 10 days after the date on which the application was filed and shall inform the obligor that an adjustment in payments will become effective on the date specified in the order or, if no date is specified in the order, 10 days after the date on which the notice is sent. The obligor may, after receipt of notice and before the effective date of the adjustment, request a hearing on the issue of whether the adjustment should take effect, in which case the adjustment shall be held in abeyance pending the outcome of the hearing. The family court commissioner shall hold a hearing requested under this subsection within 10 working days after the request. If at the hearing the obligor establishes that extraordinary circumstances beyond his or her control prevent fulfillment of the adjusted child-support obligation, the family court commissioner may direct that all or part of the adjustment not take effect until the obligor is able to fulfill the adjusted obligation. If at - the hearing the obligor does not establish that extraordinary circumstances beyond his or her control prevent fulfillment of the adjusted obligation, the adjustment shall take effect as of the date it would have become effective had no hearing been requested. Either party may, within 15 working days of the date of the decision by the family court commissioner under this subsection, seek review of the decision by the court with juris-diction over the action.

History: 1981 c. 20; 1983 a. 27; 1993 a. 481; 1995 a. 27 s. 9126 (19); 1995 a. 404; 1997 a. 27.

767.45 Determination of paternity.

(1) The following persons may bring an action or motion, including an action or motion for declaratory judgment, for the purpose of determining the paternity of a child or for the purpose of rebutting the presump-tion of paternity under s. 891.405 or 891.41 (1):

(a) The child.

(b) The child's natural mother.

(c) Unless s. 767.62 (1) applies, a man presumed to be the child's father under s. 891.405 or 891.41 (1).

(d) A man alleged or alleging himself to be the father of the child.

(e) The personal representative of a person specified under pars. (a) to (d) if that person has died.

(f) The legal or physical custodian of the child.

(g) This state whenever the circumstances specified in s. 767.075 (1) apply, including the delegates of the state as specified in sub. (6).

(h) This state as provided under sub. (6m).

(i) A guardian ad litem appointed for the child under s. 48.235, 767.045 (1) (c) or 938.235.

(j) A parent of a person listed under par. (b), (c) or (d), if the parent is liable or is potentially liable for maintenance of a child of a dependent person under s. 49.90 (1) (a) 2.

(k) In conjunction with the filing of a petition for visitation with respect to the child under s. 767.245 (3), a parent of a person who has filed a declaration of paternal interest under s. 48.025 with respect to the child or a parent of a person who, before April 1, 1998, signed and filed a statement acknowledging paternity under s. 69.15 (3) (b) 3. with respect to the child.

(2) Regardless of its terms, an agreement made after July 1, 1981, other than an agreement approved by the court between an alleged or presumed father and the mother or child, does not bar an action under this section. Whenever the court approves a agreement in which one of the parties agrees not to commence an action under this section, the court shall first determine

whether or not the agreement is in the best interest of the child. The court shall not approve any provision waiving the right to bring an action under this section if this provision is contrary to the best interests of the child.

(3) If an action under this section is brought before the birth of the child, all proceedings shall be stayed until after the birth, except that service of process, service and filing of pleadings, the first appearance and the taking of depositions to preserve testi-mony may be done before the birth of the child.

(4) The child may be a party to any action under this section.

(5) (a)   In this subsection, "any alleged father" includes any male who has engaged in sexual intercourse with the child's mother during a possible time of conception of the child.

(b)   An action under this section may be joined with any other action for child support and shall be governed by the procedures specified in s. 767.05 relating to child support, except that the title of the action shall be "In re the paternity of A.B." The petition shall state the name and date of birth of the child if born or that the mother is pregnant if the child is unborn, the name of any alleged father, whether or not an action by any of the parties to determine the paternity of the child or rebut the presumption of paternity to the child has at any time been commenced, or is pending before any judge or court com missioner, in this state or elsewhere. If a paternity judgment has been rendered, or if a paternity action has been dismissed, the petition shall state the court which rendered the judgment or dismissed the action, and the date and the place the judgment was granted if known. The petition shall also give notice of a party's right to request a genetic test under s. 49.225 or 767.48.

(c)   If a matter is referred under s. 48.299 (6) (a) or 938.299 (6) (a) to an attorney designated under sub. (6) (a), that attorney shall also include in the petition notification to the court that the matter was referred under s. 48.299 (6) (a) or 938.299 (6) (a).

(5m) Except as provided in ss. 767.458 (3), 767.465 (2) and (2m), 767.477, 767.62 and 769.401, unless a man is presumed the child's father under s. 891.41 (1), is adjudicated the child's father either under s. 767.51 or by final order or judgment of a court of competent jurisdiction in another state or has acknowledged him-self to be the child's father under s. 767.62 (1) or a substantially similar law of another state, no order or temporary order may be entered for child support, legal custody or physical placement until the man is adjudicated the father using the procedure set forth in ss. 767.45 to 767.60. Except as provided in ss. 767.477, 767.62 and 769.401, the exclusive procedure for establishment of childsupport obligations, legal custody or physical placement rights for a man who is not presumed the child's father under s. 891.41 (1), adjudicated the father or acknowledged under s. 767.62 (1) or a substantially similar law of another state to be the father is by an action under ss. 767.45 to 767.60 or under s. 769.701. No person may waive the use of this procedure. If a presumption under s. 891.41 (1) exists, a party denying paternity has the burden of rebutting the presumption.

(6)(a) The attorney responsible for support enforcement under s. 59.53 (6) (a) shall provide the representation for the state as specified under s. 767.075 (1) in cases brought under this section.

(b) The attorney under s. 59.53 (6) (a) is the only county attor-ney who may provide representation when the state delegates its authority under sub. (1) (g).

(c) The attorney under s. 59.53 (6) (a) or any state attorney act-ing under par. (b) may not represent the state as specified under s. 767.075 (1) in an action under this section and at the same time act as guardian ad litem for the child or the alleged child of the party.

(6m) The attorney designated under sub. (6) (a) shall commence an action under this section on behalf of the state within 6 months after receiving notification under s. 69.03 (15) that no father is named on the birth cer-tificate of a child who is a resident of the county if paternity has not been acknowledged under s. 767.62 (1) or a substantially similar law of another state or adjudicated, except in situations under s. 69.14 (1) (g) and (h) and as provided by the department by rule.

(6r)(a) The attorney designated under sub. (6) (a) who receives a referral under s. 48.299 (6) (a) or 938.299 (6) (a) shall do all of the following:

1. Give priority to matters referred under s. 48.299 (6) (a) or 938.299 (6) (a), including priority in determining whether an action should be brought under this section and, if the determina-tion is that such an action should be brought, priority in bringing the action and in establishing the existence or nonexistence of paternity.

2. As soon as possible, but no later than 30 days after the date on which the referral is received, notify the court that referred the matter of one of the following:

a. The date on which an action has been brought under this sec-tion or the approximate date on which such an action will be brought.

b. That a determination has been made that an action should not be brought under this section or, if such a determination has not been made, the approximate date on which a determina tion will be made as to whether such an action should be brought.

c. That the man designated in s. 48.299 (6) (a) or 938.299 (6) (a) has previously been excluded as the father of the child.

3. If an action is brought under this section, notify the court that referred the matter as soon as possible of a judgment or order determining the existence or nonexistence of paternity.

(b)   The attorney designated under sub. (6) (a) who receives a referral under s. 48.299 (7) or 938.299 (7) may bring an action under this section on behalf of the state and may give priority to the referral and notify the referring court in the same manner as is required under par. (a) when a matter is referred under s. 48.299

(6) (a) or 938.299 (6) (a).

(7) The clerk of court shall provide without charge, to each person bringing an action under this section, except to the state under sub. (1) (g) or (6m), a document setting forth the percentage standard established by the department under s. 49.22 (9) and list-ing the factors which a court may consider under s. 767.25 (1m).

History: 1979 c. 352; 1981 c. 20 s. 2202 (20) (m); 1983 a. 447; 1985 a. 29; 1987 a. 27, 355, 399, 413; 1989 a. 31, 212; 1993 a. 326, 481; 1995 a. 27 s. 9126 (19); 1995 a. 68, 100, 201, 275, 404; 1997 a. 191; 1999 a. 9.

A paternity proceeding may not be maintained posthumously. In re Estate of Blumreich, 84 Wis. 2d 545, 267 N.W.2d 870 (1978). See also Paternity of N.L.B. 140 Wis. 2d 400, 411 N.W.2d 144 (Ct. App. 1987).

Under the facts of the case, the nonbiological father was not equitably estopped from denying paternity or child support. Marriage of A. J. N. & J. M. N., 141 Wis. 2d 99, 414 N.W.2d 68 (Ct. App. 1987).

A posthumous paternity action is allowable where it is brought by the personal representative of the deceased putative father. Le Fevre v. Schreiber, 167 Wis. 2d 733, 482 N.W.2d 904 (1992).

A paternity action may not be used to challenge paternity previously decided in a divorce action. That paternity was not challenged in the divorce is irrelevant where it could have been litigated. In Re Paternity of Nathan T. 174 Wis. 2d 352, 497 N.W.2d 740 (Ct. App. 1993).

The full faith and credit clause of the U.S. Constitution did not bar a petition to determine paternity where a paternity decree of another state would have been subject to collateral attack in that state. In Re Paternity of R.L.L. 176 Wis. 2d 224, N.W.2d (Ct. App. 1993).

Because a child has a right to bring an independent action for paternity under sub. (1) (a), where the child was not a party to an earlier paternity action, it would be a violation of the child's due process rights to preclude the child from litigating the paternity issue. Mayonia M.M. v. Kieth N. 202 Wis. 2d 461, 551 N.W.2d 34 (Ct. App. 1996).

An alleged father has a statutory right to a determination of paternity. A hearing to determine whether the child's best interests would be served by a paternity proceeding is not authorized by statute. Thomas M.P. v. Kimberly J.L. 207 Wis. 2d 390, 558 N.W.2d 897 (Ct. App. 1996).

767.475 Paternity procedures.

(1)(a)   Except as provided in par. (b), the court may appoint a guardian ad litem for the child and shall appoint a guardian ad litem for a minor parent or minor who is alleged to be a parent in a paternity proceeding unless the minor parent or the minor alleged to be the parent is represented by an attorney.

(b)   The court shall appoint a guardian ad litem for the child if s. 767.045 (1) (a) or (c) applies or if the court has concern that the child's best interest is not being represented.

(2) Presumption of paternity shall be as provided in ss. 891.39, 891.405 and 891.41 (1).

(2m) If there is no presumption of paternity under s. 891.41 (1), the mother shall have sole legal custody of the child until the court orders otherwise.

(3) Evidence as to the time of conception may be offered as provided in s. 891.395.

(4) Discovery shall be conducted as provided in ch. 804, except that no discovery may be obtained later than 30 days before the trial. No discovery may solicit information relating to the sexual relations of the mother occurring at any time other than the probable time of conception.

(5) The statute of limitations for commencing actions con-cerning paternity is as provided in s. 893.88.

(6) The respondent in a paternity action may be arrested as provided in s. 818.02 (6).

(7) The court may appoint a trustee or guardian to receive and manage money paid for the support of a minor child.

(7m) The court shall give priority to an action brought under s. 767.45 whenever the petition under s. 767.45 (5) indicates that the matter was referred under s. 48.299 (6) (a) or 938.299 (6) (a) by a court assigned to exercise jurisdiction under chs. 48 and 938.

(8) In all other matters, paternity proceedings shall be governed by the procedures applicable to other actions affecting the family.

History: 1979 c. 352; 1981 c. 391; 1983 a. 447; 1989 a. 212; 1993 a. 481; 1995 a. 275; 1997 a. 191; 1999 a. 9.

A trust under sub. (7) is not restricted to where the custodial parent is a spendthrift. Paternity of Tukker M.O., 189 Wis. 2d 440, 525 N.W.2d 793 (Ct. App. 1994). See also Paternity of Tukker M.O., 199 Wis. 2d 186, 544 N.W.2d 417 (1996).

767.477 Temporary orders.

(1) At any time during the pendency of an action to establish the paternity of a child, if genetic tests show that the alleged father is not excluded and that the statistical probability of the alleged father's parentage is 99.0% or

higher, on the motion of a party, the court shall make an appropriate temporary order for the payment of child support and may make a temporary order assigning responsibility for and directing the manner of payment of the child's health care expenses.

(2) Before making any temporary order under sub. (1), the court shall consider those factors that the court is required to consider when granting a final judgment on the same subject matter. If the court makes a temporary child-support order that deviates from the amount of support that would be required by using the percentage standard established by the department under s. 49.22 (9), the court shall comply with the requirements of s. 767.25 (1n).

History: 1997 a. 191; 1999 a. 9.

767.48 Genetic tests in paternity actions.

(1)(a)   The court may, and upon request of a party shall, require the child, mother, any male for whom there is probable cause to believe that he had sexual intercourse with the mother during a possible time of the child's conception, or any male witness who testifies or will testify about his sexual relations with the mother at a possible time of conception to submit to genetic tests. Probable cause of sexual intercourse during a possible time of conception may be established by a sufficient petition or affidavit of the child's mother oran alleged father, filed with the court, or after an examination under oath of a party or witness, when the court determines such an examination is necessary. The court is not required to order a person who has undergone a genetic test under s. 49.225 to submit to another test under this paragraph unless a party requests additional tests under sub. (2).

(b)   The genetic tests shall be performed by an expert qualified as an examiner of genetic markers present on the cells of the specific body material to be used for the tests, appointed by the court. A report completed and certified by the court-appointed expert stating genetic test results and the statistical probability of the alleged father's paternity based upon the genetic tests is admissible as evidence without expert testimony and may be entered into the record at the trial or pretrial hearing if all of the following apply:

1. At least 10 days before the trial or pretrial hearing, the party offering the report files it with the court and notifies all other parties of that filing.

2. At least 10 days before the trial or pretrial hearing, the department or county child-support agency under s. 59.53 (5) notifies the alleged father of the results of the genetic tests and that he

may object to the test results by submitting an objection in writing to the court no later than the day before the hearing.
3. The alleged father, after receiving the notice under subd. 2., does not object to the test results in the manner provided in the notice under subd. 2.

(1m) If genetic tests ordered under this section or s. 49.225 show that the alleged father is not excluded and that the statistical probability of the alleged father's parentage is 99.0% or higher, the alleged father shall be rebuttably presumed to be the child's parent.

(2) The court, upon request by a party, shall order that independent tests be performed by other experts qualified as examiners of genetic markers present on the cells of the specific body material to be used for the tests. Additional tests performed by other experts of the same qualifications may be ordered by the court at the request of any party.

(3) In all cases, the court shall determine the number and qualifications of the experts.

(4) Whenever the results of genetic tests exclude an alleged father as the father of the child, this evidence shall be conclusive evidence of nonpaternity and the court shall dismiss any paternity action with respect to that alleged father. Whenever the results of genetic tests exclude any male witness from possible paternity, the tests shall be conclusive evidence of nonpaternity of the male witness. Testimony relating to sexual intercourse or possible sexual intercourse of the mother with any person excluded as a possible father, as a result of a genetic test, is inadmissible as evidence. If any party refuses to submit to a genetic test, this fact shall be disclosed to the fact finder. Refusal to submit to a genetic test ordered by the court is a contempt of the court for failure to produce evidence under s. 767.47 (5). If the action was brought by the child's mother but she refuses to submit herself or the child to genetic tests, the action shall be dismissed.

(5) The fees and costs for genetic tests performed upon any person listed under sub. (1) shall be paid for by the county except as follows:
(a)   Except as provided in par. (b), at the close of the proceeding the court may order either or both parties to reimburse the county if the court finds that they have sufficient resources to pay the costs of the genetic tests.
(b)   If 2 or more identical series of genetic tests are performed upon the same person, regardless of whether the tests were ordered under }l this section or s. 49.225 or 767.458 (2), the court shall require the person requesting the 2nd or subsequent series of tests to pay for it in advance, unless the court finds that the person is indigent.

(6) Any party calling a male witness for the purpose of testifying that he had sexual intercourse with the mother at any possible time of conception shall provide all other parties with the name and address of the witness 20 days

before the trial or pretrial hearing. If a male witness is produced at the hearing for the purpose stated in this subsection but the party calling the witness failed to provide the 20-day notice, the court may adjourn the proceeding for the purpose of taking a genetic test of the witness prior to hearing the testimony of the witness if the court finds that the party calling the witness acted in good faith.

(7) The court shall ensure that all parties are aware of their right to request genetic tests under this section.

767.50 Trial.

(1) The trial shall be divided into 2 parts. The first part shall deal with the determination of paternity. The 2nd part shall deal with child support, legal custody, periods of physical placement and related issues. At the first part of the trial, the main issue shall be whether the alleged or presumed father is or is not the father of the mother's child, but if the child was born to the mother while she was the lawful wife of a specified man there shall first be determined, as provided in s. 891.39, the prior issue of whether the husband was not the father of the child. The first part of the trial shall be by jury only if the defendant verbally requests a jury trial either at the initial appearance or pretrial hear-ing or requests a jury trial in writing prior to the pretrial hearing. The court may direct, and if requested by either party, before the introduction of any testimony in the party's behalf, shall direct the jury, in cases where there is a jury, to find a special verdict as to any of the issues specified in this section except that the court shall make all the findings enumerated in s. 767.51 (2) to (5) [s. 767.51 (2) to (4)]. If the mother is dead, becomes insane, cannot be found within the jurisdiction or fails to commence or pursue the action, the proceeding does not abate if any of the persons under s. 767.45 (1) makes a motion to continue. The testimony of the mother taken at the pretrial hearing may in any such case be read in evi-dence if it is competent, relevant and material. The issues of child support, custody and visitation and related issues shall be determined by the court either immediately after the first part of the trial or at a later hearing before the court.

(2) If a jury is requested under sub. (1), the jury shall consist of 6 persons. No verdict is valid or received unless agreed to by at least 5 of the jurors.

History: 1979 c. 352 s. 10; Stats. 1979 s. 767.50; 1983 a. 27, 447; 1987 a. 27, 355, 403; 1993 a. 481.

A preponderance of the evidence standard of proof in paternity actions meets due process requirement. Rivera v. Minnich, 483 U.S. 574 (1987).

767.51 Paternity judgment.

(1) A judgment or order of the court determining the existence or nonexistence of paternity is determinative for all purposes.

(2) The clerk of court shall file with the state registrar, within 30 days after the entry of a judgment or order determining paternity, a report showing the names, dates and birth places of the child and the father, the social security numbers of the mother, father and child and the maiden name of the mother on a form designated by the state registrar, along with the fee set forth in s. 69.22 (5), which the clerk of court shall collect.

(3) A judgment or order determining paternity shall contain all of the following provisions:

(a) An adjudication of the paternity of the child.

(b) Orders for the legal custody of and periods of physical placement with the child, determined in accordance with s. 767.24.

(c) An order requiring either or both of the parents to contribute to the support of any child of the parties who is less than 18 years old, or any child of the parties who is less than 19 years old if the child is pursuing an accredited course of instruction leading to the acquisition of a high school diploma or its equivalent, determined in accordance with s. 767.25.

(d) A determination as to which parent, if eligible, shall have the right to claim the child as an exemption for federal tax pur-poses under 26 USC 151 (c) (1) (B), or as an exemption for state tax purposes under s. 71.07 (8) (b).

(e) An order requiring the father to pay or contribute to the reasonable expenses of the mother's pregnancy and the child's birth, based on the father's ability to pay or contribute to those expenses.

(f) An order requiring either or both parties to pay or contribute to the costs of the guardian ad litem fees, genetic tests as provided in s. I 767.48 (5) and other costs.

(g) An order requiring either party to pay or contribute to the attorney fees of the other party.

(4)(a) Subject to par. (b), liability for past support of the child shall be limited to support for the period after the day on which the petition in the action under s. 767.45 is filed, unless a party shows, to the satisfaction of the court, all of the following:

1. That he or she was induced to delay commencing the action by any of the following:

a. Duress or threats.

b. Actions, promises or representations by the other party upon which the party relied.

c. Actions taken by the other party to evade paternity proceedings.

2. That, after the inducement ceased to operate, he or she did not unreasonably delay in commencing the action. (b) In no event may liability for past support of the child be imposed for any period before the birth of the child.

(6) Sections 767.24, 767.245, 767.263, 767.265, 767.267, 767.29, 767.293, 767.30, 767.305, 767.31, 767.32 and 767.325, where applicable, shall apply to a judgment or order under this section.
(7) The court may order the attorney for the prevailing party to prepare findings of fact, conclusions of law and a judgment for the approval of the court.

767.52 Right to counsel.
(1) At the pretrial hearing, at the trial and in any further proceedings in any paternity action, any party may be represented by counsel. If the respondent is indigent and the state is the petitioner under s. 767.45 (1) (g), the petitioner is represented by a government attorney as provided in s. 767.45 (6) or the action is commenced on behalf of the child by an attorney appointed under s. 767.045 (1) (c), counsel shall be appointed for the respondent as provided in ch. 977, and subject to the limitations under sub. (2m), unless the respondent knowingly and voluntarily waives the appointment of counsel.
(2) An attorney appointed under sub. (1) who is appearing on behalf of a party in a paternity action shall represent that party, subject to the limitations under sub. (2m), in all issues and proceedings relating to the paternity determination. The appointed attorney may not represent the party in any proceeding relating to child support, legal custody, periods of physical placement or related issues.
(2m) Representation by an attorney appointed under sub. (1) shall be provided only after the results of any genetic tests have been completed and only if all of the results fail to show that the alleged father is excluded and fail to give rise to the rebuttable pre- sumption under s. 767.48 (1m) that the alleged father is the father of the child.
(3) This section does not prevent an attorney responsible for support enforcement under s. 59.53 (6) (a) or any other attorney employed under s. 49.22 or 59.53 (5) from appearing in any pater-nity action as provided under s. 767.45 (6).
History: 1979 c. 352; 1983 a. 27; 1987 a. 355; 1989 a. 31; 1993 a. 16, 481; 1995 a. 27, 100, 201, 404; 1997 a. 35, 191.
A paternity respondent does not have a constitutional right to effective assistance of counsel. A paternity action is not a criminal prosecution. In re Paternity of P.L.S. 158 Wis. 2d 712, 463 N.W.2d 403 (Ct. App. 1990).

767.53 Paternity hearings and records; confidentiality.
Any hearing, discovery proceeding or trial relating to paternity determination shall be closed to any person other than thosenecessary to the action or proceeding. Any record of pending proceedings shall be placed in a closed file, except that:

(1) Access to the record of any pending proceeding involving the paternity of the same child shall be allowed to all of the follow-ing:
(a) The child's parents.
(b) The parties to that proceeding and their attorneys or their authorized representatives.
(c) If the child is the subject of a proceeding under ch. 48 or 938, all of the following:
1. The court assigned to exercise jurisdiction under chs. 48 and 938 in which the proceeding is pending.
2. The parties to the proceeding under ch. 48 or 938 and their attorneys.
3. The person under s. 48.09 or 938.09 who represents the interests of the public in the proceeding under ch. 48 or 938.
4. A guardian ad litem for the child and a guardian ad litem for the child's parent.
5. Any governmental or social agency involved in the proceeding under ch. 48 or 938.
(2) The clerk of circuit court shall provide information from court records to the department under s. 59.40 (2) (p).
(3) Subject to s. 767.19, a record of a past proceeding is open to public inspection if all of the following apply:
(a) Paternity was established in the proceeding.
(b) The record is filed after May 1, 2000.
(c) The record relates to a post-adjudication issue.
History: 1979 c. 352; 1983 a. 447; 1985 a. 29; 1995 a. 27 s. 9126 (19); 1995 a. 201, 275, 404; 1997 a. 80, 252; 1999 a. 9.

767.60 Determination of marital children.

In any case where the father and mother of any nonmarital child shall enter into a lawful marriage or a marriage which appears and they believe is lawful, except where the parental rights of the mother were terminated prior thereto, that child shall thereby become a marital child, shall be entitled to a change in birth certificate under s. 69.15 (3) (b) and shall enjoy all the rights and privileges of a marital child as if he or she had been born during the marriage of the parents; and this section shall be taken to apply to all cases prior to its date, as well as those subsequent thereto but no estate already vested shall be divested by this section and ss. 765.05 to 765.24 and 852.05. The issue of all marriages declared void under the law shall, nevertheless, be marital issue.
History: 1979 c. 32 ss. 48, 92 (2); Stats. 1979 s. 765.25; 1979 c. 352; Stats. 1979 s. 767.60; 1981 c. 314 s. 146; 1983 a. 447; 1985 a. 315.

767.62 Voluntary acknowledgment of paternity.

(1) CONCLUSIVE DETERMINATION OF PATERNITY. A statement acknowledging paternity that is on file with the state registrar under s. 69.15 (3) (b) 3. after the last day on which a person may timely rescind the statement, as specified in s. 69.15 (3m), is a conclusive determination, which shall be of the same effect as a judgment, of paternity.

(2) RESCISSION OF ACKNOWLEDGMENT.

    (a)   A statement acknowledging paternity that is filed with the state registrar under s. 69.15 (3) (b) 3. may be rescinded as provided in s. 69.15 (3m) by a person who signed the statement as a parent of the child who is the subject of the statement.

    (b)   If a statement acknowledging paternity is timely rescinded as provided in s. 69.15 (3m), a court or family court commissioner may not enter an order specified in sub. (4) with respect to the man who signed the statement as the father of the child unless the man is adjudicated the child's father using the procedures set forth in ss. 767.45 to 767.60.

(3) ACTIONS WHEN PATERNITY ACKNOWLEDGED.

    (a)   Unless the statement acknowledging paternity has been rescinded, an action affecting the family concerning custody, child support or physical placement rights may be brought with respect to persons who, with respect to a child, jointly signed and filed with the state registrar under s. 69.15 (3) (b) 3. as parents of the child a statement acknowledging paternity.

    (b)   Except as provided in s. 767.045, in an action specified in par. (a) the court or family court commissioner may appoint a guardian ad litem for the child and shall appoint a guardian ad litem for a party who is a minor, unless the minor party is represented by an attorney.

(4) ORDERS WHEN PATERNITY ACKNOWLEDGED. In an action under sub. (3) (a), if the persons who signed and filed the statement acknowledging paternity as parents of the child had notice of the hearing, the court or family court commissioner shall make an order that contains all of the following provisions:

    (a)   Orders for the legal custody of and periods of physical placement with the child, determined in accordance with s. 767.24.

    (b   An order requiring either or both of the parents to contribute to the support of any child of the parties who is less than 18 years old, or any child of the parties who is less than 19 years old if the child is pursuing an accredited course of instruction leading to the acquisition of a high school diploma or its equivalent, determined in accordance with s. 767.25.

    (c)   A determination as to which parent, if eligible, shall have the right to claim the child as an exemption for federal tax purposes under 26

USC 151 (c) (1) (B), or as an exemption for state tax purposes under s. 71.07 (8) (b).

(d) An order requiring the father to pay or contribute to the reasonable expenses of the mother's pregnancy and the child's birth, based on the father's ability to pay or contribute to those expenses.

(e) An order requiring either or both parties to pay or contribute to the costs of the guardian ad litem fees and other costs.

(f) An order requiring either party to pay or contribute to the attorney fees of the other party.

(4m) LIABILITY FOR PAST SUPPORT.

(a) Subject to par. (b), liability for past support of the child shall be limited to support for the period after the day on which the petition, motion or order to show cause requesting support is filed in the action for support under sub. (3) (a), unless a party shows, to the satisfaction of the court, all of the following:

1. That he or she was induced to delay commencing the action by any of the following:

a. Duress or threats.

b. Actions, promises or representations by the other party upon which the party relied.

c. Actions taken by the other party to evade proceedings under sub. (3) (a).

2. That, after the inducement ceased to operate, he or she did not unreasonably delay in commencing the action.

(b) In no event may liability for past support of the child be imposed for any period before the birth of the child.

(5) VOIDING DETERMINATION.

(a) A determination of paternity that arises under this section may be voided at any time upon a motion or petition stating facts that show fraud, duress or a mistake of fact. Except for good cause shown, any orders entered under sub. (4) shall remain in effect during the pendency of a proceeding under this paragraph.

(b) If a court in a proceeding under par. (a) determines that the man is not the father of the child, the court shall vacate any order entered under sub. (4) with respect to the man. The court shall notify the state registrar, in the manner provided in s. 69.15 (1) (b), to remove the man's name as the father of the child from the child's birth certificate. No paternity action may thereafter be brought against the man with respect to the child.

(6) APPLICABILITY.

(a) This section does not apply unless all of the following apply to the statement acknowledging paternity:

       1. The statement is made on a form prescribed by the state reg-istrar for use beginning on April 1, 1998.

       2. The statement was signed and filed on or after April 1, 1998.

       3. The statement contains an attestation clause showing that both parties, before signing the statement, received oral and written notice of the legal consequences of, the rights and responsibilities arising from and the alternatives to, signing the statement.

(b)   Parties who signed and filed a statement acknowledging paternity before April 1, 1998, may sign and file a new statement that fulfills he requirements under par. (a). Such a statement supersedes any statement previously filed with the state registrar and has the effect specified in this section.

(c)   The notice requirements under s. 69.15 (3) (b) 3. apply to this section beginning with forms for the acknowledgment of paternity that are prescribed by the state registrar on April 1, 1998.

History: 1993 a. 481; 1995 a. 100; 1997 a. 191; 1999 a. 9. Wisconsin's Custody, Placement and Paternity Reform Legislation. Walther. Wis.Law. April 2000.

INDEX